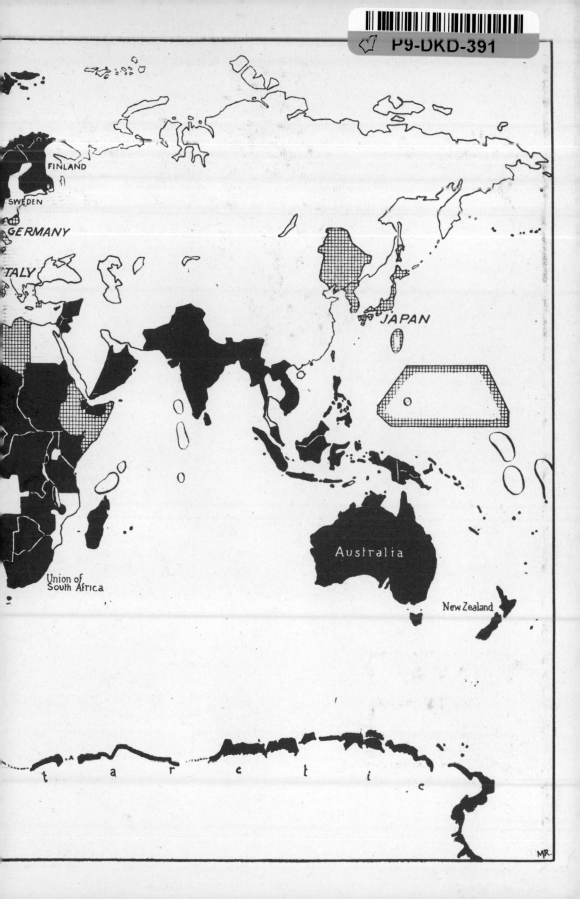

UNION NOW

A Proposal — Man's Union
A Philosophy — Man's Freedom
A Poem — Man

This book was first made public in essence in three Cooper Foundation lectures at Swarthmore College.

UNION NOW

A Proposal for a Federal Union of the Democracies of the North Atlantic

By

Clarence K. Streit

*For the Great Republic, For the Principle
It Lives By and Keeps Alive, For
Man's Vast Future. - Lincoln*

HARPER & BROTHERS PUBLISHERS

New York   1939   London

UNION NOW

Fourth Printing

Printed in the United States of America

To the Memory of Emma Kirshman, My Mother

And to all those for whom she spoke when with two sons away in the war she wrote:

Surely some great good will come out of so much suffering... Our home is broken and empty, but I am not without hope. Some day you will return improved by this awful experience, for by experiences we grow bigger and get a deeper insight in life and its mysteries.

Foreword

Today the problem of securing individual freedom, democracy, peace and prosperity is a problem in organizing world government, and to that problem this book brings a fresh solution backed by fresh analysis. Its essence may be found in the first chapter. This may lead some to assume that in writing this book I began with this chapter, too. The opposite occurred. The first chapter was written last. The conclusions it expresses are not to be taken as a thesis which the book was written to prove. Instead I have drawn them from it and have sought for the reader's convenience to say at the start as concisely as I could the essence—not the summary—of what I have to say.

I have drawn these conclusions from much more than this book, in fact from all my experience. They have grown in me since youth— "this is what I have learnt from America"—and especially since the war, particularly during the period since 1920 which I have spent working as an American newspaper correspondent in a score of countries of the Old and New Worlds, and more particularly since 1929. This last period I have spent reporting mainly from Geneva and Basle the efforts of mankind to solve the problem of living together less precariously and meanly, to organize and apply world government and law. I have followed these efforts day in and out for more than 3,000 days; I would give in this book not my experiences but what I have learned from them.

In writing this book, however, I was unable to begin with the gist of what experience had taught me. I had first to write this book through four times, not to mention revisions. When I began it in 1933 as a newspaper article most of these convictions were as vague and formless as the old prospector's conviction, "There's gold in them thar hills!" I count the writing and rewriting of this book as no small part of my experience. It was the part of finding the mother lode amid the rocks and fool's gold, of digging down to it, of separating it from the quartz, of reducing "them thar hills" down to a form where the man in the street might recognize the gold in them, and of blazing a trail back. I could not find my gold as nuggets of pure logic nor by the divining rod of mysticism.

In reporting what I have found I have followed broadly the American rules of my profession which require the reporter to pick out, boil down and tell at the start in the order of importance the essentials he has to tell. My method may be criticized as journalistic, but the quantity of speeches and documents and volumes I have had to wade through in my daily newspaper work in order to find the essentials their authors had to say has convinced me that the ideal for the presentation of all serious thought is the ideal that American news reporters seek, far from it though we fall. In a world so full and with a life so short as ours it seems to me to be highly in the interest of everyone—layman or expert—to get and give his essentials in every field as quickly as the dangers of over-simplifying permit. Since everyone reads much more than he writes and has far more to learn than teach, it seems to me that this journalistic method is to the general advantage—though it does make the writer's work much harder. Certainly I have encountered the difficulty that Pascal expressed long ago: "The last thing that we find in making a book is to know what we must put first."

And having mentioned one of my difficulties, I would mention too that I have enjoyed the enduring advantage of my wife's unending help and firm faith, and generous encouragement from a number of friends at times when I most needed it.

Oct. 14, 1938.   C. K. S.

Introduction by de Tocqueville

Among the new things that drew my attention during my sojourn in the United States none struck me so strongly as the equality of conditions . . . The more I studied American society the more I saw the equality of conditions as the generating fact from which each detail descended . . . Then I turned my thoughts to our hemisphere, and it seemed to me that I distinguished something similar to the spectacle the new world offered . . .

A great democratic revolution is at work among us. Some hope still to stop it. Others judge it to be irresistible because it seems to them the most continuous, ancient and permanent fact known to history . . .

The crusades and the English wars decimated the nobles and divided their lands, the institution of the communes introduced democratic liberty in the bosom of feudal monarchy; the discovery of firearms equalized the villain and the noble on the battlefield; the printing press offered equal resources to their intelligence; the postman came to bring light to the door of the poor man's hut as to the palace gate; protestantism maintained that all men are equally qualified to find the road to heaven. The discovery of America presented a thousand new roads to fortune . . .

Everywhere we have seen the divers incidents of the life of peoples turn to the profit of democracy . . .

Shall democracy stop now that it is so strong and its adversaries so weak? . . .

The grandeur already achieved keeps us from seeing what yet may come.

The entire book one is about to read has been written in a sort of religious awe produced in the author's soul by the sight of this irresistible revolution which has marched on through so many centuries and through every obstacle, and which we see today yet advancing . . .

The . . . peoples seem to me to present today a terrifying spectacle; . . . their fate is in their hands; but soon it will escape them.

To instruct the democracy, to revive, if possible, its beliefs, purify its practices, regulate its movements; to replace little by little its inexperience with science and its blind instincts with knowledge of its true interests; to adapt its government to the times and conditions, to modify it according to circumstances and men: such is the first of the duties our times impose on those who lead society.

A world quite new needs a new political science . . .

This book does not follow precisely in the wake of any one. In writing it I have sought neither to serve nor combat any party; I have sought to see not other but farther than the parties, and while they were busy with tomorrow I have tried to think of the future.—Alexis de Tocqueville, in the Introduction to his *Democracy in America*, 1835.

Contents

xiii

MAP AND SPHERE BY *MARTHE RAJCHMAN*.

PROPOSAL

CHAPTER I

What This Book Is About

Now it is proposed to form a Government for men and not for Societies of men or States.—George Mason in the American Union's Constitutional Convention.

I am convinced that this is the safest course for your liberty, your dignity and your happiness . . . I frankly acknowledge to you my convictions, and I will freely lay before you the reasons on which they are founded . . . My arguments will be open to all, and may be judged of by all. They shall at least be offered in a spirit which will not disgrace the cause of truth.—Alexander Hamilton, opening *The Federalist*.

UNION

Now when man's future seems so vast catastrophe threatens to cut us from it. The dangers with which depression, dictatorship, false recovery and war are hemming us in have become so grave and imminent that we no longer need concern ourselves with proving how grave and near they are, certainly not since the September that reeled from Nuremberg through Berchtesgaden and Godesberg to end at Munich. We need concern ourselves instead with the problem of escaping them and the cruel dilemma Munich found and left democracy facing: Whether to risk peace or freedom? That is the problem with which this book is concerned. I believe there is a way through these dangers, and out of the dilemma, a way to do what we all want, to keep both peace and freedom, and keep them securely and be done with this nightmare. It promises not only escape but life such as I, too, never hoped could be lived in my time.

It is not an easy way—who expects one?—and to many it will seem at first too hard to be practical. But this is because its difficulties are greatest at the start; other ways that seem easier and more obvious to begin with grow increasingly hard and lead to frustration. How could we feel hemmed in if the way through were so easy to take or even see at first? For my part to find it I had to stumble on it, but once found it soon opened so widely as to make me wonder how I had ever failed so long to see it. I shall not be surprised then if you begin by being

1

skeptical or discouraged by the difficulties at the start, but I ask you
to remember that the essential question is: Which way will really lead
us through, not, which way starts most like a valley, least like a crack
in the wall?

Since 1933 when I stumbled on this way I have been exploring it
all I could and trying, in the writing of this book, to clear away the
things hiding it. By all the tests of common sense and experience I
find it to be our safest, surest way; it proves in fact to be nothing new
but a forgotten way which our fathers opened up and tried out successfully long ago when they were hemmed in as we are now. I believe
it will lead us through in time to avoid catastrophe if only we make the
most of the brief respite gained at Munich to agree to set out on it
without delay.

*The way through is Union now of the democracies that the North At-
lantic and a thousand other things already unite—Union of these few
peoples in a great federal republic built on and for the thing they share
most, their common democratic principle of government for the sake of
individual freedom.*

This Union would be designed (a) to provide effective common government in our democratic world in those fields where such common
government will clearly serve man's freedom better than separate governments, (b) to maintain independent national governments in all other
fields where such government will best serve man's freedom, and (c)
to create by its constitution a nucleus world government capable of
growing into universal world government peacefully and as rapidly as
such growth will best serve man's freedom.

By (a) I mean the Union of the North Atlantic democracies in these
five fields:

    a union citizenship
    a union defense force
    a union customs-free economy
    a union money
    a union postal and communications system.

By (b) I mean the Union government shall guarantee against all
enemies, foreign and domestic, not only those rights of man that are
common to all the democracies but every existing national or local right
that is not clearly incompatible with effective union government in the
five named fields. The union would guarantee the right of each democracy in it to govern independently all its home affairs and practise
democracy at home in its own tongue, according to its own customs
and in its own way, whether by republic or kingdom, presidential, cabinet
or other form of government, capitalist, social or other economic system.

By (c) I mean the founder democracies shall so constitute the Union as to encourage the nations outside it and the colonies inside it to seek to unite with it instead of against it. Admission to the Union and to all its tremendous advantages for the individual man and woman would from the outset be open equally to every democracy, now or to come, that guarantees its citizens the Union's minimum Bill of Rights.

The Great Republic would be organized with a view to its spreading peacefully round the earth as nations grow ripe for it. Its Constitution would aim clearly at achieving eventually by this peaceful, ripening, natural method the goal millions have dreamed of individually but never sought to get by deliberately planning and patiently working together to achieve it. That goal would be achieved by Union when every individual of our species would be a citizen of it, a citizen of a disarmed world enjoying world free trade, a world money and a world communications system. Then Man's vast future would begin.

This goal will seem so remote now as to discourage all but the strong from setting out for it or even acknowledging that they stand for it. It is not now so remote, it does not now need men so strong as it did when Lincoln preserved the American Union "for the great republic, for the principle it lives by and keeps alive, for man's vast future." It will no longer be visionary once the Atlantic democracies unite. Their Union is not so remote, and their Union is all that concerns us here and now.

THE AMERICAN WAY THROUGH

These proceedings may at first appear strange and difficult; but, like other steps which we have already passed over, will in a little time become familiar and agreeable.—Thomas Paine in *Common Sense.*

One hundred and fifty years ago a few American democracies opened this union way through. The dangers of depression, dictatorship and war, and the persuasiveness of clear thinking and courageous leadership led them then to abandon the heresy into which they had fallen. That heresy converted the sovereignty of the state from a mere means to individual freedom into the supreme end itself and produced the wretched "League of Friendship" of the Articles of Confederation. Abandoning all this the democrats of America turned back to their Declaration of Independence— of the independence of Man from the State and of the dependence of free men on each other for their freedom, the Declaration:

That all men are created equal, that they are endowed by their creator with certain inalienable rights, that among these are life, liberty and the pursuit of happiness, that to secure these rights governments are instituted among men, deriving their just powers from the consent of the governed, that whenever any form of government becomes destructive of these ends it is the right of the people to alter or to abolish it, and to institute new government, laying its foundations on such principles and organizing its powers in such form as to them shall seem most likely to effect their safety and happiness.

Finding they had wrongly applied this philosophy to establish Thirteen "free and independent States" and organize them as the League of Friendship so that "each State retains its sovereignty, freedom and independence," they applied it next as "We the people of the United States" to "secure the blessings of liberty to ourselves and our posterity." To do this they invented and set up a new kind of inter-state government. It has worked ever since as the other, league type has never worked. It has proved to be an "astonishing and unexampled success," as Lord Acton said, not only in America but wherever democracies have tried it regardless of conditions,—among the Germans, French and Italians of Switzerland, the English and French of Canada, the Dutch and English of the Union of South Africa. It is the kind of inter-state government that Lincoln, to distinguish it from the opposing type of government of, by and for states, called "government of the people, by the people, for the people." It is the way that I call Union.

To follow this way through now our Atlantic democracies—and first of all the American Union—have only to abandon in their turn the same heresy into which they have fallen, the heresy of absolute national sovereignty and its vain alternatives, neutrality, balance of power alliance or League of Nations. We the people of the Atlantic have only to cease sacrificing needlessly our individual freedom to the freedom of our nations, be true to our democratic philosophy and establish that "more perfect Union" toward which all our existing unions explicitly or implicitly aim.

Can we hope to find a safer, surer, more successful way than this? What democrat among us does not hope that this Union will be made some day? What practical man believes it will ever be made by mere dreaming or that the longer we delay starting to make it the sooner we shall have it? All it will take to make this Union—whether in a thousand years or now, whether long after catastrophe or just in time to prevent it,—is agreement by a majority to do it. Union is one of those things which to do we need but agree to do, and which we can not possibly ever do except by agreeing to do it. Why then can we not do it now in time for us to benefit by it and save millions of lives? Are we so much feebler than our fathers and our children that we can not do what our fathers did and what we expect our children to do? Why can not we agree on Union now?

Are not liberty and Union, now and forever, one and inseparable as in Webster's day? We can not be for liberty and against Union. We can not be both for and against liberty and Union now. We must choose.

DEFINITIONS

Democracy I would define more closely than the dictionary that defines it as "government by the people" (though I would not attempt needless precision and would indicate an ideal rather than an average). I would add with Lincoln, and I would stress, that democracy is also government for the people and of the people—the people being composed of individuals all given equal weight in principle.

Democracy to me is the way to individual freedom formed by men organizing themselves on the principle of the equality of man. That is, they organize government of themselves in the sense that their laws operate on them individually as equals. They organize government by themselves, each having an equal vote in making law. They organize government for themselves, to secure equally the freedom, in the broadest possible sense of the term, of each of them. By democracy I mean government of the totality by the majority for the sake equally of each minority of one, particularly as regards securing him such rights as freedom of speech, press and association. (If merely these three rights are really secured to all individuals they have the key, I believe, to all the other rights in all the other fields, political, juridical, economic, etc., that form part of individual freedom.)

Union to me is a democracy composed of democracies—an interstate government organized on the same basic principle, by the same basic method and for the same basic purpose as the democracies in it, and with the powers of government divided between the union and the states the better to advance this common purpose, individual freedom.

Union and *league* I use as opposite terms. I divide all organization of inter-state relations into two types, according to whether man or the state is the unit and the equality of man or the equality of the state is "the principle it lives by and keeps alive." I restrict the term *union* to the former, and the term *league* to the latter. To make clearer this distinction and what I mean by unit, these three points may help:

First, a league is a government of governments: It governs each people in its territory as a unit through that unit's government. Its laws can be broken only by a people acting through its government, and enforced only by the league coercing that people as a unit, regardless of whether individuals in it opposed or favored the violation. A union is a government of the people: It governs each individual in its territory directly as a unit. Its laws apply equally to each individual instead of to each government or people, can be broken only by individuals and can be enforced only by coercing and punishing individuals found guilty of having not simply favored but caused the violation.

Second, a league is a government by governments: Its laws are made by the peoples in it acting through its government, or the delegate of that government, as a unit of equal voting power regardless of the number of individuals in it. A union is a government by the people: Its laws are made by the individuals in it acting each through his representatives as a unit of equal voting power in choosing and changing them, each state's voting power in the union government being ordinarily in close proportion to its population. A union may allow in one house of its legislature (as in the American Senate) equal weight to the people of each state regardless of population. But it provides that such representatives shall not, as in a league, represent the state as a unit and be under the instructions of and subject to recall by its government, but shall represent instead the people of the state and be answerable to them.

Third, a league is a government for governments or states: It is made for the purpose of securing the freedom, rights, independence, sovereignty of each of the states in it taken as units equally. A union is a government for the people: It is made for the purpose of securing the freedom, rights, independence, sovereignty of each of the individuals in it taken as units equally. To secure the sovereignty of the state a league sacrifices the rights of men to justice (as in the first point) and to equal voting power (as in the second point), whereas a union sacrifices the sovereignty of the state to secure the rights of men: A league is made for the state, a union is made for man.

This may suffice to explain the sense in which the terms *democracy*, *union* and *league* are meant in this book.

FIFTEEN FOUNDER DEMOCRACIES

In the North Atlantic or founder democracies I would include at least these Fifteen (or Ten): The American Union, the British Commonwealth (specifically the United Kingdom, the Federal Dominion of Canada, the Commonwealth of Australia, New Zealand, the Union of South Africa,

Ireland), the French Republic, Belgium, the Netherlands, the Swiss Confederation, Denmark, Norway, Sweden and Finland.

These few include the world's greatest, oldest, most homogeneous and closely linked democracies, the peoples most experienced and successful in solving the problem at hand—the peaceful, reasonable establishment of effective inter-state democratic world government. Language divides them into only five big groups and for all practical political purposes, into only two, English and French. Their combined citizenry of nearly 300,000,000 is well balanced, half in Europe and half overseas. None of these democracies has been at war with any of the others for more than 100 years. Each now fears war, but not one fears war from the others.

These few democracies suffice to provide the nucleus of world government with the financial, monetary, economic and political power necessary both to assure peace to its members peacefully from the outset by sheer overwhelming preponderance and invulnerability, and practically to end the monetary insecurity and economic warfare now ravaging the whole world. These few divide among them such wealth and power that the so-called world political, economic and monetary anarchy is at bottom nothing but their own anarchy—since to end it they need only unite in establishing law and order among themselves.

Together these fifteen own almost half the earth, rule all its oceans, govern nearly half mankind. They do two-thirds of the world's trade, and most of this would be called their domestic trade once they united, for it is among themselves. They have more than 50 per cent control of nearly every essential material. They have more than 60 per cent control of such war essentials as oil, copper, lead, steel, iron, coal, tin, cotton, wool, wood pulp, shipping tonnage. They have almost complete control of such keys as nickel, rubber and automobile production. They possess practically all the world's gold and banked wealth. Their existing armed strength is such that once they united it they could radically reduce their armaments and yet gain a two-power standard of armed superiority over the powers whose aggression any of them now fears.

The Union's existing and potential power from the outset would be so gigantic, its bulk so vast, its vital centers so scattered, that Germany, Italy and Japan even put together could no more dream of attacking it than Mexico dreams of invading the American Union now. Once established the Union's superiority in power would be constantly increasing simply through the admission to it of outside nations. A number would no doubt be admitted immediately. By this process the absolutist powers would constantly become weaker and more isolated.

POWER AND RESPONSIBILITY

Tremendous world power brings with it tremendous responsibility for the world. It is no use blaming today's chaos or tomorrow's catastrophe on Mussolini and Hitler and the Japanese militarists. It is still less use to blame the Japanese and German and Italian peoples. It has never been in their combined power to establish law and order and peace in the world. They are not the source of the danger our whole species now faces, they are only its first victims. They are already living on war bread, going without butter and meat, dressing in shoddy, suffering censorship, hysterical patriotism, propaganda, forced loans, loss of liberty. They are today where we dread to be tomorrow. The anarchy among the democracies is already costing Germans, Italians and Japanese what it will cost us only if we let it go on. As Ambassador Bullitt put it in inaugurating the Lafayette monument at La Pointe-de-Grave Sept. 4, 1938:

It is not enough to observe with a sense of superiority the worst mistakes of the new fanaticisms. The origins of those fanaticisms lie in part in our own unwisdom. If our effort for peace is to achieve anything, it must be based on our ability to put ourselves in other men's shoes, and recognize the truth of the saying, "There, but for the grace of God, go I."

When the really powerful members of a community refuse to organize effective government in it, when each insists on remaining a law unto himself to the degree the democracies, and especially the United States, have done since the war, then anarchy is bound to result and the first to feel the effects of the chaos are bound to be the weaker members of the community. When the pinch comes the last to be hired are the first to be laid off, and the firms working on the narrowest margin are the first to be driven to the wall or to desperate expedients. That makes the pinch worse for the more powerful and faces them with new dangers, with threats of violence. It is human for them then to blame those they have unwittingly driven to desperation, but that does not change the source of the evil.

So it has been in the world. The younger democracies have been the first to go. The first of the great powers driven to desperate and violent measures have been those with the smallest margin. There is no doubt that their methods have since made matters worse and that there is no hope in following their lead. Their autocratic governments are adding to the world's ills but they are not the real cause of them. They are instead an effect of the anarchy among the powerful democracies.

The dictators are right when they blame the democracies for the world's condition, but they are wrong when they blame it on democracy. The anarchy comes from the refusal of the democracies to renounce enough of their national sovereignty to let effective world law and order be set up. But their refusal to do this, their maintenance of the state for its own sake, their readiness to sacrifice the lives and liberties of the citizens rather than the independence of the state,—this we know is not democracy. It is the core of absolutism. Democracy has been waning and autocracy waxing, the rights of men lessening and the rights of the state growing everywhere because the leading democracies have themselves led in practising *beyond* their frontiers autocracy instead of democracy.

Now many argue that the democracies must organize themselves or at least arm more heavily because the autocracies have formed the Triangular Pact. It is true that the rising power of autocracy increases the need for Union just as the spread of a contagious disease increases the need for quarantine and for organizing the healthy. But it is essential to remember that though the victims carry the disease they did not cause it, and that quarantine of the victims and organization of the healthy are aimed not against the victims but against the epidemic, the purpose being to end it both by restricting its spread and by curing its victims. Union does not seek to put the autocracies even in quarantine in any material sense; it seeks primarily to organize the healthy so as to overcome the disease.

It is wrong, all wrong, to conceive of Union as aimed against the nations of the Triangle. There is a world of difference between the motives behind Union and those behind either the present policy in each democracy of arming for itself or the proposals for alliance among the democracies. For such armament and such alliance are meant to maintain the one thing Union does attack in the one place Union does attack it—the autocratic principle of absolute national sovereignty in the democracies. Unlike armament and alliance policies, Union leads to no crusade against autocracy abroad, to no attempt to end war by war or make the world safe for democracy by conquering foreign dictatorship. Union is no religion for tearing out the mote from a brother's eye— and the eye, too—while guarding nothing so jealously, savagely, as the beam in one's own eye.

Union calls on each democracy to remove itself the absolutism governing its relations with the other democracies, and to leave it to the people of each dictatorship to decide then for themselves whether they will maintain or overthrow the absolutism governing them not only externally but internally. Union provides equally for the protection of the democracies against attack by foreign autocracy while it remains and for the admission of each autocratic country into the Union once it becomes a democracy in the only possible way—by the will and effort of its own people.

The problems the Triangular powers now raise,—equality, treaty revision, raw materials, a place in the sun, the have and have-not struggle, —Union would put on a new basis, that of equality among individual men instead of nations, thereby rendering these problems infinitely simpler and less dangerous. To attain the equality they crave the citizens of these absolutist nations would no longer need to sacrifice their individual freedom to their nation's military power, they would need instead to sacrifice dictatorship and military power to the restoration of their own individual liberties. By gaining membership for their nation in the Great Republic they would gain the equality they now demand and more, for they would enjoy precisely the same status, rights and opportunities as all citizens of this Union just as do the citizens of a state admitted to the American Union. But, to become thus equal sovereigns of the world, they would first have to prove, by overthrowing their autocrats and establishing democracies at home, that they believe in and hold supreme the equality and freedom of individual Man, regardless of the accident of birth. The attraction membership in the Union would have for outsiders would be so powerful and the possibility of conquering the Union would be so hopeless that once Union was formed the problem the absolutist powers now present could be safely left to solve itself. As their citizens turned these governments into democracies and entered the Union the arms burden on everyone would dwindle until it soon completely disappeared.

Thus, by the simple act of uniting on the basis of their own principle, the democracies today could immediately attain practical security while reducing armaments, and could proceed steadily to absolute security and absolute disarmament.

They could also increase enormously their trade and prosperity, reduce unemployment, raise their standard of living while lowering its cost. The imagination even of the economic expert can not grasp all the saving and profit democrats would realize by merely uniting their democracies in one free trade area.

They need only establish one common money to solve most if not all of today's more insoluble monetary problems, and save their citizens the tremendous loss inherent not only in depreciation, uncertainty, danger of currency upset from foreign causes, but also in the ordinary day-to-day monetary exchange among the democracies. The Union's money would be so stable that it would at once become the universal medium of exchange—a world money far more than was the pound sterling before the war.

Merely by the elimination of excessive government, needless bureaucracy, and unnecessary duplication which Union would automatically effect, the democracies could easily balance budgets while reducing taxation and debt. To an appalling degree taxes and government in the democracies today are devoted only to the maintenance of their separate sovereignties as regards citizenship, defense, trade, money and communications. To a still more appalling degree they are quite unnecessary and thwart instead of serve the purpose for which we established those governments and voted those taxes, namely the maintenance of our own freedom and sovereignty as individual men and women.

By uniting, the democracies can serve this purpose also by greatly facilitating the distribution of goods, travel and the dissemination of knowledge and entertainment. With one move, the simple act of Union, the democrats can make half the earth equally the workshop and the playground of each of them.

Establishment of Union involves difficulties, of course, but the difficulties are transitional, not permanent ones. All other proposals in this field even if realizable could solve only temporarily this or that problem in war, peace, armaments, tariffs, monetary stabilization. These proposals would be as hard to achieve as Union, yet all together they could not do what the one act of Union would—permanently eliminate all these problems. These are problems for which the present dogma of nationalism is to blame. We can not keep it and solve them. We can not eliminate them until we first eliminate it.

WHICH WAY ADVANCES FREEDOM MORE?

This does not mean eliminating all national rights. It means eliminating them only where elimination clearly serves the individuals concerned, and maintaining them in all other respects,—not simply where maintenance clearly serves the general individual interest but also in all doubtful cases. The object of Union being to advance the freedom and individuality of the individual, it can include no thought of standardizing or regimenting him, nor admit the kind of centralizing that increases governmental power over him. These are evils of nationalism, and Union would end them. Union comes to put individuality back on the throne that nationality has usurped.

Everywhere nationalism in its zeal to make our nations instead of ourselves self-sufficing and independent is centralizing government, giving it more and more power over the citizen's business and life, putting more and more of that power in one man's hands, freeing the government from its dependence on the citizen while making him more and more dependent on it—on the pretext of keeping him independent of other governments. Everywhere the national state has tended to become a super-state in its power to dispose of the citizen, his money, job and life. Everywhere nationalism has been impoverishing the citizen with taxes, unemployment, depression, and it is poverty—it is the desert, not the jungle,—that stunts variety in life, that standardizes. Everywhere nationalism is casting the citizen increasingly in militarism's uniform robot mold.

Union would let us live more individual lives. Its test for deciding whether in a given field government should remain national or become union is this: Which would *clearly* give the individual more freedom? Clearly the individual freedom of Americans or Frenchmen would gain nothing from making Union depend on the British converting the United Kingdom into a republic. Nor would the British be the freer for making Union depend on the Americans and French changing to a monarchy. There are many fields where it is clear that home rule remains necessary for individual freedom, where the maintenance of the existing variety among the democracies helps instead of harms the object of Union.

It is clear too that a Union so secure from foreign aggression as this one would be would not need that homogeneity in population that the much weaker American Union feels obliged to seek. Our Union could afford to encourage the existing diversity among its members as a powerful safeguard against the domestic dangers to individual freedom. Just as the citizen could count on the Union to protect his nation from invasion or from dictatorship rising from within, he could count on his nation's autonomy to protect him from a majority in the Union becoming locally oppressive. The existence of so many national autonomies in the Union would guarantee each of them freedom to experiment politically, economically, socially and would save this Union from the danger of hysteria and stampede to which more homogeneous unions are exposed.

Clearly, individual freedom requires us to maintain national autonomy in most things but no less clearly it requires us to abolish that autonomy in a few things. There is no need to argue that you and I have nothing to lose and much to gain by becoming equal citizens in the Union while retaining our national citizenship. Clearly you and I would be freer had we this Great Republic's guarantee of our rights as men, its security against the armaments burden, military servitude, war. It is self-evident that you and I would live an easier and a richer life if through half the world we could do business with one money and postage, if through half the world we were free to buy in the cheapest market what we need to buy and free to sell in the dearest market what we have to sell.

In five fields—citizenship, defense, trade, money, and communications —we are sacrificing now the individual freedom we could safely, easily have. On what democratic ground can we defend this great sacrifice? We make it simply to keep our democracies independent of each other. We can not say that we must maintain the state's autonomy in these few fields in order to maintain it in the many fields where it serves our freedom, for we know how to keep it in the latter without keeping it in the former. We have proved that in the American Union, the Swiss Union, and elsewhere.

What then can we say to justify our needless sacrifice of man to the state in these five fields, a sacrifice made only to maintain the nation for the nation's sake? How can we who believe the state is made for man escape the charge that in these five fields we are following the autocratic principle that man is made for the state? How can we plead not guilty of treason to democracy? Are we not betraying our principles, our interests, our freedom, ourselves and our children? We are betraying too our fathers. They overthrew the divine right of kings and founded our democracies not for the divine right of nations but for the rights of Man.

Clearly absolute national sovereignty has now brought us to the stage where this form of government has become destructive of the ends for which we form government, where democrats to remain democrats must use their right "to abolish it, and to institute new government, laying its foundations on such principles and organizing its power in such form, as to them shall seem most likely to effect their safety and happiness."

Clearly prudence dictates that we should lay our new government's foundations on such principles and organize its powers in such form as have stood the test of experience. Clearly democracy bids us now unite our unions of free men and women in one world Union of the free.

THE ALTERNATIVES TO UNION

Fantastic? Visionary? What are the alternatives? There are only these: Either the democracies must try to stand separately or they must try to stand together on some other basis than union, that is, they must organize themselves as a league or an alliance.

Suppose we try to organize as a league. That means seeking salvation from what Alexander Hamilton called "the political monster of an *imperium in imperio*." We adopt a method which has just failed in the League of Nations, which before that led the original thirteen American democracies to a similar failure, and failed the Swiss democracies, the Dutch democracies, and the democracies of ancient Greece. We adopt a method which has been tried time and again in history and has never worked, whether limited to few members or extended to many, a method which, we shall see, when we analyze it later, is thoroughly undemocratic, untrustworthy, unsound, unable either to make or to enforce its law in time. Is it not fantastic to expect to get the American people, after 150 years of successful experience with union and after their rejection of the League of Nations, to enter any league? Can any but the visionary expect us to go through the difficulty that organization of the democracies on any basis entails—all for what we know to be a political monstrosity?

Suppose we try to organize instead an alliance of the democracies. But an alliance is simply a looser, more primitive form of league, one that operates secretly through diplomatic tunnels rather than openly through regular assemblies. It is based on the same unit as a league, —the state,—and on the same principle,—that the maintenance of the freedom of the state is the be-all and the end-all of political and economic policy. It is at most an association (instead of a government) of governments, by governments, for governments. It has all the faults of a league with most of them intensified and with some more of its own added.

Though possible as a temporary stopgap an alliance, as a permanent organization, has never been achieved and is practically impossible to achieve among as many as fifteen states. The fact that the states are democracies makes a permanent alliance among them not less but more impractical and inconceivable. For the more democratic a state is, then the more its government is dependent on public opinion and the more its people are loath to be entangled automatically in the wars of governments over which they have not even the control a league gives, and the more its foreign policy is subject to change. But the more all this is true of a state the harder it is either for it to enter an alliance or for its allies to trust it if it does.

A big alliance being looser than a league, the fact that the democracies preferred the former would show the strength of their desire to keep apart. That would further encourage their enemies to gamble on exploiting this separatist tendency till they overcame them and their satellites one by one. It would not encourage them so much as the existing nationalism among the democracies which has already led the autocrats to invade China, Ethiopia, Spain, Austria and, practically, Czechoslovakia, but the difference would not be enough to matter.

The best way to prevent war is to make attack hopeless. It will not be hopeless while the autocrats, who by their nature are gamblers with abnormal confidence in themselves and their luck, have any ground left to gamble either that the democracies can be divided or that the inter-democracy organization is too cumbersome and loose to resist surprise attack. An alliance can not long make this gamble hopeless.

The basic flaw in an alliance of democracies is the nationalist philosophy responsible for it. If the desire to avoid commitments is strong enough to prevent a democracy from forming a union or even a league with the others, it will also prevent its allying with them until the danger is so great and imminent that the alliance comes too late to prevent war. The alliance may come in time to promise to win a war that pure nationalism could not hope to win, and to win it at greater cost than could a league. But it can not promise, as Union can, to prevent the war—and that is the main thing.

Even the war danger before 1914 failed to drive the British and French democracies into a real alliance; they got no further than a "cordial understanding." It took three years of war then to bring them to agree on a supreme command. Now the war danger has driven the British to a much closer understanding with the French than in 1914, and they have already agreed on a supreme command. But by the time the rising threat from the other side drove them to this, Germany, Italy and Japan already felt too strong to be discouraged by it. And so the Anglo-French accord has utterly failed to remove the war danger.

Even the world war after it engulfed the United States could not persuade the United States to ally with the other democracies; it would only "associate" itself with them. If it is not visionary to expect the United States to enter an "entangling alliance" now, what is it?

"It is necessary," declared Secretary Hull, Aug. 16, 1938, "that as a nation we become increasingly resolute in our desire and increasingly effective in our efforts to contribute along with other peoples—always within the range of our traditional policies of non-entanglement—to the support of the only program which can turn the tide of lawlessness and place the world firmly upon the one and only roadway that can lead to enduring peace and security." By excluding all solutions contrary to "our traditional policies of non-entanglement" this champion of world law and order did not exclude union, for there can be no more tradi-

tional American policy than this; no American considers as an entanglement the union of the Thirteen democracies nor the union of their Union
with the Republic of Texas. By entanglement Americans mean alliances
and leagues; these are the solutions which Secretary Hull warns are
excluded.

But suppose the United States could be brought into an alliance. On
what reality rests the belief that this would prevent war with the opposing alliance? The lack of machinery for reaching and executing international agreement in the economic and financial and monetary fields
in time to be effective did much to throw the world into the depression
that led us through Manchuria and Hitler and Ethiopia to where we
are today. What could be more fantastic than the hope that any conceivable alliance could provide this machinery, or that without this machinery we can long avoid depression and war?

THE WORST ALTERNATIVE

Only one thing could be more visionary and fantastic, and that is the
third possible alternative to Union, the one that would seek salvation
in rejecting every type of interstate organization and in pursuing a policy
of pure nationalism,—the policy of isolationism, neutrality, of each trusting to his own armaments, military and economic. For if the democracies
are not to try to stand together by union or league or alliance, the only
thing left for them is to try to stand alone. Consider the experience of
the powers that have tried this alternative.

Once each of the Triangular powers believed so much in its ability
to stand alone and insisted so much on its right to be a law unto itself
that each defied the League and left it. Each seemed at first to prove
its case and win by the operation. Yet in fact they proved and won so
little that they have all had to recant their principle of standing alone and
organize themselves in a Triangular pact. They found that neither the
things they seized alone—Chinese territory, Ethiopian territory, Austria,
the demilitarized Rhineland and the right to arm without limit,—nor the
fact that they acted each for self made them more secure. Each instead
now feels much more exposed than it did before. That has been shown
by the way they each sought security, first, by increasing their armaments and then, when that failed to give them security, by organizing
themselves more and more. When Mussolini took care to step into the
Triangular pact before daring to step out of the Geneva Covenant he
gave a vivid example of how impossible nationalism has become and how
much nations need to work together.

At most the efforts of the Triangular powers to become politically and economically independent are not making them more independent, they are simply making them less dependent on one group of states, the democracies, and more dependent on another group, the Triangle. The more they develop these relations among themselves the more they will need to organize them. Every state they succeed in adding to this group can only involve them more deeply in the problem of how to organize it,—and they too have only these alternatives: alliance, league or union.

The experience of the United States shows that even the most powerful nations can not get what they want by isolationism. The United States sought through the nineteen twenties to preserve its peace and prosperity by isolationism. It did remain in peace, but isolationism can not be given the credit for this since Britain and France followed the opposite policy of cooperation through the League of Nations and they, too, kept out of war. As for prosperity, isolationism failed to preserve it; depression struck the United States hardest.

Hard times led to war dangers which the United States in 1935 sought to lessen by the neutrality variation of isolationism. It adopted the policy of advising potential aggressors and victims that it not merely would not attempt to distinguish between them but would furnish supplies only to the belligerent who could come, get and pay cash for them. What has happened since this policy was adopted? Italy invaded Ethiopia and conquered with poison gas. Militarism and fascism began fighting it out with democracy and communism in Spain. Japan invaded a huge part of China, bombing almost indiscriminately. Germany violated the Locarno treaty, and got by bullying all of Austria and much of Czechoslovakia. The naval limitation treaties broke down, the League broke down, the Peace Pact and the Nine Power Pact broke down, all the world's peaceful machinery broke down, and "recovery" sagged into "recession."

No "peaceful" years in modern times, not even those preceding 1914, have been so full of war and so charged with accumulating dangers to peace as those since 1935. Even if it could be argued that the adoption of the American neutrality policy did not help bring on the disasters that followed, the point is that it was adopted to lessen the war danger. It must be admitted that there is much more danger of war now than there was when this policy was adopted, and so it must be admitted that it has already failed.

The neutrality policy, moreover, was designed to require the least armaments; it left only the American continent to be protected against the raids of belligerents who had the ships to carry off American goods but lacked the gold with which to pay for them. Yet the United States has never armed so heavily in peace time as it has since it adopted this policy. And the end is not near.

In proposing, Jan. 4, 1938, that Congress spend $990,000,000 on armaments, President Roosevelt referred "specifically to the possibility that, due to world conditions over which this nation has no control, I may find it necessary to request additional appropriations for national defense."

Clearly he did not expect this huge expenditure to remove the cause for it and put under control those "world conditions over which this nation has no control." By the time Congress adjourned in June this expenditure had not only passed the billion dollar mark but the Vinson Act had called for another billion to be spent on naval construction alone. By Oct. 14 the press was reporting Washington's intention to add another and bigger increase to this program. Yet has the United States come nearer to controlling world conditions? What reason is there to hope that it will gain control of them by spending still more on its armaments? Need it not fear the opposite? It is now spending twice as much on arms as it did in 1933 and its control over world conditions has meanwhile lessened.

"Furthermore," President Roosevelt added in his January message, "the economic situation may not improve and if it does not I expect the approval of Congress and the public for additional appropriations"—additional to those of $1,138,000,000 he then proposed for "recovery and relief." Again there was no promise, only fear of failure. Within a few months President Roosevelt had tripled this figure, but still without a promise of success. What promise could there be since obviously the billions already spent had not achieved their purpose? Plainly those world conditions beyond the control of even the United States endanger it economically as well as politically, plainly the only hope for recovery as well as for security lies in gaining control over them, and plainly there is no hope of gaining it by national action alone.

Here is a policy which has had the overwhelming support of the American people, most of all in its basic isolationist principle. It has resulted in the national debt reaching $38,000,000,000 while the national and world situations have darkened, and so it is proposed to add more billions to the debt—and the proposal is accompanied with a warning that the failure may continue. Is not this proposal "fantastic," and is it not sane to propose instead that the democracies gain control of their common world by organizing effective government in it, by each bringing its part of the conditions now outside the control of the others under the common control of them all through Union?

THE MUNICH METHOD

I for one am firmly resolved to hold to this vow: So long as I am where I am there shall not be war. Aristide Briand, addressing the Assembly of the League of Nations, Sept. 11, 1930.

We are in the presence of a disaster of the first magnitude . . . There was no difficulty at all in having cordial relations between the British and German peoples . . . Never could there be friendship between the British democracy and the Nazi Power, that power which spurned Christian ethics, which cheered its onward course by a barbarous paganism, which vaunted the spirit of aggression and conquest, which derived strength and perverted pleasure from persecution, and used with pitiless brutality the threat of murderous force . . . The policy of submission will carry with it restrictions upon the freedom of speech and debate in Parliament, on public platforms, and discussions in the Press.—Winston Churchill, House of Commons, Oct. 6, 1938.

Suppose we dilute this policy so that only some democracies, such as the United States, Switzerland, Belgium, Holland, Denmark, Norway, Sweden and Finland seek peace and freedom in neutrality while others, notably Britain and France, depend on alliance. This is what we are now doing. Suppose we continue on this road that led to Munich and put our trust in a Four Power pact or any other variant of the balance of power theory.

Those to whom Munich brought hope of peace in our time seem to have gained it chiefly from these sources: The intense desire for peace and dread of war every people showed in the Sudeten crisis, the part this feeling played in preventing war, and the belief that Munich removed the most dangerous of the European causes for war. This belief seems based on Chancellor Hitler's statement that this was his last European territorial demand, or on belief that all the remaining questions can be settled now by further great power "consultations" or by a "general settlement" through conference of everyone on everything, or on belief that since the great democracies would not fight for Czechoslovakia they will not fight for states which do not have that democracy's claim on their sympathies and which are now in the line of German expansion,— Poland, Lithuania, Hungary, Rumania, Russia.

There is no doubt that the immediate popular reception of Prime Minister Chamberlain's flight to Berchtesgaden and of the Munich agreement proved the existence everywhere of a powerful desire for peace. This helped prevent war then, and it remains a power that must be taken into account in future as contributing both positively to facilitate the trend toward appeasement and negatively to brake the trend toward war. But if the mere existence of power sufficed to get results we could run our factories simply by making water steam; we would not need to bother about making machinery to center the steam on the piston-head. If the quantity of power available is the main thing we should be satisfied with turbines so crude that they will work only when the river is at flood.

The Sudeten German crisis proved how deeply defective is our machinery for harnessing to peace mankind's will for peace. It was so defective that time and again that month millions thought war inevitable. Each time they found themselves saved by a miracle only to find themselves next week in need of a greater miracle to save them from its consequences. The magician who pulls rabbit after rabbit from an empty hat is sure to be applauded by the famished, and when he has nothing left to pull out except a rabbit's foot the applause will be greater because the hunger and the willingness to believe in magic have grown greater too.

By returning repeatedly to tremble on the brink of an abyss we may learn to balance better but we do not avoid the danger of falling. As Pope wrote of vice:

> *War is a monster of so frightful mien,*
> *As to be hated needs but to be seen;*
> *Yet seen too oft, familiar with her face*
> *We first endure, then pity, then embrace.*

The fact is that as the war danger has grown the readiness of every people to plunge into it has grown, too. When Germany occupied the Rhineland with a relatively small force in 1936 France did not call two classes to the colors, Britain did not mobilize the fleet and the United States did not intervene to pin responsibility on Chancellor Hitler. They made these moves in 1938 after all the horrors of war in Spain and China had been drummed into them and after they faced a semi-mobilized Germany. How can we hope that we shall avoid war because we lived all September with the spectre of war, when the American people was not kept out of war but drawn into it by living for three years with world war itself?

Not only psychologically but militarily the world is readier for war now than it was before the Munich meeting. No aggressor will go to war in the hope of its being long-drawn-out; to attack he must gamble on winning quickly by overwhelming surprise. This gamble has proved wrong in Spain and China but that will no more keep others from trying their luck than deaths of climbers kept other men from trying to scale the Eiger Wall until they did succeed.

To win a lightning war one must have a military force that is at once exceptionally well-prepared, exceptionally well-trained and exceptionally numerous; to defeat a lightning war all this is needed, too. Because this is the kind of war for which Europe must prepare and because neither side had had the dress rehearsal that is the *sine qua non* of success in such a fast and dangerous enterprise, I said to any who asked my opinion before and at the worst of the September crisis that I believed there would be no general European war this year but a dress rehearsal that would leave the danger of war next year much greater. Where governments once could be content with the practice given by war games on the scale of a division or an army corps, they must now practice on a far greater scale and test out too their machinery for mobilizing their army, their industry and their public opinion. The Sudeten German crisis allowed every great power in Europe to make these tests. Since then leaders in every country have been showing that Prime Minister Chamberlain spoke for them all when he told Parliament Oct. 6, 1938:

One good thing at any rate has come out of this emergency through which we have passed. It has thrown a vivid light on our preparations for defence, on their strength and their weakness. I would not think we were doing our duty if we had not already ordered that a prompt and thorough inquiry should be made to cover the whole of our preparations, military and civil, in order to see, in the light of what happened during these hectic days, what further steps may be necessary to make good our deficiencies in the shortest possible time.

I do not say that the September scene was consciously staged by Machiavellians, nor do I mean that it was never in danger of getting out of hand. I say only that the underlying situation tended at that time to produce a dress rehearsal and to keep it one, and that as one result every government is now correcting the faults this test revealed in its war machine. Each is already much better prepared than it was in July for the lightning war it seeks to save itself with or from.

There remains the belief that Munich ended the most dangerous European cause for war. How can democrats base their hope for peace in our time on Chancellor Hitler's statement that the Sudetenland is his last European territorial demand? Before *anschluss* he promised to respect Austrian independence, during *anschluss* he had Marshall Goering reassure President Benes as he himself reassured the British Prime Minister in September—and then at Saarbruecken Oct. 9, 1938 he boasted that he had made a New Year's vow to himself to bring both Austria and

Sudetenland into Germany. "At the beginning of this year," he said, "I reached the determination to bring back to the Reich the 10,000,000 Germans who stood apart from us." How can one trust a man who can keep his secret vows to himself only by breaking his public vows to others?

Suppose that despite such questions as the Polish corridor we can trust Herr Hitler this time; can we reasonably expect one in his shoes to trust that Mr. Chamberlain will long remain Prime Minister? Does he not have reason for his fear in that Saarbruecken speech that "a Duff Cooper or an Eden or a Churchill" may come to power? Herr Hitler obviously does not believe that even the Germans would keep his own regime in power were they free to choose; how can he trust the British people not to use their freedom to choose leaders who will stand against him? How can peace be made on a basis of mutual trust between democracies and dictatorships when the democracies can have no guarantee that the dictator will keep his word, and the dictator can have no guarantee that the democracies will keep in power those whose word strengthens him?

Shall we depend on Four Power pacts and/or conferences to impose and/or negotiate a general settlement of all remaining questions? A Four Power pact excludes Russia from the meeting room but not from the world that the pact must work in. The same is true of Japan and the United States. To omit Russia from the pact practically means removing Russia's weight from the Franco-British side while neither replacing it with the United States nor removing Japan's weight from the other side. It also means freeing Germany and Japan to absorb as much of Russia as they can. This would seem to be making not peace but the kind of power against which Mr. Chamberlain himself said he would fight. And what faith can we Americans have in such a method, even if it leaves us on the sidelines at our own demand?

LEAVING "EUROPE" TO THE EUROPEANS

It is important that our people should not overlook problems and issues which, though they lie beyond our borders, may, and probably will, have a vital influence on the United States of the future.—President Franklin D. Roosevelt, Aug. 14, 1936.

In "leaving Europe to the Europeans," do we not leave our peace and freedom to them too? We see that if peace is upset in Europe we shall suffer too, but we do not seem to see that by the present policy we entrust our future blindly to Britain and France, we depend on their statesmanship to keep us out of war and on their arms to keep autocracy from invading America. We see the advantage of keeping our peace and freedom, but from the way we talk about never fighting again off American soil it is clear we do not see the advantage of the policy that has kept invasion from British soil since 1066. That is a policy of not waiting till the conqueror comes to lay waste one's home but of going out to stop him while he is far away and relatively weak. If we think it wise to warn the world that we will fight for our freedom, is it not still wiser to add the warning that we will begin to fight for it on its European frontiers? It is better not to fight if one can help it, but if one must fight is it not better to fight away from home?

If we could trust the British and French governments to preserve our peace and freedom safely for us, yet to leave the burden to them alone would still be unworthy of us. And can we have this faith in them? Obviously we do not have it. We made that clear after what we called the "Hoare-Laval deal." But did we improve things for ourselves by the paradoxical policy we then adopted of leaving our fate all the more in their hands by keeping ours tied with the neutrality act? Has it not led us straight to Munich?

We may prove to the hilt that the European democracies are not up to our standards, but if so is that an argument for trusting the future of our freedom to them as we are doing? It may be that we are in position to sit by and find fault with others who are at the danger point, it may be that it is better that those in our position should find fault than keep still—after all, if those who are in the most secure position do not speak out for what is right, who will?—all this may be true, but the position it leaves us in is not always becoming to a man.

I can not say the British and French "sold out" Prague when they sought nothing for it except a peace that benefits me too. I can only say that if they sacrificed Czechoslovakia to save themselves from war they followed a lead we gave them long before. For was it not partly to save ourselves from having to go to war for Czechoslovakia that we refused the Wilsonian Covenant? I can not condemn Messrs. Chamberlain and Daladier, but I must ask those Americans who condemn them as being both knaves and fools how they can then urge on us an isolationist policy that means trusting more than ever Europeans to save us from the consequences of war?

Suppose that, instead of everyone depending for peace on a Four Power pact, we all turn back to the general conference method. It failed before under easier circumstances, but suppose it will succeed now— though this is supposing to the point of dreaming. Success means the restoration to Germany of the Polish corridor, Memel, Eupen, colonies, also the restoration of the international gold standard, the return to normal trade barriers, and so on. What guarantee of peace is all that dream if realized? All that dream was already real once—in July, 1914.

We come to those who believe that the corner is turned for better or worse since democracies that would not fight for the only democracy east of Switzerland can not go to war to protect the oil wells of Rumania, or to save a Poland that resorts to partition from perishing again by partition. Is this idea well-founded either as fact or as a basis for expecting peace in our time? Consider but one thing:

Munich leaves Europe with two "Belgiums," No. 1 southwest and No. 2 southeast of Germany, and Britain has now promised to guarantee the neutrality and integrity of No. 2—though it is almost surrounded by Germany—as well as the frontiers of No. 1. Belgium No. 2 is stripped down now on the moral side to a democracy that is purely Czechoslovak. The self-determination principle is now all on its side and it is strengthened by its self-sacrificing acceptance of the wrongs done it for the sake of peace. On the strategic side it is stripped down to the bones of the Bohemian quadrilateral round Prague of which Bismarck said, "Who holds that, holds Europe." That is why Czechoslovakia is to be neutralized. Its neutrality is made and is liable to be broken for the same considerations that led to the creation and then to the violation of the neutrality of Belgium No. 1.

Czechoslovakia remains a strongly armed base in position to endanger on the left flank German aggressive expansion toward Rumania and the Ukraine and to endanger on the right flank German aggressive expansion toward the Polish corridor. Czechoslovakia can be turned in a twinkling into an air base from which the warplanes of Russia—excluded at Munich from the pledge to respect Czech neutrality—can attack the heart of Germany and harass or cut the communications of a German force attacking Russia through Rumania or Poland. At the teeth of the upper jaw of Germany lies the great mining and industrial area of Silesia, at the teeth of the lower jaw lies Vienna. The distance between these teeth—if they cut violently through Czechoslovakia—is about ten times shorter than their line of communications while they go respectfully round the Bohemian quadrilateral. In these circumstances can one reasonably expect Chancellor Hitler, who has openly proclaimed his aggressive intentions against Russia, to treat his Czech neutrality pledge as other than a scrap of paper the day his war with Russia starts?

If he violates Czech neutrality Britain must then either follow suit and treat as a scrap of paper its own guarantee of Czech neutrality against this very danger, or it must go to war against the violator. If it does the former its moral position is almost as bad as Germany's and its political and military positions become much worse than Germany's. Its position as the chief bulwark of democracy in Europe goes down, down and down. By this course it is accepting the one thing that Prime Minister Chamberlain in his moving radio broadcast Sept. 27, 1938, said he himself would go to war rather than accept:

I am myself a man of peace to the depths of my soul. Armed conflict between nations is a nightmare to me. But if I were convinced that any nation had made up its mind to dominate the world by fear of its force, I should feel that it must be resisted. Under such a domination life for people who believe in liberty would not be worth living; but war is a fearful thing and we must be very clear, before we embark on it that it is really the great issues that are at stake.

By the other course Britain and France would fight—but they would be fighting no more for Rumania or Poland than they fought in 1914 for Serbia. They would be fighting for the neutrality of the Czech democracy, for the respect of treaties, for the defense of individual freedom everywhere. Can we really base our hopes for peace in our time on the assumption that there is now nothing left for which the great democracies would fight?

THE PERIL RETURNS—ONLY GREATER AND NEARER

For our own people the issue becomes terrifying. They desire peace ardently and sincerely. They are ready to make sacrifices in order to strengthen the foundations of peace. They seek freedom of thought, of race, of worship, which every week become more restricted in Europe. The conviction is growing that continual retreat can only lead to ever-widening confusion. They know that a stand must be made. They say "Let it be not made too late."—Anthony Eden, speaking at Stratford-on-Avon, Sept. 21, 1938.

How can we but be alarmed at the Munich method of appeasement when its German partner who rose to power by tracing the evils we suffer to the Treaty of Versailles seeks to remedy them by practising in turn what he condemned? Germany was at least consulted at Versailles before the signature of the treaty; Czechoslovakia was not even invited to Munich. If Versailles can be called a *diktat*, what must Munich be called? How can those who believe events have proved that peace can not be made by *diktat*, believe that peace in our time can be secured by the Munich method?

How can we but be still more alarmed when the great champions of the Munich method have themselves made clear that their alarm now is greater than it was before Munich? When in indorsing Munich Lord Baldwin came out in favor of the mobilization of British industry for war? When the great London newspaper that opened September, 1938, with a plea for a plebiscite in Sudetenland ended September by announcing and upholding the Munich accord in one column while opening in the adjoining column a campaign for conscription in Britain? Most alarming of all, Mr. Chamberlain himself told the House of Commons Oct. 4, 1938: "For a long period now we have been engaged in this country on a great program of rearmament which is daily increasing in pace and in volume. Let no one think that because we have signed this agreement between the four Powers at Munich we can afford to relax our efforts in regard to that program at this moment."

In finishing the debate Oct. 7 all he could answer to the comments this provoked was to edge closer to conscription ("I would not like to commit myself now until I have had a little time for reflection as to what further it may seem good to ask the nation to do"), after saying:

"I am told that the policy which I have tried to describe is inconsistent with the continuance, and much more inconsistent with the acceleration, of our present program of armaments. I am asked how I can reconcile an appeal to the country to support the continuance of this program with the words which I used when I came back from Munich the other day and spoke of my belief that we might have peace for our time.

"I hope that hon. members will not be disposed to read into words used in moments of some emotion, after a long and exhausting day, after I had driven through miles of excited, enthusiastic, cheering people, something more than they were intended to convey. (Ministerial cheers.) I do indeed believe that we may yet secure peace in our time (No cheers), but I never meant to suggest that we would do that by disarming until we can induce others to disarm too."

How is this to be done? In the same speech Mr. Chamberlain said, "I say that it is no use to call a conference of the world, including these totalitarian Powers, until you are sure that they are going to attend, and not only that they are going to attend but that they are going to attend with the intention of aiding you in the policy on which you have set your heart." Apart from trusting in "the universal aversion to war" as "the strongest argument against the inevitability of war," Mr. Chamberlain in this speech based his hopes as regards disarmament and peace in general on the following policy:

"What is the alternative to this bleak and barren policy of the inevitability of war? In my view it is that we should seek, by every means

in our power, to avoid war by analyzing its possible causes and by trying to remove them by discussing in a spirit of collaboration and good
will. I can not believe that such a program would be rejected by the
people of the country even if it does mean the establishment of personal
contact with dictators, and talk, man to man, on the basis that each is
free to maintain his own ideas of the internal government of his country,
willing to allow that other systems may suit better other people."

This is the sort of thing in which British peace-lovers put their trust
before the World War. They were arming then too, they were talking,
then too, with Berlin man to man about disarmament and trying to remove the causes of war—by, for example, secretly dickering to satisfy
Germany's demand for "a place in the sun" with part of the colonies of
Portugal, Britain's oldest ally. The parallel today with the period that
preceded World War once before in our time is only too clear.

There is the same political and strategic balance between the war-
breeding grounds of eastern Europe and the western Mediterranean, between the Danube valley and the Straits of Gibraltar. But where peace
then trembled between the annexation of Bosnia and the Balkan wars to
the East and the conflict over Morocco in the West, it now trembles between Czechoslovakia and Spain. The main difference is that the danger
has moved North, closer to the heart of civilization.

There are the same dramatic "peace" agreements, reached only more
melodramatically now because of more modern methods of communication and mass propaganda, with the same net results. But where
the Agadir peace resulted in France making service for three years oblig-
atory for every man, the Munich peace is no sooner signed than Britain
itself moves toward conscription. The main difference is that military
servitude is moving West, closer to the heart of individual freedom.

There are the same frantic and vain last minute appeals for a conference by a power that allows the aggressor to hope that it will not fight
against him if he goes to war. But where these appeals were made in
1914 by London, they are made now by Washington. This time they
succeeded? When did Chancellor Hitler answer President Roosevelt's
second appeal? When was the "conference of all the nations directly interested in the present controversy" that he then suggested held? The
main change is that this time to get even to Agadir a President West of
the Atlantic instead of a Foreign Minister West of the Channel had to beg
for a conference.

The outstanding change is that all along the line the catastrophe is
developing on a greater scale and at a faster rate and moving North and
West,—nearer, nearer, nearer to ourselves.

BALANCE OR UNBALANCE OF POWER?

Never in post-war history has the menace that hangs over European economy made itself felt more, the menace of grave disorders capable, if we do not promptly remedy them, of leading us in the end to a dangerous rupture of the balance to the detriment of all . . .

At this moment the hope of millions expects from us more than an affirmation, it expects the demonstration of a will for peace, effective and constructive . . . —Aristide Briand, addressing the Commission of Enquiry for European Union, Jan. 16, 1931.

The balance of power theory that is preparing catastrophe now as then—there is no more sterile, illusory, fantastic, exploded and explosive peace policy than the balance of power. Look at it. Take it apart. What does it mean in common words? It means seeking to get stability by seeking to equalize the weight on both sides of the balance. One can conceive of reaching stability this way—but for how long and at the cost of what violent ups and downs before? And when the scales do hang in perfect balance it takes but a breath, only the wind that goes with a word spoken or shrieked in the Hitlerian manner, to end at once the stability, the peace that has been achieved. Stability can never be more in danger, more at the mercy of the slightest mistake, accident or act of ill will than at the very moment when the ideal of the balance of power is finally achieved.

Who would ever suggest that we seek to keep the peace in our town or state or nation by striving to arrange a perfect balance of power between law-keepers and law-breakers, between G-men and gangsters? It is only when we let our fancies roam beyond the nation and out into the world that we indulge in such blundering buncombe— and it is precisely in this great field that a mistake is worse than a murder.

We do not and can not get peace by balance of power; we can and do get it by *unbalance* of power. We get it by putting so much weight surely on the side of law that the strongest possible law-breaker can not possibly offset it and is bound to be overwhelmed. We get lasting stability by having one side of the balance safely on the ground and the other side high in the air.

Even the moment's stability which the balance of power may theoretically attain is a delusion since each side knows it can not last. Therefore neither can believe in it and the nearer they come to it the harder both must struggle to prevent it by adding more weight on their side so as to enjoy the lasting peace that unbalance of power secures,—and the race is to the strongest.

The race is to the strongest, and the democracies, by scrapping all this balance of power and neutrality nonsense and directly seeking peace in the unbalance of power that Union alone can quickly and securely give them, can still win, for they need but unite their strength to be by far the strongest.

The problem facing the democracies is simply one of uniting their existing power, but the problem before the autocracies is to get that much power, and more, to unite. The speed at which Germany, Japan and Italy have increased their power in recent years has blinded many to this basic difference, and to the fact that despite all their gains the power of the three put together remains feeble compared to the combined power of the fifteen democracies.

The democracies can secure world control overnight without doing violence to any one or to any democratic principle. They need merely change their own minds, decide to stand together as the Union instead of apart, accomplish this simple act of reason. The autocracies can do nothing of the kind. They can not possibly gain world control overnight. None of them can add to its territory without doing violence to some one, and thereby offsetting the gain by making possession precarious and increasing opposition everywhere, as each of them has been doing. None of them can keep the power they have gained nor even that which they began with except by force,—not one of them can stand free speech even in his own capital.

The autocracies can not unite their power under a common government without each violating the totalitarian state's basic principle of the supremacy of the state above all else. Their problem in gaining world control is infinitely harder than ours, and they can not possibly solve it by their own strength, reason or genius. They are like an outclassed football team that can not hope to score—let alone win—except through the errors of the other side.

Now that I have said why I am convinced that there is no hope for peace in the Chamberlain policy, I would express my admiration for his courage and sincerity and my gratitude to him for having gone to Berchtesgaden and Godesberg and Munich. I would express this no less strongly to Premier Daladier who encouraged and supported him and to President Benes and the Czech people who paid the bill. If I have my own reasons for believing that the continuance of this policy will be fatal both to our peace and freedom, I have also reasons others do not have for being grateful that this policy was followed in September.

Its great merit then was the reasoning in which Messrs. Chamberlain,

Daladier and Benes really placed their faith,—that we all want both our peace and freedom, that we shall have sacrificed our peace once we go to war for our freedom, that by averting war this time there will still remain the possibility of finding somehow a means of saving our peace and freedom both together. That reasoning is unanswerable, but it means that we must lose no time now in finding that way through.

The greatness of Mr. Chamberlain will be judged in the end by whether the catastrophe is definitely averted or only made greater in the breathing space he gained. It will be a tragedy if the courage Mr. Chamberlain showed in rescuing a drowning world in September should come to be forgotten through his having then finished it off by doing the wrong thing when he sought to revive it. I who believe I know the way to revive it must remain grateful to him and to all the others who have kept open the possibility of preserving peace and freedom through Union now.

THE TEST OF COMMON SENSE

Who knoweth not such things as these?—Job

Because Union is a fresh solution of the world problem it appears to be something new. The deeper one goes into it, however, the better one may see that there is in it nothing new, strange, untried, nothing utopian, mystic. The fact is that we democrats have already strayed away from the road of reason and realism into the desert of make-believe and mysticism. We have strayed away seeking the mirage utopia of a world where each nation is itself a self-sufficing world, where each gains security and peace by fearing and preparing war, where law and order no longer require government but magically result from keeping each nation a law unto itself, where the individual's freedom is saved by abandoning at the national frontier the principle that the state is made for man and adopting there the dogma that man is made for the nation. It is proposed here that we have done with these dangerous delusions, that we return to the road of reason and seek salvation by tested methods, by doing again what we know from experience we can do. I ask nothing better than that we stick to the common interests of us individual men and women and to the simpler teachings of common sense.

Common sense tells us that it is in our individual interest to make the world safe for our individual selves, and that we can not do this while we lack effective means of governing our world.

It tells us that the wealthier, the more advanced in machinery, the more civilized a people is and the more liberties its citizens enjoy, the greater the stake they have in preventing depression, dictatorship, war. The more one has, the more one has to lose.

Common sense tells us that some of the causes of depression, dictatorship, war, lie inside the nation and that others lie outside it. It tells us that our existing political machinery has let us govern strongly the conditions of life within the nation but not outside it, and that all each people has done to overcome the dangers inside it has been blighted by its failure to reach the dangers outside it, or remains at the mercy of those ungoverned forces.

Common sense advises us to turn our attention now to finding means of governing the forces still beyond our control, to constituting effective world government. It warns us that no matter how strong or perfect we each make our national government, it can never end those outside dangers, and that we individuals can not know how long we can wait to end those dangers before they end us.

Common sense reminds us Americans that we are part of the world and not a world apart, that the more we keep our lead in the development of machines the more important to us we make the rest of the world, that we can not, without catastrophe, continue through good times and bad improving these machines while refusing to develop political machinery to govern the world we are thus creating. It tells us that the principles of this Union of the free are the principles that America was born to champion, that Americans can not deny them and still remain Americans. For the loyalty of the American is not to soil or race. The oath he takes when he enters the service of the American Union, is altogether to the principles of Union, "to support and defend the Constitution,"— a constitution that is already universal in its scope, that allows for the admission to its Union of any state on earth, that never even mentions territory or language, and that mentions race and color only to provide that freedom shall never on that account be denied to any man.

THE AMERICAN EXAMPLE

Common sense may seem to say that the American example does not apply, that it was much easier for the Thirteen States to unite than it would be for the Fifteen Democracies today, that the possibility of their forming a Union is now too remote to justify practical men trying to solve the immediate problem this way. It may seem to say that one needs only consider current American public opinion to realize that unlike 1787 Union now is a dream that cannot possibly be realized for many years, let alone in time to save us now. This seems convincing but is it so?

American opinion has always been remarkable for seeing from afar danger to democracy and quickly adopting the common sense solution, however remote and radical and difficult and dangerous it seemed to be. What other people ever revolted at less oppression? Independence was so remote from American thought at the start of 1776 that it was not even proposed seriously until January 10, when Paine came out for it. Yet his *Common Sense* then so swept the country that within six months the Declaration of Independence was adopted.

To understand how difficult and remote the Union of the Thirteen States really was when 1787 began and how encouragingly the example they set applies to our democracies today, common sense suggests that we turn back and see the situation then as contemporaries saw it.

"If there is a country in the world where concord, according to common calculation, would be least expected, it is America," wrote Paine himself. "Made up as it is of people from different nations, accustomed to different forms and habits of Government, speaking different languages, and more different in their modes of worship, it would appear that the union of such a people was impracticable."

Conditions among the American democracies of the League of Friendship were if anything worse than among ours today. As John Fiske put it, "By 1786, under the universal depression and want of confidence, all trade had well-nigh stopped, and political quackery, with its cheap and dirty remedies, had full control of the field." Trade disputes threatened war among New York, Connecticut and New Jersey. Territorial disputes led to bloodshed and threat of war among New York, New Hampshire and Vermont, and between Connecticut and Pennsylvania. War with Spain threatened to break the League of Friendship in two camps. The League could not coerce its members. Threats of withdrawal from it were common. Its Congress often had no quorum, rarely had any money in the treasury, could no longer borrow. The states issued worthless currency, misery was rife, and courts were broken up by armed mobs. When these troubles culminated early in 1787 with the attempt of Shays's rebels to capture the League arsenal in Massachusetts so strong was state sovereignty and so feeble the League that Massachusetts would not allow League troops to enter its territory even to guard the League's own arsenal. Washington had already written to Jay in 1786, "I am uneasy and apprehensive, more so than during the war." Everything seemed to justify the words of the contemporary liberal philosopher, Josiah Tucker, Dean of Gloucester:

As to the future grandeur of America, and its being a rising empire under one head, whether republican or monarchical, it is one of the idlest and most visionary notions that ever was conceived even by writers of romance. The mutual antipathies and clashing interests of the Americans, their differences of governments, habitudes, and manners, indicate that they will have no centre of union and no common interest. They never can be united into one compact empire under any species of government whatever; a disunited people till the end of time, suspicious and distrustful of each other, they will be divided and sub-divided into little commonwealths or principalities, according to natural boundaries, by great bays of the sea, and by vast rivers, lakes, and ridges of mountains.

The idea of turning from league to union was so remote in 1787 that it was not even seriously proposed until the end of May when the Federal Convention opened. How remote it was may be inferred from the fact that the opening of the Convention had to wait ten days in order to have even the bare majority of the Thirteen States needed for a quorum. The Convention itself had been called by Congress merely to reform the League—"for the sole and express purpose of revising the Articles of Confederation." It was not deflected away from patching and into building anew until the eve of its session,—and then only thanks to George Washington's personal intervention. Even then Union as we know it now was more than remote: It was unknown, it still had to be invented.

Yet once the Convention decided to build anew it completed this revolutionary political invention within 100 working days. Within two years— two years of close votes and vehement debate in which Hamilton, Madison and others, now called "men of vision," were derided as "visionary young men" even by Richard Henry Lee, the revolutionist who had moved the Declaration of Independence in 1776,—within two years the anarchy-ridden, freedom-loving American democracies agreed to try out this invention on themselves. Twenty months after they read its text the American people established the Constitution that still governs them,—but now governs four times as many democracies and forty times as many free men and women.

Is it really visionary to believe that the American people can still be trusted quickly to understand and act upon the common sense of Union?

Can it be hard-headed reason that holds it easier for the American democracies to invent and agree to try out Union in the infancy of self-government than it is for our more mature democracies to adopt it now?

It does seem practical to ask first how all the difficulties in changing from national sovereignty to Union are to be met. Yet the makers of the first Union were not delayed by such considerations. They abolished each State's right to levy tariffs, issue money, make treaties, and keep an army, and they gave these rights to the Union without waiting for a plan to meet the difficulties of changing from protection to free trade, etc. They did not even bother trying to work out plans to meet all these difficulties of transition. And they were right in treating all this as secondary and leaving it to the Union itself to solve, for the lack of such plans neither prevented the swift adoption of Union nor caused any serious difficulty thereafter.

Yet they lived in a time when New York was protecting its fuel interests by a tariff on Connecticut wood and its farmers by duties on New Jersey butter, when Massachusetts closed while Connecticut opened its ports to British shipping, when Boston was boycotting Rhode Island grain and Philadelphia was refusing to accept New Jersey money, when the money of Connecticut, Delaware and Virginia was sound, that of all other States was variously depreciated and that of Rhode Island and Georgia was so worthless that their governments sought to coerce the citizens into accepting it. In those days New York was massing troops on its Vermont frontier while the army of Pennsylvania was committing the atrocities of the "Wyoming massacre" against settlers from Connecticut.

Can it still be said that the difficulties of transition to Union were simpler then than now? That it was then more practical to risk establishing Union without a transition plan than to risk delaying Union until such a plan was made? That it is now more practical to delay Union at the risk of catastrophe than to adopt it at the risk of having some transition difficulties? Common sense answers, No.

Some factors, of course, made Union easier for the American democracies than it is for us just as others made it harder for them. Though it seems to me on balance that Union is much easier now than then, I would grant that it is hard to strike such a balance. But we can not have it both ways. Those who say that I am wrong, that conditions were so much more favorable to union of the American democracies then than they are for Union now, they are also saying implicitly that conditions then were also much more favorable than now to all the alternative solutions—league, alliance, or isolationism. If a common language, a common mother country, a common continent and all the other things the American democracies had in common made union easier for them than us, they also made it easier for them to make a league succeed. If even they could not make a league work, then how in the name of common sense can we expect to do better with a league than they did? Even if Union is harder now than then we know, at least, that we can succeed with it.

Common sense leads to this conclusion: If we the people of the American Union, the British Commonwealth, the French Republic, the Lowlands, Scandinavia and the Swiss Confederation can not unite, the world can not. If we will not do this little for man's freedom and vast future, we can not hope that others will; catastrophe must come and there is no one to blame but ourselves. But the burden is ours because the power is ours, too. If we *will* Union we can achieve Union, and the time we take to do it depends only on ourselves.

.　　.　　.　　.　　.　　.　　.

In the democracies of Europe—in the little democracies in the danger zones; in the more fortunate democracies of Scandinavia; above all, in the great democracies of France and Britain—the average American finds a way of life which he knows instinctively to be the way of life which he himself has chosen.

He knows that these democracies are the outposts of our own kind of civilization, of the democratic system, of the progress we have achieved through the methods of self-government and of the progress we still hope to make tomorrow. He knows that if these outposts are overrun by the dictatorships of either Right or Left we shall find ourselves deprived of friends. He knows that, despite geographical remoteness and a traditional desire to avoid entanglement in other peoples' quarrels, we are inevitably the natural allies of the democracies of Europe . . .

In any ultimate test of strength between democracy and dictatorship, the good-will and the moral support—and in the long run more likely than not the physical power of the United States—will be found on the side of those nations defending a way of life which is our own way of life and the only way of life which Americans believe to be worth living.—The New York Times, editorial, *A Way of Life*, June 15, 1938.

CHAPTER II

Public Problem No. I: World Government

Transport, education and rapid development of both spiritual and material relationships by means of steam power and the telegraph, all this will make great changes. I am convinced that the Great Framer of the World will so develop it that it becomes one nation, so that armies and navies are no longer necessary.—President Grant, 1873.

During my journey in Europe I have been more deeply impressed than ever with the gravity of the situation with which we are faced. When I perceive that in one or two days a degree of devastation can be effected which no lapse of time could ever make good, again I realize that we must make provision for a form of security which is dynamic and not static, and which rests on reason and not on force.—Lindbergh, at the German Air Ministry, July 24, 1936.

Is the future of the world to be determined by universal reliance upon armed force and frequent resort to aggression, with resultant autarchy, impoverishment, loss of individual independence and international anarchy? Or will practices of peace, morality, justice and order under law, resting upon sound foundations of economic well-being, security and progress, guide and govern in international relations? As modern science and invention bring nations ever closer together, the time approaches when, in the very nature of things, one or the other of these alternatives must prevail. In a smaller and smaller world it will soon no longer be possible for some nations to choose and follow the way of force and for other nations to choose and follow the way of reason. All will have to go in one direction and by one way . . . The re-establishing of order under law in relations among nations has become imperatively necessary.—Secretary of State Hull, Aug. 16, 1938.

PLAN OF CHAPTER

The proposition we begin with is this: The most urgent problem of civilized mankind is to constitute effective means of governing itself where its civilization has already made its world practically one.

We reach this conclusion in this chapter by examining first the relation between the development of machinery and the needs of government.

We find that the characteristic of the machine is, as it develops, to bring the individual man into closer relation with the rest of mankind and both to enlarge the circle of men with whom he needs to reach agreements in order to govern his conditions of life and also to speed the tempo with which the instrument for reaching such agreements, government, must work. We find this process has already reached the point requiring constitution of effective government on a world scale, and that the urgency of this problem is greatest for the peoples most advanced in the development of the machine. To find whether this world or external problem in government is more urgent to them than the national or internal problem in government which the development of the machine also raises, we then consider both problems from the standpoints of experience and theory.

The objections of those who find other things more urgent than the problem of constituting effective world government are then examined. Special attention is paid to the argument that the economic problem, particularly the conflict between capital and labor, is more urgent than the world constitutional problem.

THE MACHINE THAT REQUIRES WORLD GOVERNMENT

Politics can be separated from the machine no more than can civilization. The machine I would define broadly as anything made by man that frees man even a little from any of his natural limitations or that extends his powers. The machine's nature is such that to use it or make the most of it men need more of the world than they needed before its invention. To do their work well or to exist an increasing number of machines today need the whole planet.

A wooden plow needs little land, and few men, whether to make it, work it or consume the harvest. A steel plow needs more land, a bigger world. It needs many men to make—prospectors, miners, iron puddlers, blast-furnace men, tool-makers, transporters, salesmen. It brings greater surplus than the wooden plow: It needs more consumers. A tractor gang plow requires a still wider world. Horses may feed on the farm, but one may need to bring fuel to a tractor thousands of miles. And one needs a world of consumers if tractor wheat is to be sold.

Any one can make himself a megaphone and extend his voice a little. But to make a telephone that will extend his voice anywhere one needs generations of inventors and scientists of many nations. One needs to comb the world to get all the little things required to make a telephone. If a man could find them all in his backyard and invent the whole thing himself, to use it he would need another man, and to make the most of it he would need all mankind. One can telephone round the world today but one does not telephone to oneself. The more civilized and civilizing the machine, the more we must depend on all the planet and all mankind to make and use it.

In the world our machines have made us, distance is no more a thing of miles, but of minutes. New York is closer to England now than to Virginia in George Washington's time. Men fly round the globe today in one tenth the time once needed to send news of the Monroe Doctrine from the White House to Buenos Ayres. Rumor, panic and millions in money can now cross oceans even faster—in a flash.

Our world is now practically one in many respects. Even the Ethiopians who rate low in machines and civilization have had this fact forced upon them. An early Ethiopian statement to the League lamented the hopelessness of making their case known to the world: Italy had all the machinery for reaching daily mankind's eye and ear and Ethiopia had none. Yet such is the world we live in that it spent millions merely to satisfy its own need of knowing the Ethiopian side. The League broadcast it round the world while Americans carried a microphone to the Emperor. New York overnight became willing to pay many times more for a word from Addis Ababa than from Washington. Suddenly it became possible to see in Paris the bombing of the then unheard of down of Dessié only a few days after it happened. While the Ethiopians were learning that there was a vast incalculable world outside, the more civilized world was learning that there was a backward Ethiopia and that it could upset many a plan made far from it. We all live in the same world now, but the more civilized we are the more we live together in it, the more we depend on each other, the more our world is one.

Does this bring to civilized mankind the problem of constituting effective means of governing itself?

We can not give our world the tendons that mass production and consumption give it, the blood circulation that steamships, railways, automobiles and airplanes supply, and the nervous system with which electricity permeates it, and expect it still to function as it did before we made it one organism. When our common organism begins to ail we can not reasonably expect to cure it by each nation seeking to cure its portion of the nerves, blood and tendons separately, whether by its own devices or its own dervishes.

Nor can we now dispense with tendons, blood and nerves. True, we got on without them once. That was when we were, politically, like the amoeba—one-celled creatures. But once the germ from which we start develops tendons, blood, nerves, we can no longer live without them, nor without a head, an effective means of governing the whole. These are thereafter vital.

The idea that we need not bother much about these connecting common things while they are relatively small is as unsound as the idea that since we did without them once we can do without them again. Those who argue that we can do without world trade because it is a mere fraction of national trade should argue too that we can do without the tendons because they are smaller than the muscles. The blood and nervous systems do not give the body its weight, but so long as they remain the rest can be starved down almost to skin and bones, and yet recover. It is the fraction that pours over the spillway that keeps a whole lake fit to drink, and it is the lack of even a trickling outlet that makes the Dead Sea. Except under penalty of stagnation poisoning us we can no more dispense with world trade, communications, contact, than we can uninvent our steam, gasoline, electric and other machines.

These world-machines, these world-made, world-needing and world-making machines, inevitably bring our nations many problems in living together. Such problems in human relations can be solved only (a) by one imposing his solution on the rest by force, or (b) by mutual agreement. While machines were crude the way of force was possible. There is no possibility now of some modern Rome imposing law on all mankind. Our choice is not between law through conquest and law through agreement. It is between agreed law and no law, between self-government and no government. Before we can agree on how to solve any of the problems of living together, we need to agree on how to reach and enforce and interpret and revise such agreements or laws in time. Our first problem in mutual agreement is the constitutional problem of creating effective world government.

THE INTERNAL OR THE EXTERNAL PROBLEM?

The more intelligent among civilized people seem ready to agree that we do face a problem in world government. They question only whether this is the most urgent problem now, particularly for themselves. Many deny that it is, and more act as if it could wait more safely than other problems.

It is true that there is no end of problems, world, national, local, individual crowding in on us. We can neither give them all equal attention nor safely drop all but one to concentrate on it. We need to give our best attention to what is most urgent, without letting the rest get out of hand. But first we need to decide which problem is really most urgent.

Problems in living can be divided in two, internal and external. Whether we are concerned with a nation, or any organized group in it, or with the individual, or with any single organic cell, there is always this division. To live it is not enough that a cell should be so organized that all within works together, there is also the problem of its relations with other cells, with all the outside world. For the individual man life depends on keeping healthy not simply the relations among the cells in his body but also his relations with other men, with all his outside world. We turn from physiology to economics when we turn from man to the nation, and we speak of self-government where we spoke of self-control; the words change, not their meaning. We can then boil down our choice to this: Which is the more urgent, the internal or the external side of our problem in government?

Before answering, one general remark: The degree to which the external directly affects cells, men or nations, is in proportion to their reach, that is to say, to their powers of movement and communication. The machines that are said to make the world smaller really make it larger. They extend to the antipodes the world within reach of a man's eye, ear, tongue, and thought. They free him from barriers that hemmed in his fathers. The world that was small was that of the cave man: His world was his cave and as far as he could reach, throw, walk, look, listen, yell. Machines have made the civilized man's world today the planet. Men have never had anything like the reach that men have today. That means that the external side of human problems has never been nearly as great as it is now.

Europe was no problem to the men of America nor America to the Europeans until the machines of the fifteenth century let Columbus establish communication between them, and made the Old and New worlds one. But this did not make them one world to all men at once, but at first only to those whose machines gave them the greatest reach. America was no more a part of the external problem of the Tibetans in 1692 than in 1491. One can concede that the internal problem remains even now more important than the external one for the Tibetan, and certainly his world is smaller and his life less dependent on the rest of mankind than are, say, the American's.

It seems safe to formulate the rule that the poorer, weaker, remote and more backward generally a people is, the more self-sufficing it therefore is, the higher the ratio of its internal to its external problem and the less urgent the problem of world government to it. Conversely, the richer, stronger, the faster in communications and generally the more developed mechanically and more educated and civilized a people is, the less self-sufficing it therefore is, the more dependent on all mankind, the higher the ratio of its external to its internal problem and the more urgent its need of world government.

If this problem is not more urgent than the national one for us who are citizens of the advanced nations it can not be for any one else. We can confine to ourselves, then, the question: Which is the more urgent, the problem in national or in world government?

WHAT THE RECORD SHOWS

To answer it, consider first the record. At the start one thing stands out. The one important problem that has nowhere been accorded urgent treatment is the problem of world government. It came nearest to urgent status, perhaps, in 1919 when the Covenant was drafted. But even then when catastrophe was still smouldering President Wilson was damned everywhere, and not least in the United States, for delaying what the world generally deemed most urgent—the winding up of that particular war—in order to secure the establishment of a first attempt at world government, the League. The Covenant had to be drafted after office hours and such men as Lloyd George and Clemenceau never had time for it.

Since the League's foundation what has been done about this world constitutional problem? Briand's committee to inquire into European Union was merely an attempt to establish European government along League lines. What little political discussion his committee dared indulge in added nothing new to inter-state or world constitutional thinking. The Bank for International Settlements was, like the League, a by-product of the conference that gave it birth. Thereafter there was no sign of political activity in the constitutional field of world government until the 1936 League Assembly, and it showed little evidence of any fresh thinking about this problem.

External affairs generally have received much more attention than has this constitutional problem, but even they have not been treated as most urgent since the war. The relative importance everywhere attached to national and to world government is reflected by budgets; the whole world has never spent more than $10,000,000 a year on all the activities of the League. For the equal of the League budgets one has to get down to such budgets as that of the tiny canton of Geneva.

Many international meetings have attempted to solve this or that specific external problem by the existing machinery. Not even in such great ones as the Disarmament Conference and the Monetary and Economic Conference did the attempt at a world solution receive as urgent treatment as the attempt at a national solution simultaneously made by each nation. Compare the effort and money spent on arming by each power in any day, month or year of the Disarmament Conference with the amount it spent seeking disarmament agreement. Here was a thing that had always defied man, success in it was worth immeasurably more than victory in war, yet governments, press, and public seemed to assume that disarmament could be had for only a shade of the attention they would give to winning a war. There seems no need to draw the contrast between the noisy show the nations gave at the London Monetary and Economic Conference and the huge efforts they were making at the same time to strengthen national policies. Still less need is there to contrast the energy governments are devoting now to reform at Geneva and to rearmament at home.

On the other hand the theory that the internal side of our problem deserves the most urgent treatment has had as fair a trial as any theory can hope to have. The record may thus be summarized:

First, in the golden middle nineteen twenties when times were good and war danger relatively small all the nations acted as if the urgent thing was (a) to extract, each for itself, the most profit from the situation at the least cost in preparations to meet the changes, internal and especially external, this golden age was rapidly making, and (b) to try to continue this golden age by maintaining unchanged whatever national constitution laws, administration, machinery or general political condition happen to be accompanying prosperity.

Second, when this policy crashed in 1929, the nations acted on the theory that the most urgent thing for each was to make national laws to meet each emergency as it rose. This was a policy of seeking recovery by concentrating on bringing the national statutes in line with the changed conditions machines had produced, as far as this could be done while keeping the national constitution static and foreign policy passive or retrograde.

Third, as nations reached their limits in constitutionally changing their national laws, administrations and policies, they proceeded on the theory that the national problem, which had grown worse under this treatment, was more than ever the urgent one and now required this treatment to be carried beyond constitutional limits, but only temporarily, as in much New Deal legislation.

Fourth, where this policy has failed to bring relief, nations have simply carried further the theory behind it, and have given urgent attention to the question of changing their constitution, peacefully or by revolution.

THE WIDENING GAP

The depression showed that the internal machinery in every state was already far better made than its external machinery for that swift, strong, responsive action which the machine age demands. Political machinery to be effective must be able to act quickly when an emergency rises. Compare the action the American Union got through its national political machinery in 1933 with its failure to get action through its external machinery on the same problem. The mechanism governing the relations of the people of the forty-eight states of the American Union enabled them in a few months to do and undo a vast amount of important legislation. Meanwhile neither the mechanism governing the relations of the people of the fifty odd states of the League nor all the diplomatic machinery has yet enabled them to agree on any important constructive action.

When the emergency rose Britain's internal political machinery was so responsive that the British could reverse overnight in 1931 even their historic policies of gold money and free trade. The machinery of the German Republic proved capable of extraordinarily swift, radical action without Hitlerian purges or press control. The government of the French Republic has shown during the franc crisis in 1926, the Paris riots and the 1936 strikes, remarkable power to meet quickly the gravest emergencies without suspending constitutional methods or the rights of man. Everywhere one finds that the internal machinery allowed people swiftly to reach agreement and act—whatever one may think of some of the actions taken—while the external machinery failed to do this. It seems safe to say that even before the depression the worst internal political machinery anywhere in the civilized world was far more efficient than the best external machinery. It would appear to follow that the more urgent need for improvement lay on the external side even in 1929.

Yet since 1929 the gap has widened. By changes in law, by the force of practice or of violence, the internal political machinery in nearly all nations has been made capable of still faster and stronger action. Meanwhile their external machinery has become even weaker, even slower. Within the nations many checks on governmental action have been weakened or removed: Political checks, such as free speech, free press, free assembly, free elections, the necessity of taking into account powerful minorities and of bowing to local self-government and to genuine majorities. Juridical checks, such as independent courts and the need to submit to process of law. Economic checks, such as private property rights. Psychological checks, such as rugged individualism and prejudices against being dependent on the government, against politicians "managing" money, against deficits, against bureaucracy, against centralization, against concentrating tremendous powers in the hands of one man.

Nearly all these checks have already been removed in some nations, as Germany; in others, such as Britain, only a few have gone or been weakened. But no nation has escaped the trend toward removing the brakes on the national government, nor the accompanying trend toward increasing its motive power with more cylinders, whether by giving it new legal rights, or huge funds to spend, or control over domestic and foreign exchange or trade, or great armed force. In every nation one finds men advocating or practising all kinds of perilous experiments in state reorganization, and an increasing number preaching the sacrifice of individual freedom in the interests of these experiments. Few seem even to ponder whether the desired results might not be more easily or safely gained by a milder readjustment of external political machinery.

The point here is not whether some or all of these changes are good or bad. Still less do I mean that there is no need for change in national political machinery. The point is simply that the political machinery has been and is being changed to make its action stronger and swifter, and that there exists not only recognition of the need of such change but powerful demand for it,—but always mainly on the internal side.

On the external side the trend has been toward strengthening still more the political, juridical, economic, psychological brakes on the machinery and weakening still more the motor.

Americans can estimate the efficiency of the world's political machinery in 1929 by considering what the Washington machinery would have been worth if each of the forty-eight states had an army, a high tariff, and a money all its own, and reserved the right of veto on the ground that Aim No. 1 was not agreement with the others but independence from them. Americans can measure the deterioration in the world's political machinery since 1929 by considering what would be left of Washington's machinery if each state then had a bigger army, a higher tariff and a more dubious money, while Pennsylvania and California seceded and Indiana successfully invaded Arkansas, and every state insisted more than ever on its right to veto all agreement.

Another American example may make the point clearer. In 1933 Washington was at least suggesting a definition for aggression and considering conditionally consulting other law-abiding powers in the event of war. Now—except in Latin America where it hardly matters—the United States is applying a policy of unconditional refusal to consult or even to try to distinguish between aggressor and victim, no matter how flagrant the offense. The American attitude toward the external problem has thus changed from refusal to agree that world government needs to be strong and effective to complete negation of the first principle on which all government depends, namely, that offenses against the law will be judged by the law-abiding neutrals. During this American trend toward anarchy on the outside what has been the trend on the inside?

Many of those who sought in 1933 to bring political development in line with machine development by changing only the internal laws and practices of the United States now seem mentally ready to change its fundamental law, the Constitution, as being out of date. Many of those who are temperamentally most open to new ideas, the liberals, radicals, revolutionists, seem even more conservative and reactionary now regarding the problem of external relations than they were in 1933. They seem willing to face the dangers of revolution in internal American government, but they remain blind to the need of even moderate change in the government of American relations with the rest of the world.

They would scrap the Constitution before they would scrap neutrality or isolationism. That Constitution has been for 150 years the world's outstanding success in inter-state government, but the idea that Americans, before doing violence to it, might study whether they could attain their ends better by applying its principles to the problem of world inter-state government,—that idea seems to be too revolutionary even to occur to today's American revolutionists.

Everywhere the gap has widened. The means of doing business within the nation have been speeded, the means of doing business outside it have been slowed. But is the problem of living together being solved? Has the policy of giving the national side of the problem most urgent treatment justified the hopes placed in it, the sacrifices made for it? Is the world farther from catastrophe now than it was? Does any people on earth feel the richer, the safer, the freer for its stronger means of agreeing swiftly with itself on its own plan of action and its weaker means of agreeing with other peoples? The fact is that the problem has been getting harder to solve not only externally, but internally and as a whole.

WHAT REASON SHOWS

Yet the very fact that the situation has grown worse under this treatment continues to make people act as if the national side of the problem deserved still more immediate attention. It is true that the more a man takes poison the more urgently he needs to take something—but is it more poison? The record allows no hope that continuance of the present policy will bring anything but disaster. If, however, we will not accept the answer that the past has given, we must turn to logic to know what the future will reply.

Suppose then that we continue to act on the assumption that the most urgent problem is the internal one. What does success and what does failure bring? Suppose first that all countries recover by this method. Suppose the exponents of planned and managed nationalism get their hearts' desire, and that we can wait long enough for it. Suppose miracles. Suppose the governments plan so well that each achieves the ideal of the self-subsisting nation, that the Americans succeed in turning their surplus cotton into rubber (without causing a surplus in rubber), the Swiss their surplus cheese into cotton, the Germans their potash into nickel, the British their ships into soil, the Japanese their silk into oil and every people their leisure into toil. Can the point be reached by all nations where there is no further monetary, trade or communication problem to solve because there is no longer any exchange among them? If it could, would this end the need of world government?

The need for world government rises for every people from two movements; its own outward movement into the world and the world's inward movement into it. Recovery is bound to increase the importance of both these movements for each nation that enjoys it. It is bound to mean greater development of and dependence on the world-made and world-making machines, and that means still greater inter-dependence of peoples, still greater need of world government.

For what are we going to do with our prosperity? Spend it trying to keep in our Lindberghs and keep out the Einsteins? Prosperity means having more than we want at home and therefore having the means of getting other things elsewhere. Will that not increase our desire for them? Do we not usually want most what we haven't got? If we want merely to travel, to see new sights and old ruins and get fresh ideas, we are buying abroad and to buy we must sell, and once we are doing all this we have fallen from the nationalist ideal of self-subsistence, we are no longer independent but inter-dependent. If we are to enjoy our prosperity we are bound to use it to trade, travel, invest—and to develop those interests in the world whose enjoyment and protection require world law and order. If we are not to enjoy these things, if we can not spent our money abroad, if we can not get about the world as we please, if each nation is a prison no citizen can leave, where on earth is the individual freedom for which democratic states were made, the freedom which this national planning and managing has also promised us?

Germany has reached the point in self-subsistence where citizens can not freely buy a foreign newspaper or travel abroad, but even without prosperity to stimulate the outward movement Germany has been unable to end that movement. Russia, paradoxically, came closest to self-subsistence when it was suffering famine; as Russia has risen from famine the outward movement has grown, and the importance of foreign affairs. Even if nationalism succeeded with Germans and Russians who are accustomed to autocracy, even if its prisons could be gilded with prosperity as they are papered with patriotism, would men accustomed to freedom tolerate it?

If they did, the nation would still remain more concerned with the outside world than it was before it gained prosperity because it could not, by becoming richer, lessen the world's inward movement into it. It is prosperity, not poverty, that attracts the world. Our supposition that each nation really recovers by nationalism can not possibly mean that they all attain the same level of prosperity. Just as the rich man needs protection against kidnapping and robbery more than does the poor man, the rich nation needs more than the poor nation protection against invasion or other form of aggression. This protection can be gained only through effective government or through each keeping his own bodyguard.

The nationalist method, if it brings us this need of protection, rules out our gaining it through world government. Its cardinal principle is that we must depend on ourselves alone, whereas the cardinal principle of government is that we depend on the community and the community depends on us. To suppose that nations gain prosperity by devotion to the nationalist principle is to suppose that they become still more devoted to it, and less inclined to abandon it for the opposite principle of world government. And so, the more successful national recovery is the more it makes world government not only necessary but the harder to achieve.

Moreover, the nationalist principle that we must depend only on ourselves rises largely from fear and suspicion of others. We readily depend on those we trust—indeed, one synonym of *trust* is *depend on*. One cannot teach a nation that it must depend on itself for everything without teaching it to distrust other nations and regard them as potential enemies. If, then, nationalism leads to prosperity it must also lead to suspicion, and the more it gives the nation to protect, the more it leads the nation to suspect sinister designs against it in the outside world. The more nationalism profits a nation the more insecure the nation must feel and the less inclined to have that trust in others needed for security through government.

To make all this worse, the development of the machine which prosperity brings means that each nation has more nations to fear, for more come within range to strike it. The value of its natural defences, such as oceans, mountains, rivers, is lowered and the need of artificial defences, armaments, increased. Even if a nation could prevent all outward movement of its civilian fliers in peace time, it would still face the problem of keeping out the inward movement of enemy fliers attacking by surprise before peace time ended in formal declaration of war.

Nationalist recovery, even if successful, does not end the problem of security, it merely makes it worse. It makes nations need protection more than ever, it forces them to seek that protection in armaments instead of law, in each of them building up their own bodyguard instead of common government. It leads them to speed a process which, with them as with prosperous gangsters, inevitably ends in self-destruction.

Since we can not make the problem of world government less urgent by succeeding in recovering through purely national measures, let us consider the other alternative. Suppose we fail to recover by the national route. Will failure make us need world government less urgently? Failure involves depression, poverty, war, destruction. They can put us back far. There is no doubt that the problem of world government was much less acute before the steamship, railroad and telegraph created such things as world prices and world markets only some seventy years ago. It was still less acute before simpler machines led to the discovery of the New World. It did not exist in the area of the wooden plow. But this road back to the wooden plow is marked with wooden crosses, every foot. It is no road out of the problem of living together.

MORE URGENT THAN TREATY OR ECONOMIC ISSUES

There remain the objections of those who have still other problems that they would put before the problem of world government.

One school holds it more urgent to get certain concrete improvements in the world situation than to improve the machinery for getting such results. To this popular school belong those who reject the League because of the Versailles Treaty: They would defer the establishment of the machinery for removing injustice till injustice is removed without it. Here we find all those pacifists and liberals who devote their energies to discovering or stressing existing injustices and inequalities and expatiating on the need of redressing them. They talk as if the crying evil were blindness to the existence and effects of evil, lack of will to obtain prosperity and do away with war, and not lack of effective machinery for harnessing the world's will for peace and prosperity to the attainment of these ends.

"Justice, disarmament and a basic economic readjustment of our present order, not legality, are the only true hopes of peace," they preach, but they bend their efforts neither to building up patiently the League of Nations mechanism for obtaining these nor to working out an alternative to it. Some of them assume that these objectives can be gained by a sort of spontaneous creation if only sufficient desire for them is expressed. Others assume that the war they see coming will be a just war. Because it seeks to wipe out the injustices of the last one they depend on it to leave no injustices of its own. The more realistic members of this school admit that "steps must be taken to secure equality of economic opportunity for all nations" or even smaller objectives. But they seem never realistic enough to consider just how these steps shall be taken. When pressed they suggest a world conference, or a small conference of great powers, or the League, or diplomatic channels, or armaments, or that "just war." They propose, in short, to leave it to machinery whose failure to achieve such results they themselves have announced and denounced at the time of its last trial.

The most flourishing section of this school is now the economic one. To it belong those who divide the nations into two classes, the haves and the have-nots, or the static and dynamic, and then split on what to do about it. Some turn hopefully to a conference to end this phenomenon before it results in war. The conference to prevent war by reducing the means of holding and gaining possessions by arms failed, for both haves and have-nots preferred even the unlimited risks of war to the risk to their holdings or their dreams which they saw in disarmament. The conference to prevent war by freeing trade and thus lessening the importance of having or not having possessions also failed. What hope can then remain for a conference called to end the whole issue through the haves handing over to the have-nots the possessions themselves? Even if some territory changes hands, will that make matters better? Even if all Germany's colonies were re-stored, and the Polish Corridor, Alsace-Lorraine and everything else, why should that decrease instead of increase the war danger? When Germany had all that in 1914, and Britain was trying to soothe her with half of Portugal's colonies, Germany was demanding only more imperiously than now "a place in the sun."

Others, agreeing there is no hope of our existing machinery adjusting peacefully the difference between the haves and have-nots, advise us to leave it to war. But war can not end this struggle; it can only change the line-up, the units and the prizes. The aim is to keep this struggle, whether among nations or individuals, from ending in violence, and the only hope of doing so is to provide effective means of making, enforcing, interpreting and revising law,—to provide effective means of governing human relations.

Another group finds the root of all war in the venerable practice of turn-ing public passion into private profit. For this group the most urgent thing is to abolish or control profit in armaments. Since I myself wrote a pamphlet attacking this traffic* a dozen years before it became fashionable to do so, it can not be said that I have failed to give its claims for most urgent treatment sympathetic consideration. It need only be added that even if we could succeed better than Soviet Russia in abolishing war merely by abolishing profit in armaments, there would remain the previous question: How to get world agreement to abolish it since all the conferences so far have failed to get agreement even to control this evil?

We come next to those for whom the machine age's most urgent problem is the world-wide struggle between capital and labor. Whichever side of it they are on, it seems so urgent to them that they have no time for the problem of organizing world government. They dismiss it as remote and visionary, or as unnecessary or impossible to solve before they have had their revolution, or counter-revolution.

There is no doubt that men everywhere are deeply torn into hostile groups

* *"Where Iron Is, There Is the Fatherland."* B. W. Huebsch, New York, 1920.

by the economic issue and that it needs attention. But there is no doubt either that they are still more deeply torn into enemy camps by the political dogma of nationalism. Both if left to themselves will end inevitably in explosion dangerous not simply to civilization but to each man's life. But it is not civil war, it is war that threatens to strike most of us first. Indeed, the only real danger of civil war lies nearly everywhere in its following war—at least among the vanquished, for though both sides lose in war one side loses more. Only in Spain do men now seem so torn by the issue of capital and labor that the dogma of nationalism can not unite, in the service of its wars, both these classes against both of them beyond the frontier. Even in the special case of Spain, the issue is far from being purely economic, or domestic.

Capital denounces the efforts of the Red Internationals to unite labor throughout the world. Labor denounces the attempts of the international bankers, the munition makers, the steel cartels, the shipping pools and all the Yellow International of gold, to overcome the national divisions of capital. But despite all the efforts of Red or Yellow mankind remains more miserably and murderously divided into nations that into labor and capital. Whether one admits for heart's desire the more abundant life or the more abundant profit, he has much less to fear from delaying fulfilment of that desire than from delaying the establishment of law and government among nations. No sweatshop can be so inhuman as the cold sweatshop of war. No profit can buy back a son once slain.

Some argue that it is the capitalist system that causes war, that the first thing to do therefore is to remove it and that if each nation will only do this for itself all the nations will then live in peace, and world government will either be easy to establish or unnecessary. Whether or not the capitalist system is one of the causes of war, it is true that the problem of organizing peaceful relations among the nations was not solved when all the world was capitalistic. It may possibly be that if all the world were communistic the problem would be solved. No one can say. But one can say this: The capitalist system is not going to be eradicated soon nor is the whole world going to become communist at once. Any movement in this direction will be that of one nation after another and if each acts separately it is quite probable that there will be wide differences in their conception and application of communism. Consequently, even if we grant the argument, the practical questions remain: How long can you and I afford to wait for war to be thus eliminated? What of the period meanwhile? National divisions are bound to be made more miserable and murderous when to them is added the condition of some nations being on a capitalist basis and others on a Marxist basis. Once Germany, Russia and Japan all shared the same economic system, capitalism, combined with absolutism. They still have absolutism but now each has a different solution of the capital-labor problem, and their quarrels are the more envenomed. When our democracies no longer all share their present basic economic system, they too will need more urgently than ever world law and order, and they too will be much more liable to suffer war than to enjoy world government. And whatever solution of the capital-labor question they may have reached before that war begins is liable to be upset in it, especially if they lose.

Their safest, surest way of solving wisely and enduringly the problems of capital and labor is to solve first the problem of their international relations by uniting while they have so much in common to help bring them together. Union, far from preventing any democracy from continuing whatever social or economic experiments it desires, will, by making them safer, encourage such experiments to be made, and to be made by ballots instead of bullets.

Finally, there are those who know that nationalism is wrong and who admit the need of world government, but who find the times unpropitious, the price of peace too high. Will the price ever be lower? Are the times growing less dangerous? What keeps us waiting? It is the fear of war. There is no worse unwisdom than to fear that war is coming and stop one's fearing there. Wars never end where they begin. Can we trust war to make times safer for organizing world law and order? Can we hope that it will leave that problem less difficult? Even so, it's true solution then must be its true solution now. Since we must in the end truly solve this problem of living together, surely the urgent thing is to solve it now in time to keep alive. Conditions can not possibly be more favorable than they are now for us to unite to save our freedom and our lives, for now we still have our free governments and our lives. More than all else the looming dangers of war make the establishment of effective world government our most urgent problem now.

.   .   .   .

There is no worse tyrant than ungovernment.

.   .   .   .

The extreme parts of the inhabited world somehow possess the most excellent products.—Herodotus, III, 106.

.   .   .   .

We are an overseas people and we are dependent upon Europe for market for the surplus products of our farmers and laborers. Without order in Europe we will at best have business depression, unemployment, and all their train of troubles. With renewed disorganization in Europe, social diseases and anarchy thrive, and we are infected by every social wind that blows from Europe. We are forced to interest ourselves in the welfare of the world if we are to thrive. No American who has spent the last ten months in Europe does not pray that we should get out of the entanglement in the sordid selfishness, the passions, the misery of the world. Our expansion overseas has entangled us for good or ill, and I stand for an honest attempt to join with Europe's better spirits to prevent these entanglements from involving us in war.—Herbert Hoover, addressing Stanford University, Oct. 2, 1919.

CHAPTER III

Urgent Most for Americans

Can it be that Providence has not connected the permanent felicity of a nation with its virtue?—Washington, *Farewell Address.*

The question before the world today, Mr. Chancellor, is not a question of errors of judgment or of injustices committed in the past. It is a question of the fate of the world, today and tomorrow. The world asks of us who at this moment are the heads of nations the supreme capacity to achieve the destinies of the nations without forcing upon them as the price the mutilation and death of millions of citizens. . . . The Government of the United States has no political involvements in Europe. . . . Yet in our own right we recognize our responsibilities as part of a world of neighbors.—President Roosevelt, *Appeal to Chancellor Hitler,* Sept. 28, 1938.

Not only has the rebuilding of a sound economic structure become absolutely essential but the re-establishment of order under law in relations among nations has become imperatively necessary. . . . When the dignity of the human soul is denied in great parts of the world, and when that denial is made a slogan under which propaganda is set in motion and armies take the field, no one of us can be sure that his country or even his home is safe.—Secretary of State Hull, Aug. 16, 1938.

PLAN OF CHAPTER

We consider here the peculiar urgency for Americans of the problem of organizing effective world government. We examine the policies of isolationism and neutrality which deny this and find that they are leading us away from the great line of American history. This deviation we trace to an interpretation of contemporary American history which holds that the mistake accounting for our present plight was our decision to enter the struggle to make the world safe for democracy. We find that this view is based on failure even to consider whether the mistake was not, instead, our decision to quit that struggle after two years. We conclude that whatever the mistake was, it has left us facing a grave situation and that failure to solve it in time can cost no people so much economically, politically, and morally as it will cost us, particularly our generation.

53

THE PRESENT AMERICAN POSITION

A people . . . which remain among the graves and . . . say, Stand by
thyself, come not near to me; for I am holier than thou. These are a smoke
in my nose. . . . Ye shall all bow down to the slaughter . . . ye shall
be hungry . . . ye shall be ashamed . . . and leave your name for a
curse. . . . He who blesseth himself in the earth shall bless himself in
the God of truth. . . . For, behold, I create new heavens and a new earth.
—Isaiah, 65: 3-17.

What has been said of the urgent need for world government applies
with peculiar force to the United States. Yet nowhere is it more denied
or ignored. This and the fact that practically there can be no effective
world government without the United States require us to pay special attention to the present American position.

According to it the urgent thing for the United States to do is to attempt, not to keep out of war by organizing a world government capable
of preventing its outbreak, but to organize instead a heavily armed neutrality with a view to keeping out of war after it starts. This policy aims
to foresee and block in advance everything capable of drawing the United
States into war. It would provide by legislation so that no political, legal,
economic, financial, or moral motive should ever lead the American people
to help either the victim or the aggressor,—the neutrality law in its ma-
jestic equality (to paraphrase Anatole France) aiming to safeguard the
United States no less against aiding the invader than against aiding the
invaded. That is its aim, at any rate, though in practice it has fallen so
far short of safeguarding us against helping the aggressor that the government has found it more neutral not to apply the neutrality law to
Japan's invasion of China.

A wave must run its course to the froth in which it ends, and this
neutralism is but the old isolationism gone to foam. Isolationism refused
to help organize law and order in the world, but it refused on the ground
that the American people should not commit themselves in advance while
conceding that they must deal with each disturbance of the peace when
it rose. Isolationism thus implicitly committed the United States to judging in each given case whether to aid one side or remain neutral. Neutralism carries this philosophy to its ultimate chaos by seeking to commit
the American people never to stand for law and order outside their hemisphere. It requires them to refuse in advance to judge even in the most
flagrant cases. There can be no worse negation of law than absolute negation of the duty of judging. There can be no law where there is no judg-

ing; there must be violent anarchy where the leading men refuse to judge not because they find the case too hard but because they fear to risk their own skins for what they know is right.

A position more opposed to world government could hardly be imagined. Its popular strength now would seem to make Union hopeless. But a wave always reaches its peak and seems most imposing precisely at the moment when it breaks into froth and starts foaming down. This neutralism which shudders even at the thought of parallel action with other democracies to protect our individual freedom never won for us that freedom; it was won only thanks to alliance with France. It was kept only by the constitution of effective inter-state government among thirteen democracies.

Isolationism, it is true, has on its side such Americans as Patrick Henry, who, placing the independence of their state above the freedom of the people in it, opposed the Constitution of the American Union. Neutralism does not have behind it even Patrick Henry. Like isolationism it has against it the basic American conception of government as applied in the Constitution and proclaimed in the Declaration of Independence.

It was not to neutralism or isolationism that the American people dedicated themselves at Gettysburg. It was "to the great task remaining before us: that from these honored dead we take increased devotion to that cause for which they gave the last full measure of devotion; that we here highly resolve that these dead shall not have died in vain; that this nation, under God, shall have a new birth of freedom; and that government of the people, by the people, for the people, shall not perish from the earth."

The present deviation from the great line of American history stands and falls on an interpretation of the last few years of that history. This interpretation results partly from some able, upright and very persuasive American thinkers and leaders seeing imperfectly one might-have-been while remaining blind to other might-have-beens. They are impressed by how much better off the United States might have been (they imagine) had we only kept out of the World War. They overlook, among other things, how much better off we might have been, too, if the United States, having been drawn into the war, had not been drawn out of the peace. The only American mistakes they see were made before the Versailles Treaty reached the Senate; they either insist or imply that none was made thereafter. If they do not trace the present situation entirely to the sins of Morgan and Wilson, it is only to put some of the blame on the Europeans or Japanese; it is not to attach responsibility to the post-war policy of the United States nor to Lodge, Borah, Johnson, Harding, Hearst, Huey Long and Coughlin.

Prominent in the school that teaches that our mistake was to have entered the war are those who lay it mainly to economic factors. They have been disillusioned and overwhelmed by the discovery that the war to end war and make the world safe for democracy has resulted instead in a depression-and-dictator-and-war-breeding situation, and that the economic factors in our entry in the war were much stronger than they had thought. They conclude and teach that the moral and political factors were mere Wilsonian window-dressing and propaganda to hide the real sordid motives and dupe the people into war.*

The failure to win the ideals President Wilson proclaimed is, however, the true father of the belief that our entry in the war was a mistake. The theory that we were duped into fighting for democracy and must safeguard ourselves against being duped again began really to flourish only after calamities thickened and the League failed and dictatorships spread and the war danger came galloping back. The economic interpretation of our entry in the war became the fashion only after hard times began. It and the resulting neutralism, like the Nazi interpretation of the same war and post-war period and the resulting Hitlerism, are the product of the belly, not the brain. It has been said of old, "An empty belly makes a bad counsellor."

The failure to achieve the ideals for which we fought can not be denied, but what was the cause of the failure? To argue that we failed because we entered the war is to argue that we might have succeeded if only we had never tried. This argument implies that had the United States kept on struggling year in, year out, since 1919 to organize peace the world would be even further from this goal. That is a singular thing for American patriots to argue.

The record shows that we fought for two years to organize the world effectively for peace and democracy, and that then we quit. If our dead died this time in vain, who this time abandoned in the hour of victory the cause for which they died? Does any American believe that their sacrifice will continue to be vain when once again from our honored dead we take increased devotion as at Gettysburg to that cause for which they gave the last full measure of devotion? Our fathers fought seven years to make half the Atlantic coast of North America safe for democracy. What sons are we to quit because we fail to make the whole world safe for it in two?

It is at least possible that the mistake that accounts for our present plight was made in quitting this struggle, not in beginning it. Why, then,

---

* Those who find I do not give this viewpoint sufficient attention or sympathy are requested to read Annex 5 of this book, which gives my own personal evolution in thought. They will find there documentary proof that I was alive to the economic and propaganda sides of the war during the war itself and stressed them when fewer did.

have our debunkers concentrated on how we were drawn in and ignored how we were drawn out, charting the road to the war to end war but not the road to isolationism and neutralism though it is the road to unending war? If we were capable of being so badly duped as they say we were in 1917, how can they or we be sure that we have never been duped since then? How can we safely assume that such undupers are not duping us now, after having duped themselves first of all?

Why do those who trace our entry in the war to profit and propaganda fail to put our post-war policy to their tests? What is so sacred in the Harding Administration and our nineteen twenties that they are taboo? Whatever the motive for suppressing nine-tenths of the record and applying microscope and megaphone to the rest, the effect is to justify ourselves in our own eyes for having quit the struggle to make peace. Is that not a troubling fact? What propaganda is more dangerous than self-propaganda, self-deception?

Few enterprises start so badly that nothing can be salvaged from them, none start so well that they can not be ruined by mistakes later. If proving a war was tarnished at the source proves that no good could come from it, it also proves that a muddy stream can never clear with time, and that the fair can never mend the foul. Such reasoning would deny bread because of the manure in the wheatfield. Yet what on earth is good that was untarnished at the start or made without the bad?

Whether we should have stayed out of the struggle or stayed in till we won what we fought for, the facts are that we did neither and that we, like everyone else, are now in a grave situation, and the overriding question is: What are we going to do about it? Wilson's great achievement was that he turned great evil to some good. We can do that, too. No poison is so poisonous that men—if only they keep trying—can not make it cure instead of kill.

WHERE WE ARE MORE EXPOSED THAN EUROPE

We in the Americas are no longer a far-away continent to which the eddies of controversies beyond the seas could bring no interest or no harm. Instead we in the Americas have become a consideration to every propaganda office and to every general staff beyond the seas. The vast amount of our resources, the vigor of our commerce, and the strength of our men have made us vital factors in world peace whether we choose or not.— President Roosevelt, Aug. 18, 1938.

The problem of world government is of peculiar urgency for us partly because it does not seem to be. We are less exposed than others to some of the dangers besetting mankind, but that exposes us most of all to one of the worst of dangers,—to the delusion that we shall be spared in any general calamity our species suffers. We suffer from that delusion to the point where our approach to the common problems of mankind has become habitually one of self-sacrifice rather than self-interest, of doing the world a favor rather than recognizing that we have anything to gain from the world, of donating rather than trading. We can not be safe while our thinking is wrong, and no thinking can be right that starts with the assumption that the United States is not a part of the world but a world apart.

The problem of world government is most urgent for us because the factors that expose us less than other nations—such as the ocean—belong to the past and are rapidly losing force, while the factors that expose us more than others belong to the present and future, and are rapidly gaining force. No other nation is so advanced as we are in world-needing and world-making machines. No other has so much to lose economically, politically, and morally as we by failure to solve in time the problem of world government.

We have already seen why the development of world machines makes increasingly urgent the need of world government, especially for the more advanced peoples. There seems no need to prove that we lead the world in developing these machines, and that therefore our position is particularly exposed and that we less than any other people can expect or afford to live in our world today on yesterday's political basis. But we can hardly recall too often that the depression struck no people so swiftly and savagely as it struck the people who believed what Irving T. Bush expressed in 1927: "The future destiny of America is in our hands, and is not dependent upon other nations."

No other people suffered and still suffers such per capita unemployment as the people which overwhelmingly elected President the candidate who assured them in August 11, 1928, "The poor-house is vanishing from among us," and on Sept. 17, "Were it not for sound governmental policies and wise leadership, employment conditions in America today would be similar to those existing in many other parts of the world."

There was only one people whose bank deposits shrank 20 per cent even in the first three years of depression (a rate of shrinkage 40 per cent faster than the average for the other 14 democracies and a total absolute loss twice as great as theirs combined, twelve billion gold dollars against five and a half), and then shrank during the next year 49 per cent (twenty-one billion gold dollars),—and whose banks were all forced to close. This people's present Chief Justice, Charles Evans Hughes, proclaiming its unique prosperity Oct. 24, 1928, said: "Delegations from foreign lands are visiting us to ascertain our secret."

In his last Message to Congress President Coolidge said, Dec. 4, 1928: "No Congress of the United States ever assembled, on surveying the state of the Union, has met with a more pleasing prospect than that which appears at the present time." Within four years American foreign trade had crashed down from $9,100,000,000 to $2,900,000,000. We lost 68 per cent of the gold value of our trade while the British lost only 59 per cent and the French only 53 per cent. Thereafter in one year of more energetically managed nationalism, 1933, we sank down to the level of 1902. Our trade dropped half a billion gold dollars in 1933 alone. It took a whole generation of American pioneers to add that much value to our trade, to raise it from $134 million in 1830 to $687 million in 1860.

It has cost and is costing no people anywhere so much in budget deficits, debt and monetary depreciation, to get what recovery we have gained since 1933 by strenuous nationalist measures and by Secretary Hull's strenuous efforts to add some very mild international measures to these. The color all this costly effort has brought to the American cheek—has it ever been the glow of health and not of fever?

How many times since 1929 have we been told that "prosperity is just ahead of us?" How often have our experts assured us that "the corner has been turned?" In 1930 they argued hopefully, "The farmer is flat on his back and there is no way to look, except up," and they still have that argument.

MORE THAN MONEY TO LOSE

We have a phrase that covers our position now as then: "The higher you are, the harder you fall." Whether or not we can gamble on being able to keep out of European or Asiatic war, we can not even gamble on keeping clear of the economic and financial effects of the world ungovernment to which we contribute so prodigally. Just as the war side of the catastrophe that ungovernment is bringing is more liable to strike first again in Europe or Asia and spread to us from there, its economic side is more liable to begin again with us and spread to Europe and Asia.

We have more than money to lose in depression. The Germans and Italians lost their individual freedom to no foreign aggressor but to dictators who rose from inside with hard times and unemployment brought on by world ungovernment. We can be the next great people to lose inside our state what we made it for. If we lose our freedom that way while the British and the French lose theirs to foreign autocrats, shall we be the better off? If we must risk it I would rather risk losing it to an autocrat from without than from within.

I have little fear of our losing our individual freedom through war—and none whatever if in that war we have with us all the democracies of the world. Even if we lose it to a foreign dictator whom we have allowed to fatten on the European democracies, I believe it will be relatively easy to rouse revolt against alien rule. I have no fear for the restoration of our freedom if we lose it fighting for it. But how shall we restore our freedom once we ourselves have deliberately destroyed it, stupidly or cravenly surrendering it more and more to some home-grown autocrat until all of it is gone—simply because we will not unite with European democrats to remove the source of the danger?

Under the pressure of the need of cutting costs, machines have developed tremendously since the depression,—and nowhere so much as with us. We are still marching ahead in the development of world-making and world-needing machines, and we are still keeping our political head stuck securely in volcanic ash. If to stand with one's head stuck so is folly, to go ahead with it stuck so can not be wise.

One thing more we need to note. It is that we more than others must be swift to foresee and make allowance in our political calculations for the speed of this machine development increasing in future. To do this we need to keep in mind its development during our own lives. If we compare each decade of the past thirty years with the decade before it we shall have some clue to the accumulating speed with which the machine will be making our world one during the next decade—if our failure to provide it with a governor does not meanwhile wreck machine and us.

Our generation has seen the world's worst war, its biggest inflation, its greatest boom, its deepest depression, all in quick succession. The one thing that has grown steadily through all these extremes of frost and drought is the machine that brings more and more and more of the world to the door of each of us and makes each depend increasingly for everything on all mankind. Consider how all the speed records were going down before the depression, and how all of them have been broken and broken again during the depression. Consider how much faster, safer, cheaper, better than in golden 1929 is now the automobile, radio, telephone, airplane, railway train, ocean liner, and every machine for communicating among all mankind men themselves and everything they make or say or think.

Consider too how much more this exposes us to tyranny on the tremendous scale of Hitler and Mussolini, how much closer it brings us to the evil as well as the good men do, how much more deadly it makes war.

What else except catastrophe beyond anything we yet have known can possibly prevent the world-machine from continuing its dizzying development, month on month, whether we like it or not? If we think the machine has not yet made even our North Atlantic democracies interdependent, we need to think that it is more inter-dependent today than it was yesterday and less than it will be tomorrow. If we think that the ocean still gives us enough security we need to think that that security is shrinking while our need of security is expanding and that when our natural security is gone it will be too late to replace it. It was not because we could not do without the Louisiana Territory in 1803 that we then added that great wilderness to our own. It was because we had in President Jefferson a man who looked ahead and knew that the safest, cheapest, wisest time to act is before action can not be avoided. It is only truer now than then that "to govern is to foresee," for change is faster now.

What then must we say of political thinking whose basic tenet is that we who are the most advanced and advancing in the development of world machines are the one people who can safely keep aloof from all efforts to organize the world politically? That for those who delight more than others in such things as telephoning from their Clippers flying across the Pacific to their balloons rising thirteen miles into the stratosphere the course of wisdom is to refrain from building machinery for allowing world change to proceed without war? That the more inventive and enterprising and foresighted a nation is mechanically the less it needs to be inventive and enterprising and foresighted politically? Can we say such thinking is political? Can we call it thinking?

We may set our clock back, we may set our clock ahead, but we can not set our clock back and ahead both at once.

HERMIT OR PIONEER?

We have only two choices, between struggling forward all along the line and falling backward all along it. We have only the choice between continuing the experiment we began three hundred years ago or abandoning it for the one Japan then started. In 1639 our fathers, believing that "to mayntayne the peace and union . . . there should be an orderly and decent Government established," made history's first written constitution to this end, establishing in Connecticut the federation of self-governing communities which served as a model for the American Union. In 1639, too, the Shogun, Iyemitsu Tokugawa, closed Japan, hoping to keep the world out forever by forbidding the Japanese to build ships big enough to take them overseas. For 215 years thereafter—until the federation of three Connecticut villages grew into one of 30,000,000 people stretching to and across the Pacific and knocking at Japan's door—the Tokugawas kept Japan a hermit nation with its population held down to 30,000,000.

Now the people who opened Japan in 1854 are urged to close their own country. Now while Japanese *conquistadores* carry the dogmas of divine right—both of kings and nations—through Asia, the children of the pioneers who spread the rights of man through the world are asked (often in the name of George Washington) to go the way of Iyemitsu. The modern American priests of Iyemitsu broadcast to us that no matter what happens to the rest of mankind we Americans can keep our prosperity and peace and freedom if only we will scrap the methods and the principles by which we gained them. They would keep us rich and independent by killing off our surplus pigs and making us depend on cowardice instead of courage for our freedom and our lives.

They forgot to tell us that the Shogun found some other things were needed to attain that isolationist, nationalist, neutralist paradise which Japan's hermit period represents. It was achieved and maintained only by killing off, too, the surplus Japanese by infanticide, famine and disease instead of war. More than half the 70,000,000 Japanese today owe their lives to the fact their country was finally opened to the civilization that, during their hermit centuries, had developed in the West with the doctrine of man's individual right to life and liberty. After Japan was opened to the West "prosperity and population rose by leaps and bounds" (to quote Hugh Byas). Thereafter, he points out, "the new mobility of the peasants and the introduction of chemical fertilizers doubled the food supply and abortion and infanticide ceased. Western hygienic science, favored by the traditional cleanliness of the people, reduced the toll of disease, and railways abolished regional famines." Thereafter, too, ceased the long night when the human species owed little to any Japanese. Then came the Shigas and the Hatas to serve mankind, and Noguchi to die for us all fighting the germ of yellow fever.

So it was in Japan. But it is one thing for a poverty-stricken, remote people accustomed to despotism to turn hermit in the seventeenth century and in its relatively static Orient. It is another for a rich, twentieth century western people accustomed to individual freedom to start back toward famine and infanticide. It is one thing for plants to feel the sun, another to feel the frost. It is one thing, too, for men to flourish while they let their free principles freely expand, another for them and their freedom to survive when subjected to quickening contraction.

Americans who believe they have already suffered in recent years all the ills isolationism can produce or who believe Japan's experience tells the worst they have to fear from hermithood—these Americans have many painful things left to learn. Two facts they may learn now. When Rome let freedom go it was not in Rome it slowly rose again; it was at the farthest edge of her vast empire. And when the Romans let go their freedom they fell so far that they have not climbed back to freedom yet.

. . . .

In the choice facing men today the name of no man is so much at stake as the name, *American*. Other peoples have proud traditions, but none has to continue the tradition "rooted in the future" that we Americans have to continue on the frontiers of self-government and Union.

Nor can this duty be more urgent to any Americans than to those of my own generation. The last Americans to die that this tradition might live were not the cronies of our fathers. They were not the playmates of our sons. They were the boys who played Indian and cowboy with us. They were the buddies of those who have now passed forty. They have a claim on us they have on no one else.

It is not our generation that is lost—not yet. We have only now reached that prime age when the responsibility for all that America means rests most on us. We followed when it was our turn to follow; now it is our turn to lead. We must write our own line now or never in the great record that Columbus opened with "Sail on!" The moving finger is already poised. We were lads in 1917 and we did then all that can be asked of youngsters. We are men today. Or are we? We must answer now. To us Walt Whitman calls:

> *Come my tan-faced children!* . . .
>
> *For we cannot tarry here,*
> *We must march, my darlings, we must bear the brunt of danger,*
> *We the youthful sinewy races, all the rest on us depend,*
> *Pioneers! O pioneers!*

. . . .

The New York Times *believes the American people will awake to the facts which menace this nation; and the world will learn that events are conceivable, that circumstances can arise, outside this hemisphere, which will instantly range American public opinion behind an effective peace policy and make junk overnight of the so-called Neutrality Act . . . The enemies of democracy will discover that the United States has not become so timorous and so stupid as to abandon its responsibilities and imperil its greatness and its freedom. It will be wiser to put them on notice at once.*—The New York Times, editorial, Nov. 30, 1937.

. . . .

The right is more precious than peace, and we shall fight for the things which we have always carried nearest our hearts,—for democracy, for the right of those who submit to authority to have a voice in their own Governments, for the rights and liberties of small nations, for a universal dominion of right by such a concert of free peoples as shall bring peace and safety to all nations and make the world itself at last free. To such a task we can dedicate our lives and our fortunes, everything that we have, with the pride of those who know that the day has come when America is privileged to spend her blood and her might for the principles that gave her birth and happiness and the peace which she has treasured. God helping her, she can do no other.—President Wilson, ending his speech to Congress for declaration of war against Germany, April 2, 1917.

CHAPTER IV

Patching Won't Do

No amendment leaving the states in possession of their sovereignty could possibly answer the purpose.—Hamilton.

The importance of the Federalist papers is that they expose, from experience and with unanswerable argument, why sovereignty is an insuperable obstacle to the organization of peace, and why the federal principle is the only way forward.—Lord Lothian, July 30, 1938.

PLAN OF CHAPTER

Our best post-war machinery for making, enforcing, interpreting and revising world law, the League of Nations, has failed. The trend back to pre-war methods proves this. It proves also how desperately we feel the need of change, for it is only too clear that there is no hope in turning back. Armaments, alliances, the Atlantic ocean, balancing power, proclaiming neutrality, desiring to keep out of war,—all these failed those who trusted in them before. They saved no people from war and between wars they failed to provide even a semblance of world government. The time gained by them costs fearfully in the gaining and risks making the final catastrophe only greater.

Reforming or patching the machinery we have seems to many the only practical thing to do. By reforming or, as I prefer, patching, I mean leaving basic principle intact. In patching I include any change, in law or fact, which however reached and however great, leaves the existing world machinery based on the principle of national sovereignty.

Before considering whether patching the League can suffice, we shall examine the possibility of patching one post-war international mechanism that remains in relatively good repute, the gold standard mechanism for giving the world stable money. The monetary problem has the advantage of being the least difficult of the major ones facing the world, and so, if we find it cannot be solved without sacrificing the principle of national sovereignty, we have gone far toward finding that patching won't do in any field. We need not then waste time examining other possibilities of patching things outside the League and can concentrate on the problem

65

of patching the League. To find that patching it is not enough is to conclude, as this chapter does, that we must tackle afresh the problem of organizing world government.

PATCHING THE WORLD GOLD STANDARD

Progress has been made . . . in the . . . establishment of a solid basis for exchange stability. . . . But that general confidence which is essential to international stability is not present. . . .

Adherence to a common currency system does not mean that individual countries will no longer be able to pursue internal policies of many different patterns. It does mean, however, that in doing so they will have to observe certain general principles . . . without which no monetary stability can be secured.—J. W. Beyen, President of the Bank for International Settlements, 1938 Report.

The world enjoyed stable money before the war, and it achieved this then through the gold standard even without the League of Nations or the Bank for International Settlements. To achieve it again is really a matter of agreement among a very few countries which have made considerable progress toward agreement in the Tripartite Accord; why then, can we not regain monetary stability by patching the old gold standard?

That standard, patched as the London Monetary and Economic Conference proposed, provides, I would grant, the best international money available under national sovereignty. Restoration of the gold standard on that basis, or any other basis of national sovereignty, has so far been blocked by such difficulties as the war debts problem, the question of where to fix the ratio of the pound and dollar, the disinclination in both Britain and the United States to resume foreign lending on a big scale and to reduce trade barriers to where they were when the gold standard flourished. These suffice to show how formidable are the practical difficulties facing monetary stabilization on these lines, but I do not insist on them here.

Suppose that the gold standard can be restored with all the improvements in the rules or provisions for cooperation that any one desires—so long as this leaves the principle of national sovereignty intact, with each state remaining free to leave gold by its own sovereign will and with the international gold standard differing from the national gold standard in having behind it no effective common government, common budget, common commercial policy and common gold reserve. When we get the best that is possible within these limits have we got international monetary stability? Not merely for a few years but enduringly, for otherwise it is not stability. Can we get reasonable stability and keep national sovereignty?

The first thing to be noted is that when we have thus restored the gold standard we shall not have solved our security, armament and economic problems. Even when the gold standard was functioning these other problems were accumulating the pressure that broke that standard in the world depression. That fact says all that needs to be said on the durability of any monetary stabilization that is not accompanied by solution of our political and economic problems. Mere restoration of the gold standard can not in itself cure these ills; such restoration therefore can not long remain.

The stability of the gold standard depends not only on gold reserves and budgets but, above all, on confidence—confidence particularly that the rules of the game will be observed scrupulously, especially in emergencies and by those whom this observance most endangers or hurts. One can not trust in the law when one can not trust in the policeman to risk his life to enforce the law against dangerous criminals. The restoration of the gold standard *among sovereign powers* depends for its durability upon the United States, Great Britain, France, Germany, Russia, Italy, and Japan, at least, feeling certain that the good will, good faith and enlightened self-interest of each of them will lead them all to respect scrupulously common monetary rules and cooperate loyally while accepting no strong central control and remaining political and economic rivals. Unless one can depend on them all having this mutual confidence one can not depend on the gold standard providing stability.

One plainly can not depend on this, and least of all when those very emergencies arise that stabilization is really intended to meet. In emergencies undisciplined and uncontrolled men are not governed by enlightened self-interest, good faith and good will, and in time of panic the collectivities of men called nations tend to become mobs. Moreover, the essential thing is that each of these nations, in retaining its sovereignty, retains the right to secede from the gold standard whenever it sees fit. The great powers may compel the weak ones to stay on gold, but short of war there is no way under national sovereignty to make a great power stick to any agreement on a really vital interest. To trust in the gold standard for stability in such conditions is like trusting in the law to keep the peace in a community which can not control the policeman and where each policeman reserves the right to leave the streets to bandits whenever they begin to shoot.

Recent experience is devastating to confidence in such a monetary system. It shows that central control over money is essential to confidence and that it is not possible when national sovereignty divides control among several fairly equal rivals.

The gold standard developed as an international money when world trade and finance were much less intensive, divided and swift-moving

than now and when Britain's position in world trade, finance and politics
was dominant. The gold standard developed then much more as a means
to national than to international monetary stability. Indeed, the only two
dangers to a nation's monetary stability that were foreseen before 1931
lay both inside the nation. One was the danger of domestic panic, the citizens all seeking at once to convert their paper money into gold. The other
danger was that a government which wished to balance its budget or increase its revenues without raising taxes, might issue more promises to
pay on sight in gold (that is, paper money) than it could reasonably hope
to make good. The gold standard went on the theory that both these
dangers could be met by each nation's law making its central banking
institution independent of the government as far as possible and by requiring it to maintain a certain minimum ratio (usually 40 per cent) of
gold in reserve against its paper currency or sight obligations.

Yet, when the gold standard broke down in 1931 it broke down through
neither of these causes, through no violation of the ratio rule, through no
inflationary measures, through no run on a gold reserve begun within the
nation. International, not national, factors broke it down. The people who
as voters had some control over the national budget and the national laws
had confidence everywhere in the national money. In each nation where
a run began, it began from a quite unexpected quarter, the outside world.
It would seem only natural, however, that the first man to distrust a money
when emergency loomed should be the man who had no control over it,
who had to put his trust in the good faith and enlightened self-interest of
foreigners,—not merely of the sovereign government and the men of the
country concerned but of other foreigners and their sovereign governments.

Even if the nations should agree to improve the gold standard with the
1933 London rules its essential untrustworthiness and instability would remain, for these rules do not reach the source of the trouble. They lower
the minimum ratio to 25 per cent and they improve the means of cooperation among the nations but they place no central control over them.

So long as any world money is based on cooperation alone the powers
each remain sovereign. Indeed, it is simply to allow each to remain at
bottom a law unto itself that the method of cooperation is followed. *One
can not have enduring faith in a money whose sole backers have thus
implicitly reserved the right to break their promises whenever they think
fit and have each preserved most carefully the means of violating with
impunity their undertakings to the world.* Any world money, so long as
the United States, Britain, and France retain their sovereign rights and
refuse to unite behind it as one government and make it depend on one
joint budget and one joint political economy, will sooner or later fall a

prey to precisely the same blind forces that wrecked the international gold standard in 1931. It will remain cursed by the memory of the examples set by England in 1931 and by the United States in 1933.*

It is silly to trust for stability in the supposition that the great powers have learned their lesson and can therefore be relied on to keep on gold once they have returned to it. They may all desire and they may all honestly intend to keep on gold, but not one of them will trust the others to keep from plunging the world back into monetary chaos, any more than it trusts the others, because of the experience of 1914-18, to keep from plunging the world back into war. Even if the great rival sovereign powers should not be half so nervous, alarmist and suspicious of each other on the monetary side in future as they have been politically during the past fifteen years, their distrust will still suffice to sap and to ruin whatever world gold standard they restore. It is conceivable that the world may return to gold without loss of national sovereignty, but if it does it can be thankful if this "stabilization" endures even as long as it did the last time and that was only five years, 1926-31.

THE FACT TO BE RETAINED

Before the war there was as a rule no fundamental maladjustment of currencies. . . . Not only were more peaceful relations maintained in the hundred years 1815-1914 than in any other period of modern history, but the wars that occurred caused no permanent currency depreciations. . . . There was no living memory of serious currency losses to make people fear for the substance of their savings or hesitate to grant commercial credits to foreign customers from apprehension regarding exchange and transfer difficulties. In such an age the monetary problems were mainly technical and unaffected by the current of national and international politics.

Today, on the contrary, not only the grave question of peace or war but also the general attitude of the different countries . . . has its influence; indeed, armaments and other measures that produce expansion predominantly in the national sphere may have unwonted repercussions on the foreign currency position. There is no overlooking the fact that an increase in "planned" activity creates new difficulties.—J. W. Beyen, President of the Bank for International Settlements, 1938 Report.

The fact to be retained is that when the international gold standard worked the only time it really did—in the nineteenth century and down to the war—it was based then on a factor that no longer obtains: British

* See Annex 3 for detailed study of how the principle of national sovereignty worked in practice to destroy monetary stability in and after 1931.

hegemony, especially in the industrial, commercial and financial world. It would be more accurate and enlightening to call the international gold standard then the sterling standard. Sterling then was the world money, and this was so not because sterling was on gold, but because Britain so far outdistanced all other powers that sterling had in every way the best backing of any currency, and traders everywhere prefer to do business in the stablest measure of value. The sterling note was not merely "as good as gold," but better, if only because it was also more convenient. Under the name of the gold standard the sterling standard spread abroad with the help of British prestige and British influence, the desire on one side to borrow in London as cheaply as possible and on the other to safeguard investments and promote trade. The currency in which most international business was done was sterling, even when between countries neither of which was British. While Germany, France and the United States were growing into rivals of Britain, time was also serving to fix more firmly on the world the British financial and monetary system.

The war ended this British hegemony without leaving any other power —not even the United States—in position to assume Britain's monetary role in the world. The British government sought to continue it as before, paid a high price to put sterling back on gold, and seemed at first to have succeeded in restoring the pre-war gold standard. But gold and tradition and momentum were not enough to keep it functioning in a world where the unrivalled financial predominance of one power had given way to rivalry among near equals. And so the gold standard crashed between two stools, along with the world's confidence in both the leading monetary rivals, the pound and the dollar.

There would seem to be no hope of restoring the enduringly stable money the world enjoyed in Britain's prime without restoring first its essential basis, namely, a single overwhelmingly powerful government that is responsible for it. There can be no such basis while the power which that money must have behind it remains divided among three sovereigns, Britain, the United States and France.

PATCHING THE LEAGUE OF NATIONS

No thinking person can seriously dispute that it is State sovereignty and the anarchy it creates in a shrinking world which is the basic cause of our main troubles today. . . . It is what prevents the League, for all that it represents the first attempt to organize the world for law and peace, from accomplishing its noble purpose.—Lord Lothian, July 30, 1938.

When we turn to the best existing machinery for making, enforcing, interpreting and revising international agreements, the League of Nations, we find that it is itself a patch—though a big one—on the pre-war machinery. The League's "internationalism" is often contrasted with pre-war nationalism as if it were at the other pole. It is really an extension of the same principle.

The basic principle of the pre-war system was national sovereignty: Its unit for making, enforcing, interpreting and revising agreement was the state, its equality was the equality of these units, its procedure required their unanimous consent and its highest aim was to keep each state sovereign. The drafters of the Covenant, far from rejecting this, sought to legalize and crystallize it all by converting it from the unwritten to the solemnly signed. They enthroned the pre-war principle in the League and contented themselves with patching the pre-war application of it.

Their patching affected mainly two fields, (a) the means of making and revising and interpreting agreement peacefully, and (b) the means of enforcing it. In the first field, the chief means that the pre-war system provided were the permanent diplomatic machinery, isolated conferences, and The Hague panels from which special courts might be made for special questions. To these the League added permanent machinery for regular conference, a permanent secretariat, and a permanent court for all questions. In the second field, the pre-war system provided no international means to enforce international law, or to attain its object, the preservation of national sovereignty, except regional alliances aimed against other alliances. The League patched this by providing a world-wide collective alliance to uphold its law against any state that broke it by resorting to war.

THE TWO SCHOOLS

All proposals to patch the League consist at bottom in patching either or both of these League patches on the pre-war system. The patchers may therefore be divided into those who concentrate on the conference side of the League's patch on the pre-war system, and those who concentrate on the enforcement side.

The first are fascinated by all they imagine the League might do if only the United States joined it; this thought lies at the root of their thinking. The cult of universalism at Geneva is but one of the manifestations of its suppressed desire for American membership. Those who keep saying that the League cannot work because it is not universal really mean they think it cannot work without the United States. The fact, of course, is that the League was built to work without being universal, it was meant to be limited to democracies,—to be, in President Wilson's words, "such a concert of free peoples as shall bring peace and safety to all nations and make the world itself at last free." But it was not built to work without the United States. Since, however, Americans resented being reminded of this, those who sought to bring the United States in stressed by euphemism the need of universality. This led to the idea that if only non-membership could be reduced to the United States alone, the American people could not hold out longer and would join, too. From this tortuous thinking developed the habit and then the cult of that Geneva universalism which now holds it worse for the League to lose a member than a principle.

The second school is fascinated by all the power that the League wastes. It stresses that even without the United States, Germany, Japan and Italy, the combined power of the 50 odd members of the League would be overwhelming—if only the Covenant effectively harnessed it. This school sees that one can take a much smaller number of powers and by combining better their power make their organization far more effective than a universal league based on the present Covenant, let alone one based on a looser covenant.

The first school fears that tightening the machinery will mean practically an alliance against Germany, Japan and Italy. Or it sees that no matter what assurances are given that the alliance is open to these powers the reasons that have already brought them all into conflict with the League will keep them out of it. Tightening the League seems to this school equivalent to resigning oneself to war, for how, it asks, can peace possibly be arranged if all the parties are not around the table?

The second school fears that bringing everyone around the table means resigning oneself to war by hiding head in sand, recreating in substance the pre-war situation, where all the world sat round the table at The Hague, but remained divided into prospective neutrals and prospective belligerents, with the latter divided into two great allied camps. When this led to war, the more democratic camp was forced to build up a world coalition to save itself, and the League was designed to provide permanently a democratic coalition so as to prevent the danger recurring. Why dissolve that coalition, this school asks, for another mirage of universal concord only to have to build it up again by this terrible process?

Then there are those many who share the hopes and fears of both schools and would combine all the patches in a political "crazy quilt." They would make the League universal by removing its teeth as far as they concern the United States, Japan and other overseas countries. Within this they would have continental compartments organized possibly in America and certainly in Europe on the present basis of the Covenant, except that its military commitment would be dropped and only its non-military sanctions retained. Within these continental compartments they would organize military mutual assistance pacts whereby the neighbors around every danger zone would commit themselves to enforce peace by arms against any one of them violating it.

To simplify the task all these patches will be considered under three general headings: (1) the universal conference, (2) the world or big regional collective alliance, (3) the small regional collective alliance or mutual assistance pact. In finding that they are all delusions, we shall see that the combination of them produces only delusion, too.

At the outset it may be noted that the patch that consists in bringing the United States into the League as it stands should be ruled out as practically hopeless. But all proposed patches that involve, as most do, serious amendments of the Covenant, whether to weaken or strengthen it, are no less hopeless. Many efforts have already been made to amend the Covenant; all of any importance have failed; there is no reason to expect success in future. Suppose, however, that these hurdles can be cleared, and in good time.

THE FUTILITY OF UNIVERSAL CONFERENCE

The school that stresses the conference side of the League aims to get everyone regularly around the table by sacrificing the means of enforcing the Covenant. It does not yet explain what revision of the Covenant will bring back Italy, Germany and Japan, keep out Ethiopia, bring in Manchukuo, and still attract the United States to Geneva. Bringing nations around a table does not make sure that agreement will be reached even if they are few in number and seek the same ends. Increasing their number by increasing their divergencies, as by bringing democracies and autocracies together as partners, makes sure only that agreement will be reached very slowly if at all. Could the League have done as much as swiftly as it did in condemning Italy and applying sanctions had Japan and Germany still been members?

This patching, moreover, cannot possibly reduce armaments or stop alliances. Since it provides no means of enforcing any peace agreements that do result, each nation must depend as before the war entirely on its own arms, alliances, and secret diplomacy. Finally and most important, no system of law and government has ever yet succeeded without having force, and overwhelming force, behind it. All patching of the League that ignores this is foredoomed to fail.

THE FUTILITY OF THE BIG COLLECTIVE ALLIANCE

We come to the other school which seeks to avoid the dangers both of no enforcement and of the pre-war alliance by the collective alliance backed by military staff plans for its execution. The case for this collective alliance, whether big or small, has been well put by Sir Norman Angell to whom peace owes so much. Speaking for the Executive Committee of "The Next Five Years Group" in a letter to *The Times* (London), published March 31, 1936, he wrote:

We are warned from many quarters about the danger of "making alliances with France" of conversations between the staffs, and are urged instead to "act through the League." There is certainly some danger here of falling into grave confusion owing to a careless use of words. The danger is not in an alliance—the League itself is an alliance—but in allowing an alliance designed to be the nucleus of a true European society upholding a principle of security which can be applied to all alike becoming an alliance which is in fact a challenge to that principle.

The older type of alliance was exemplified in the two groups that confronted each other at the outbreak of the War. The growing power of Germany threatened to deprive us of all means of defending our interests and rights. Germany saw the War close by a hostile preponderance which deprived her of any means of defending her interests and rights and which imposed the Treaty of Versailles. If she was secure, we were not; if we were secure, she was not. The only recourse open to a State threatened by hostile preponderance was to fight.

Collective alliances offer another alternative to a state threatened with encirclement; it can join the alliances which encircle it and claim their privileges and protections, the privilege, that is, of impartial judgment in its disputes and protection against war; a defence organized on the principle that an attack on one is an attack on all. The collective alliance offers to others the same protection of law which it claims for itself. The old alliances did not. All forms of the collective method involve the giving of guarantees, undertakings to do certain things in certain circumstances. To say that conversations beforehand as to how these undertakings may best be carried out are dangerous is to condemn the undertakings themselves to unreality. The whole method depends upon the conviction that when the time comes the undertakings really will be fulfilled.

There seems no doubt that Sir Norman Angell is right in holding that to keep the potential aggressor in awe of overwhelming opposition one must do more than pledge in advance to give military aid to his victim, one must back this up with concrete staff plans. This staff work triply protects a member of an alliance: It assures him and everyone that his allies mean business, and it tells him precisely what help in men, material, blockade or money he will get and how it is to be used.

Moreover, the secrecy of the plan coupled with the knowledge that there is a plan leaves the potential aggressor against whom it is aimed fearful of the surprises that the allies have prepared against his own surprises. Gas, the airplane, the elimination of declaration of war because of the Kellogg Pact, and other things greatly increase the danger that the aggressor will attempt swift and overwhelming surprise attack requiring swift and strong defence to meet it. This makes detailed and secret staff planning in advance by allies—whether collective or not—much more necessary than before 1914.

It is practically impossible, however, to provide this planning in a genuine collective alliance, whether it has sixty members or three. Attempts at security through this method therefore also lead inevitably to armaments, pre-war alliances and secret diplomacy.*

To save the military and non-military commitments of Article Sixteen of the Covenant from unreality by staff planning, the League would need a secret war plan to protect each of the fifty-eight members against aggression by any of the other fifty-seven through alliance of the remaining fifty-six, since each member in this system is potentially victim, aggressor and ally. It would need war plans too against each of the non-Members, and against coalitions of Members, or of non-Members, or of both. Nothing half so complicated is possible. Even if it were the plans would be of small value for they could not be kept secret.

Even were the United States in the League, the universal collective alliance must still be practically planless and therefore of no military value to any League member at the time when war begins—when military aid is most needed. It may, of course, help later, and this possibility may deter the potential aggressor. The collective alliance is by no means useless to any peaceful country, and may save it not only from attack but from defeat in the end. But the aim of every government is bound to be to avoid being, (a) overwhelmed by surprise attack, (b) drawn into so long a war that it is ruined even if it wins, or, (c) forced to fight on its own soil. To avoid all this each member of the collective alliance is obliged to depend on his own armed force, to meet the first—and surprise—attack, and to hold the fort thereafter

* This sentence, indeed all this chapter was written early in 1936. I leave it to the reader to consider how subsequent events, such as rearmament, the development of the axis and new Anglo-French Entente, and the shift from Geneva to diplomatic channels, have justified it. I included much of the substance of this chapter in a lecture to the Geneva Institute of International Relations in August, 1936, published by the Institute in the eleventh series of its *Problems of Peace*. I take this occasion to thank the Institute and its publisher, George Allen and Unwin, Ltd., for their permission to use this material here, the place for which it was originally written.

until Geneva can improvise and deliver aid of problematic character, speed and value.

Attack means that the victim's trust in the deterrent value of the League has proved unfounded, out-balanced probably by the aggressor's hope that he can sow confusion among the League members, exploit their inertia or divergent interests and delay the League's aid until it comes too late, or prevent its coming at all. These possibilities increase the victim's need of preparing to stand the first shock himself.

The upshot is that the League's collective alliance can not reduce armaments. Instead, the *League's inability to provide immediate military help together with its possibility of providing decisive help in the end if the victim can only hold out long enough combine positively to encourage each member*—or at least those most likely to be attacked—*to increase armaments*. The League thus leads back fatally to armaments racing.

This situation encourages the most exposed members to turn back to the encircling regional alliance to supply the deficiencies of the big collective alliance. Such arrangements as those of France with Belgium, Poland, Czechoslovakia, Yugoslavia and Rumania, the Little Entente and the Balkan Entente follow. Since no government, and least of all the one against which the alliance is more or less disguisedly directed, can be sure it is really a defensive and not an aggressive alliance, each must seek alliances. The League thus leads back fatally to the pre-war race for alliances.

All this encourages secret diplomacy. For these encircling alliances must be so harmonized with the collective alliance that the swift aid given by the one does not cancel the claim for the collective alliance's slower aid. All sorts of formulas have been used to this end, but it is practically impossible genuinely to harmonize the two. League governments cannot possibly avow openly that they are allying in pre-war style against one of their collective allies in the League. They must hide the real purpose of their treaty as well as the inter-staff work which forms the means to its end. The more exposed they are to attack the more deeply they are driven into secret diplomacy. For they then need the more not only to plan with their regional allies against the initial attack but also to obtain the moral support and slower material aid of the big collective alliance. The League thus leads back fatally to secret diplomacy.

THE FUTILITY OF SMALL REGIONAL PACTS

The consequences of the collective alliance can not be avoided by reducing its membership. To see this we need consider only the smallest pact, the Locarno guarantee treaty and the mutual assistance pact which has been proposed in its place. Here is the difference between them: In the Locarno treaty Britain and Italy agreed to guarantee with their military power France, Belgium and Germany against attack by any one or two of these three, but these three did not guarantee Britain and Italy. In the mutual pact all members would guarantee each other equally; they would form really a small league or collective alliance.

The effectiveness of the Locarno guarantee depended on France, Britain and Italy arranging in advance through their staffs secret war plans to repel together German attack on France by any conceivable route. It depended equally on Britain and Italy making similar secret plans with Germany to repel French attack on Germany. It is, however, clearly impossible to do both. Britain and Italy would have to know the secret war plans of both France and Germany, and they would have to divulge the French secrets to the German staff and the German secrets to the French staff. That would require new plans on each side whose secrets would then have to be divulged, and so on. The process would be worse than sterile, it would breed suspicion.

The Locarno guarantee was thus at bottom meaningless, but its members never got down to these absurdities. They were too busy with another difficulty. Britain, having no control over the policy of either France or Germany, insisted on keeping its guarantee to both ambiguous so that when a war threat actually rose it might decide for itself what if anything it would do. Before the French staff could plan with the British staff for the execution of the guarantee, the French had first to get Britain to make the guarantee unambiguous and automatic; they devoted ten years to this in vain. The Germans waited to see the result, for they knew that the British would not do more for Germany than for France. So no joint plans were made to execute either guarantee, France and Germany had to rely entirely on their own arms, the one could not reduce them nor the other ask less than equality in them, and the race began. Soon Germany found reason to fear that the French, thanks to Italy's Ethiopian challenge to Britain, had finally got the British to the verge of jointly planning to uphold Locarno's guarantee that the Rhineland should remain demilitarized and unfortified. Germany decided to move before they were ready and occupied that region by surprise March 7, 1936. The Locarno guarantee ended by not being upheld in this flagrant case.*

The result was that the British staff then made secret plans with the French staff and London unambiguously guaranteed France and Bel-

* See Annex 3 for a more detailed analysis of how the principle of national sovereignty destroyed the Locarno treaty.

gium against German attack while dropping its guarantee to Germany. That means that Britain is even more committed now than in 1914. The British government has sought to escape the danger of this situation by declaring that the commitment is strictly limited to the period needed to replace the Locarno treaty with a mutual assistance pact that would include Germany. But such a pact would make matters worse. For the mutual treaty has all the fatal defects that the Locarno guarantee type has, and it has them to a worse degree.

The rock on which Locarno foundered was not that Britain had no guarantee from France and Germany but that Britain could not give an automatic guarantee to either without practically underwriting its policies blindly. Britain does not change this by asking a blind guarantee of its own policy in return; all it does is weaken the guarantee Britain gives. For the fact that Britain asks a guarantee proves that Britain is no longer strong and impregnable enough to defend itself alone.

If the new mutual treaty should get past the rock on which Locarno foundered it would run on the rocks that Locarno escaped only by foundering beforehand: The untrustworthiness of such security pacts unless armed with secret war plans, and the impossibility of thus arming them. The basic absurdity in the Locarno treaty was that Britain and Italy had to make and could not possibly make secret war plans with France for war on Germany and with Germany for war on France. A mutual pact makes this absurdity worse for it requires secret war planing among

Britain, Italy, France,	against	Germany;
Britain, Italy, Germany,	"	France;
Britain, France, Germany,	"	Italy;
France, Germany, Italy,	"	Britain.

Could the devil himself devise anything capable of causing more frustration, intrigue and suspicion than this? If no plans are made the door is left open to surprise attack all round. If all the plans could be made they would only cancel each other out. There are only four major possibilities:

1. All explicitly agree there shall be no staff planning; this leaves each open to surprise attack and therefore requires each to arm or seek alliances or both.

2. Because of the futility and danger of this first course, all implicitly agree to plan but none does; this still leaves each open to surprise attack and encourages each to suspect that the others are planning to attack it.

3. Because of the futility and danger of the first two courses, all

the plans are made; this leaves each plan cancelling out the others, none of them secret, and all the parties back where they started.

4. Because of the futility and danger of the first three courses, any one of them is ostensibly followed, and under cover of this some members make a super-secret plan against another; this changes the pact into a pre-war alliance with all its faults compounded by super-secrecy, hypocrisy and bad faith.

Clearly if any government is to feel secure under a regional mutual assistance pact it must trust in the power of its armaments and the secrecy of its diplomacy, not in the pact.

So far we have assumed that a Rhine mutual assistance pact could stand alone. But it could not. This is so obvious that none of its supporters has seriously proposed to limit mutual assistance to one region. The idea is to have several of these pacts and to tie them together some way through the League. It consists, as "provisionally" expressed by Neville Chamberlain,* in "localizing the danger spots of the world and trying to find a more practical method of securing peace by means of regional arrangements which could be approved by the League, but which should be guaranteed only by those nations whose interests were vitally connected with these danger zones." Whether left as loose as this or made as tight as Paul-Boncour's elaborate plan, this idea involves mutual assistance pacts on the Rhine and in Eastern Europe, Central Europe, the Balkans, and the Mediterranean, at least. It merely multiplies the difficulties and absurdities of the Rhine pact. Each of these pacts has the defects of the Rhine one, and most of them to a worse degree. The Eastern Pact, for example, would require Communist Russia to plan secretly to aid Nazi Germany against France—and would require (if it is to work) Germany to trust that Russia is as sincere in planning for as in planning against Germany.

The inter-connections of these pacts cause further difficulties. When, for example, Britain and Italy interpret the Rhine pact to mean they must aid Germany against France they may find Russia and Poland interpreting the Eastern pact to mean they must aid France against Germany. Britain, Italy and Germany will not only have to make war plans against France in order to execute their pact, they must plan war against France, Poland and Russia too. The reverse is also true, of course, as are also all the other possibilities,—Britain, Italy, Poland, Germany, against France and Russia, etc., etc. This is only a beginning for there are the Central European, Balkan, and Mediterranean Pacts to be considered, too, in the planning. The possibilities are infinite, and much too bewildering for this system to give confidence to any nation. The

* In his speech before the 1900 Club, June 10, 1936.

method of simplifying by resorting to small regional pacts ends by creating even worse complications than a European or universal mutual assistance pact.

The backers of this scheme hope, of course, that all these pacts will be focused together on one state as aggressor, that when, for example, Britain and Italy decide France is aggressor against Germany, this view will be shared by Russia and Poland, so that the result will be five against France. But that possibility does not require nearly the planning that the opposite possibility does for it is not so dangerous. Consequently if Britain and Italy refuse to plan secretly with Germany to meet the greater danger, that Russia and/or Poland should aid France, Berlin must prepare otherwise against the risk of being deserted precisely when and because it needs help most,—and this means more armaments.

Moreover, this system so works that the less danger the victim runs the more likely he is to get the promised mutual assistance, and the more danger he runs the less likely he is to get help. What system of law enforcement could be more untrustworthy?

This situation forces the backers of this scheme back to the League in order to have at least some means of focusing all the regional pacts on one country as aggressor by this decision being taken simultaneously at the same table. This, however, does not guarantee that all parties will then agree—and it is the possibility of disagreement in fact if not in form that does the damage. Moreover, it is hard to tie such regional pacts to the Covenant without making them so slow and uncertain in action as to make them useless. It will be hard enough to get each of them concluded in the first place, and still harder to enforce the Covenant in any given area without the neighboring powers having planned ahead to enforce it there. One needs only read the Locarno treaty and study how the Council's role in it worked out in fact to appreciate how serious are these difficulties.

Finally each government must expect that when the moment comes to apply these pacts, either separately or through the Council, there will be, just then, such unforeseen complications as in March, 1936, when the Locarno violation found Italy playing the triple role of Locarno guarantor, condemned Ethiopian aggressor, and Council member,—sheriff, criminal and judge. One must expect something unforeseen at such times because aggressors always seek to act when such complications exist to favor them.

The hope which the idea of regional mutual assistance pacts has raised in many quarters comes from no merit in the idea itself, but simply from the promise of an alternative to a hopeless universal pact and the still more hopeless pre-war system and from the failure to think it through. It owes its favor not to what it is but to what it isn't and to what it is fancied to be. The more deeply one goes into it, the more unworkable, unreal and downright absurd it appears and the less one can escape the conclusion that either its utter futility will throw the world openly back into two armed camps as in 1914 or it will provide merely a blind to hide this fact. The regional pact is no better than the universal one; it leads as fatally to arms racing, alliance racing, secret diplomacy and war.

How could such glaring defects as these in the collective system whether on a universal or a regional basis escape so long the attention both of foes and friends of the League and Locarno? For years I have been in the thick of world discussions of this security problem by those most immersed in it without hearing these flaws brought out. I say this in no criticizing spirit but to note a fact that must interest every thinking man, for it concerns process of thought itself. I am in no position to criticize others for blindness. I have made as thorough a study of the security problem as I could and I confess that these basic absurdities of the League never occurred to me, either, until after sanctions were applied to Italy.

Looking backward I find these reasons why the world never got down to these basic absurdities of the collective system.

The foes of the League who presumably should have brought them out have not generally been very intelligent or lucid in their criticisms of it; their opposition has proceeded more from prejudice and passion than from reason. The opposition has rarely approached the subject from the premise that some form of world government is necessary and proceeded to deny the conclusion that the League form meets this need soundly. Instead it has usually denied the premise, and held that no world organization, or none with enforcing power, is needed, or is worth the sacrifice of national sovereignty. Often, indeed, the opposition has agreed, at least implicitly, that the conclusion of the League supporters followed from their premise; it has objected to the League not because it couldn't work but because it was supposed to be too strong, a superstate that would work only too well. Denial of the Geneva premise and rejection of its conclusion as too true have especially characterized opposition to the League in the United States and the British Empire, and the success of such opposition in such strong states has determined the development of the whole debate.

League supporters had no time to go deeply into the question of collective security. They were too busy defending their premise, trying to work out the problem of relations with the United States, seeking to get Britain to commit itself to the enforcement of the Covenant. They tended to assume that if only the United States would join and would consult, or if only Britain would agree unequivocally to stand by Article Sixteen, or if only the peoples were educated up to the fact that to prevent war they must be ready to assure quick overwhelming military aid to the victim no matter where,—why, then, no difficulty would be left. They knew enforcement was necessary for the maintenance of law and order, they saw no alternative to the League method of enforcement, the opposition offered none, and, being under no pressure to consider whether their method was sound, they simply jumped to the conclusion that it was sound. To get to the core of a matter one must first get below the surface, but the face that the surface is too tough to get through gives no reason to assume that the core is solid. It can still be hollow.

GEORGE WASHINGTON COULD NOT MAKE A LEAGUE WORK

The League's failure is not due to lack of leaders, lack of real statesmen. In the Geneva Assemblies that discussed the Ethiopian fiasco a number of delegates placed the blame for it not on the Covenant but on men who failed to apply it. It is very doubtful, however, that the greatest statesmen mankind has ever had could make the League of Nations work well enough to meet our needs. History has known other leagues but it has never known statesmen who could make one work successfully. The United States began as a League of Friendship and the fact that even this league worked no better than the League of Nations helps to show that the fault today lies in the system, not the statesmen.

The League of Friendship had greater power than the League of Nations, for though it lacked the explicit legal right to coerce members it enjoyed such practical powers as the right to raise its own army, make requisitions, issue money. It was made up of thirteen contiguous states, instead of nearly sixty world-scattered countries. Its member peoples, though much more divided than we now assume, had a common color (white), a common language and a dominant nationality (English), a common mother country, a common religion (Christian), a common tradition (pioneer), a common political theory (democracy). This is not true of the members of the League of Nations. The League of Friendship had a much better political instrument for common action and a far easier problem in cooperation than the League of Nations. Yet the League of Nations has been a success compared to the League of Friendship. Its failures have been in the same fields, and have been relatively no worse; and it has successes to its credit (such as maintaining order in the Saar with a League Army, settling the Yugoslav-Hungarian conflict, establishing some effective treaties, especially the narcotics convention of 1931, and restoring the finances of Austria, Hungary and other States) for which there is no parallel in the League of Friendship.

It has enjoyed, too, much more respect and good will from most of its member states. Apart from Italy's withdrawal for political reasons, no member of the League Council except Ecuador has ever failed to attend a single meeting, and only a few of the more backward and unimportant member states have ever missed the annual Assembly. No Geneva meeting has ever been even delayed for lack of a quorum. Compare this with the record of the League of Friendship. The total membership of its Congress was ninety-one delegates but the average attendance in the six years preceding Union was only about twenty-five. Often it could not sit because no quorum came. Things reached the point where Delaware, not thirty miles from Philadelphia where Congress met, decided it was no longer worth the expense to send a delegate.

Because of the contempt into which this American Assembly had fallen it was even thought necessary to insert in the new Constitution of the American Union a provision empowering the Union's Congress "to compel the attendance of absent members in such manner, and under such penalties as each House may provide." The Union Congress has not had to use this power, but the League of Nations not only has never had but has never needed the right to compel attendance.

Two things seem to account for the relatively smaller failure of the League of Nations, despite its harder problems, weaker powers and more cumbersome machinery. One is that the general standard of political intelligence and the general level of statesmanship throughout the world has risen considerably in the 150 years since the League of Friendship gave way to the American Union.

The other is that communications are now much faster. It took a month for the fastest message to reach Philadelphia, the seat of the League of Friendship, from its most remote members: a delegate took still longer. A delegate to the League of Nations can reach Geneva from any state in half that time—and Geneva can broadcast to the whole world in a flash. The Romans were right: Speed of communication is one of the greatest factors in government.

But despite these improvements the best the League can do is not good enough today. We cannot expect statesmen to succeed with it. Washington, Jefferson, Hamilton, Adams, Madison,—the men who founded so securely the American Union and made so great a success of this untried system of inter-state government,—were all alive when the League of Friendship existed. They tried first to make the league system work. They could do nothing with it. We can not reasonably hope that men even of their calibre can meet through any kind of league our swiftly growing needs today. What we can hope is that once we find the sound mechanism for world government that the American States found in 1787 we shall also find as they did then plenty of able statesmen among the very men we now condemn for failing to make a league work.

THE NEED TO START AFRESH

With the League and collective security as with the old high-wheeled bicycle we have started in the right direction but on the wrong wheel. For a generation inventors wasted ingenuity trying to make that absurd bicycle effective while carefully preserving the principle of harnessing the power directly to the front wheel axle. That seemed the easiest solution of the power problem, but it was the cause of the bicycle's absurdity, for it forced the front wheel to have a radius as long as a man's leg. When this principle was abandoned, the problem tackled afresh and the power chained to the other wheel, the bicycle became at once effective. True, had the high wheel's absurdity led men to abandon the bicycle itself in despair and content themselves with the horse they would never have solved the problem. It can not be wiser to abandon the League of Nations or any other existing machinery for world government until a better mechanism has been found. Men can not hope, however, to achieve reasonable and effective world government until they do abandon the assumptions which have led to the grotesque and unworkable, and start afresh their thinking on this problem too.

We face today the issue that the Thirteen American States faced when their attempt to organize themselves as a league had confronted them with the dangers of war, dictatorship and depression. As the delegates assembled in Philadelphia in 1787 for the Convention called to consider what to do, debate began among them on the question: Whether to attempt merely to patch the League of Friendship or to start afresh? Here is the story as Fiske tells it in his *Critical Period of American History:**

Some of the delegates came with the design of simply amending the articles of confederation by taking away from the states the power of regulating commerce, and intrusting this power to Congress. Others felt that if the work were not done thoroughly now another chance might never be offered; and these men thought it necessary to abolish the confederation, and establish a federal republic, in which the general government should act directly upon the people. The difficult problem was how to frame a plan of this sort which people could be made to understand and adopt.

* See *Critical Period of American History*, 1783-1789, p. 249 ff. Houghton Mifflin and Co., Boston and New York.

At the outset, before the convention had been called to order, some of the delegates began to exhibit symptoms of that peculiar kind of moral cowardice which is wont to afflict free governments, and of which American history furnishes so many instructive examples. In an informal discussion it was suggested that palliatives and half measures would be far more likely to find favor with the people than any thorough-going reform, when Washington suddenly interposed with a brief but immortal speech, which ought to be blazoned in letters of gold and posted on the wall of every American assembly . . . In tones unwontedly solemn he exclaimed:

"It is too probable that no plan we propose will be adopted. Perhaps another dreadful conflict is to be sustained. If, to please the people, we offer what we ourselves disapprove, how can we afterward defend our work? Let us raise a standard to which the wise and the honest can repair; the event is in the hand of God."

That settled the question then, and the results gained by following Washington's advice should make its wisdom still more persuasive to us now.

CHAPTER V

Why Start with the Democracies

We have it in our power to begin the world over again.—Paine, *Common Sense,* 1776.

PLAN OF CHAPTER

We must approach afresh the problem of organizing world government, but where shall we start? Shall we begin by trying to organize all the world at once or only a few peoples, and if so, which? This chapter shows why we should start with a nucleus composed only of democracies. Since the more the peoples composing the nucleus are naturally drawn together and the stronger their combined power the better the nucleus will be, the qualifications of fifteen democracies are then examined from both these standpoints and found unequalled. Discussion of whether it would be still better to omit a few or add a few democracies leads next to the conclusion that two things are essential, namely that the nucleus be composed of at least twelve and not more than twenty democracies, and that universality must be the ultimate goal. In this connection the problems raised by various states, such as Czechoslovakia, the Latin American republics, Soviet Russia, Germany, Italy, and Japan, are discussed, and also the general question of relations with non-members.

NEEDED: A NUCLEUS WORLD GOVERNMENT

The magnitude of the object is indeed embarrassing. The great system of Henry the IVth of France, aided by the greatest statesmen, is small when compared to the fabric we are now about to erect.—James Wilson in the American Union's Constitutional Convention.

With frustration for mainspring, the pendulum of world political thought has been swinging between the equally impractical extremes of trying to let each nation move as it pleases and trying to get all the nations to move together. The League of Nations and its still more universal disarmament and economic conferences illustrate the universal method. The first and hardest step in organizing the world is to get agreement on its constitution, and the universal method increases this difficulty (a) by increasing the number upon whose consent agreement depends, and (b) by thus inevitably lowering the average of political culture and experience available to meet the difficulty it heightens. Because universality must be the goal of any plan for world government, many think that the more members at the start the better. But one can not advance far when one tries to make the last step the first step, too.

The failures of the two extreme methods, isolationism and universalism, have led to various attempts and proposals to find some half-way ground by restricting numbers. Examples are the Pan America school, Briand's European Federation plan, and the post-war spectre of the old Concert of Powers flickering from Big Three to Big Five around Mussolini's Four Power pact proposal. They all have had two things in common: (1) They base their restriction of members on some factor, such as position on a certain continent or possession of great armed power, which keeps their membership forever restricted and excludes the possibility of growth into universal government, and (2) they have not proved satisfactory even in their restricted fields.

There remains what I call the method of the nucleus, which has not been tried. It alone combines the truth in the restricted method with the truth in the universal method, and combines them in their common sense order. It alone seeks to achieve world government through the normal principle of growth, through taking care at the start to select the best seed and then planting it well and cultivating it.

This method would have a nucleus world state organized by the peoples best qualified to organize its government soundly on a basis favorable to its peaceful extension round the world, and it would count thereafter on the vitality of this nucleus and the character of its principles for its growth to universality. The nucleus method would turn to the leaders in inter-state government for leadership toward universal government. The rearguard may become the leader when a mass reverses its movement, but if the mass is to continue forward, the vanguard must lead. Some sixty nations make the world political mass, and to count more than fifteen or twenty of them as the vanguard is to confuse the vanguard with the body and the rearguard, and deprive either one's terms of all meaning or the mass of all movement. The political character of the problem, the magnitude of the object and the need of early, sound solution all favor organizing the smallest practical number of the nations most advanced politically into a nucleus world government.

THE NUCLEUS NEEDS TO BE DEMOCRATIC

The last hope of human liberty in this world rests on us.—Jefferson.

What states shall compose the nucleus, the autocracies, the democracies, or a combination of the two? It can not be composed of autocracies alone.

They are not strong enough. Their basic political theory is opposed to organizing law and order in the world except by the method of one conquering all. Such governments as the German, the Italian, and the Japanese must organize inter-state government—if they can at all—on their common theory that the people are made for the state. They could not bring the American, British, French, and other democratic peoples under such a government except by force.

Nor can the nucleus be composed of democracies and autocracies together. We organize a tug of war, not a government, when we arrange for those who believe that government is made for the people to pull together with those who believe the opposite.

The nucleus must be composed exclusively of democracies. To start to make a world government pre-supposes belief in the democratic principle that government is made by the people. It is no accident that the desire for world law and order is strongest among the democratic peoples. It is natural that the democrats should be the ones who want world government, that they should insist on its being democratic, and that they should begin by organizing it among themselves.

One can hope, moreover, for the existing autocracies to enter eventually a democratic world government without war. Can one imagine, say, an American Napoleon overthrowing the American democracy and establishing himself as autocrat—in order to submit peacefully to the foreign autocrat ruling an autocratic world government? One can imagine a people overthrowing its autocrat and establishing a democracy in order to gain admittance to a democratic world government.

To organize world government soundly we must turn to the peoples most advanced and experienced politically, and this too turns us to the democracies. Peoples that accept dictatorships must be classified, politically, among the immature, or retarded, or inexperienced, high as they may rank otherwise. In admitting to be governed authoritatively, they admit they are not able to govern themselves freely. While men accept being governed as children they must be rated as immature.

As the world must turn to the democracies for world government, the democracies must turn to their vanguard. To begin this task in a constituent assembly composed of all the peoples that call themselves democratic is to burden the most experienced nations with those least experienced. It is as well-intentioned and foolish as trying to preserve the Bill of Rights for our children by giving children the vote.

The essential, it is worth repeating, is to get government constituted soundly and without delay. One can be sure then that those left out at the start will not be left out long. An example: When the American Union was made the glaring exception slavery formed to the Union's basic principle, *all men are created equal*, caused much argument. Such great democrats as George Mason, though himself a rich slave-owner, refused to sign the Constitution partly because it did not apply this principle thoroughly enough, and particularly because it allowed the slave traffic from Africa to continue twenty years. The Union could not have been established at all had its Constitution abolished immediately the importation of slaves, let alone extended complete political equality to the Negro, or even manhood suffrage to white men. Failure to form the Union could not have hastened manhood suffrage and the abolition of slavery; it might well have prevented them. Yet, once the American Union was firmly established by slave-owners and other men of property on the principle, *all men are created equal*, it began applying that principle to all those excluded from it at the start, and it has kept on doing so ever since.

This example suggests how all those left out of the world government at the time of its foundation may count themselves nonetheless among those who helped make it possible, for by their absence they helped reduce a hitherto insoluble problem to terms easy enough for sound solution to be reached. It indicates, too, how they gain from such solution being thus made possible. It shows how in organizing a new and democratic government in any community we need to turn to the elements in it—whether wealthy slave-owners or imperial democracies—that have, because of their possessions, the greatest interest in replacing chaos with effective government, and that are at the same time, because of their experience and ideals, best qualified to harness effective government to liberal principles.

FIFTEEN DEMOCRACIES AS NUCLEUS

Turning from the general to the concrete let us now consider the nucleus that could be formed by these fifteen democracies: The American Union, the United Kingdom, France, Australia, Belgium, Canada, Denmark, Finland, Holland, Ireland, New Zealand, Norway, Sweden, Switzerland, and the Union of South Africa. By first considering the possibilities that this group offers we can decide better whether to start the enterprise with a somewhat smaller or somewhat larger number.

The best nucleus will be composed of those peoples who already have strong natural bonds drawing them together and enough material power to provide them, as soon as they unite, with overwhelming world power in every important field. One can name groups of fifteen countries whose total power will equal or surpass that of our fifteen, but the thing that we must seek is the combination of the greatest power with the strongest natural bonds. The stronger these bonds are the easier it will be to organize the nucleus effectively, and the more effective its organization the greater its combined power will be and the less material power it needs to combine. We shall therefore examine our fifteen first from the standpoint of their natural cohesion and second from that of their material power.

THE CLOSE COHESION OF THE FIFTEEN

What other nucleus of fifteen has such natural bonds to unite such power as ours?

Geographically, they have the enormous advantage of being all grouped (with three undecisive exceptions) around that cheap and excellent means of communication, a common body of water. The Roman Empire spread round the Mediterranean and then through Europe, not through Europe and then round the Mediterranean.

But the Mediterranean was not nearly so small and convenient then as is the North Atlantic today. All the most important capitals of the North Atlantic democracies are within five days of each other by steam, one day by gasoline, less than a minute by electricity.

A government that bases itself on a continent or sea limits its possibilities of expansion, but a government that is based on the ocean is headed straight toward universality.

The culture of our fifteen is inextricably interconnected. Proceeding from the same basic Greek-Roman-Hebrew mixture grafted on the same dominant Teutonic-Celtic stock, the civilization of these democracies has reached broadly the same level. These peoples already do most of their travelling and studying and playing in the area they together own; they are more at home in it than in the outside world.

As for trade's strong tie, the fifteen already do most of their foreign commerce with each other. This is particularly true of exports, the side of trade that interests most countries most. The chief market of every one of the fifteen is formed by the other fourteen. Each of them also buys most of its supplies from the territory of the others, except Switzerland which, though situated between two of the autocracies, draws almost half its imports from the democratic group. On the whole 70 per cent of the trade of all our democracies is with each other, 73 per cent of their exports going to and 67 per cent of their imports coming from the democratic group,—while only 11 per cent of their trade is with the Triangle of autocracy.

The table on page 92 shows not only this, but also how little our democracies depend commercially on the autocracies and how much the

Triangle depends on them for its exports and imports. It shows, too, how weak are the commercial bonds binding together Japan, Germany and Italy. Only Italy does even 21 per cent of its trade with the others. Germany does only 7 per cent and Japan less than 4 per cent. This table speaks volumes.

The closest financial and business ties bind our fifteen together. They have built up each other with their savings and trust them to each other at their lowest interest rates. Most of them share the creditor's outlook and difficulties, and they include all the world's creditor powers. Ownership of many of the corporations in each is scattered among the people of the whole group, and their great corporations operate through branches in more and more of the area of the fifteen.

Not least are the fifteen bound together by the peaceful, good neighborly relations they enjoy with each other and desire to enjoy with all the world. In all that half the earth which the fifteen govern what acre causes dangerous dispute among them? Their relations in this respect are far more promising than were those among the Thirteen American States when they formed their Union. Not one of the fifteen now fears aggression for any cause from any of the others.

No two of the fifteen have fought each other since the Belgian-Dutch war of 1830. There is no parallel in all politics to this remarkable and unremarked achievement of democracy in maintaining peace so long among so many powerful, independent and often rival peoples, burdened as these were with hatreds and prejudices left behind by all the fighting among them before they achieved democracy.

Most essential of the ties binding together the fifteen is their common concept of the state. The machinery of government differs among them in detail but in all it is based on the individual as equal unit, it follows the same broad lines of free representative government of the people and by the people, and it aims to assure the same minimum guarantees of freedom to the individual, whether called the Bill of Rights, the Rights of Man, or *les Droits de l'Homme*.

All are devoted to freedom of speech, of the press, of association and of conscience, to the supremacy of civil power and of law made by common free consent of men equal before it. All share the same desire to protect the individual from the mass and assure him the utmost possible liberty within the limits that the liberty of other individuals allows.

These guarantees of men to man are "the very life-blood of democracy," as Senator Borah once said. But though he was addressing the Council on Foreign Relations he showed no awareness that at least fourteen other peoples than his own would think that he meant them when he added: "We shall find our highest service, not only to our own people, but to

DEMOCRACY AS DEMOCRACY'S MARKET

This table shows the percentage of exports sold by each of the Fifteen Democracies to the other fourteen, and of imports bought by each from the others; the percentage of their exports to and imports from the Autocratic Triangle (including Manchukuo, Ethiopia and Austria); and the same thing for each of the latter—Japan, Germany and Italy.

Country	Percentage of Trade with 15 Democracies 1936		Percentage of Trade with the Triangle 1936	
	Exports	Imports	Exports	Imports
DEMOCRACY				
New Zealand............	96	92	4	5
Ireland................	96	83	3	5
Canada................	92	86	3	3
Union of South Africa......	91	82	5	10
Finland................	82	64	12	21
United Kingdom..........	75	71	6	6
Australia...............	74	80	16	10
France................	73	66	6	9
Denmark..............	73	62	21	26
Norway................	69	68	17	18
Sweden...............	69	59	19	26
Belgium...............	68	64	13	12
Holland...............	68	51	17	25
United States...........	58	55	15	12
Switzerland.............	50	44	31	34
Average..............	76	68	13	15
Weighted Average.......	73	67	11	11
AUTOCRACY				
Japan.................	57	67	2	5
Germany..............	56	51	9	7
Italy (1934)*..........	47	51	19	23
Average..............	53	56	10	12

* 1934 figures given because the sanctions of the League of Nations made Italy's trade in-1935 and 1935 and 1936 abnormal.

General Note: This table is drawn from the League of Nations yearbook, *International Trade Statistics*, 1936. It tends to err on the conservative side because the source does not give the trade with all the colonial possessions, and the omissions are much greater for the democracies.

mankind and to the peace of the world, in transmitting these principles unimpaired to succeeding generations. That is our supreme duty."

The fifteen hold this heritage of personal liberty inextricably in common. It did not come from any one of them alone. From the highlands that sheltered the Swiss democracies to the lowlands where rose the Dutch Republic, from the Old World to the New World and back again, through the English, American and French revolutions, first one and then another has helped make possible what freedom the common man now enjoys in all their territory.* Together they have worked out and established the modern theory and practice of democracy. Could one of these free nations be where it is today had its concept of freedom been always its concept alone? Had it had always to fight singlehanded against the world for the Rights of Man? Had each had always to depend only on its own citizens and resources could any of them have handed down its free principles unimpaired? Other nations have no such debt to each other, no such bond among them, as have the free.

Geographically, culturally, commercially, financially, politically, historically, our fifteen provide a most cohesive nucleus. No other group of fifteen

---

*In his *History of Freedom* Lord Acton thus distributes the honors—and rates the freedom of the press as the keystone of democracy: "The Swiss Cantons, especially Geneva, profoundly influenced opinion in the days preceding the French Revolution, but they had had no part in the earlier movement to inaugurate the reign of law. That honor belongs to the Netherlands alone among the Commonwealths. They earned it, not by their form of government, which was defective and precarious, . . . but by the freedom of the press, which made Holland the vantage-ground from which, in the darkest hour of oppression, the victims of the oppressors obtained the ear of Europe." (p. 50.)

He amplifies this in his *Lectures on Modern History*: "They [the Dutch] made their universities the seat of original learning and original thinking, and their towns were the centre of the European press . . . It [their government] gave the right of citizenship to revolutionary principles, and handed on the torch when the turn of England came. There the sects were reared which made this country free; and there the expedition was fitted out, and the king provided, by which the Whigs acquired their predominance. England, America, France have been the most powerful agents of political progress; but they were preceded by the Dutch. For it was by them that the great transition was made, that religious change became political change, that the Revolution was evolved from the Reformation." (154.) (*Macmillan*, London, Publisher.)

"About the year 1770 things had been brought back, by indirect ways, nearly to the condition which the [English] Revolution had been designed to remedy for ever. Europe seemed incapable of becoming the home of free States. It was from America that the plain ideas that men ought to mind their own business . . . burst forth like a conqueror upon the world they were destined to transform under the title of the Rights of Man." (*History of Freedom*, p. 54-55; *Macmillan*, London, Publisher.)

is so held together by all these bonds or lends itself so easily to our purpose.

THE OVERWHELMING POWER OF THE FIFTEEN

Shall democracy stop now that it is so strong and its adversaries so weak?—De Tocqueville, 1835.

There remains the question of material power, and here the answer is even more decisively in favor of taking our fifteen for nucleus.

The following tables may suffice to show that these fifteen alone provide all the power—and more—that the nucleus needs. To bring this out more clearly I have lumped together their power on the one hand and, on the other, that of the only three states from which the democracies fear war— the aggressively absolutist trio, Germany, Italy and Japan. In most items I have also given separately the figures for Soviet Russia and for the rest of the world to help show how relatively feeble any other conceivable combination would be. To give the more conservative view of the relative power of the fifteen democracies and the three autocracies I have included Manchukuo and Ethiopia and Austria as possessions in calculating the strength of the latter but have excluded Egypt and Iraq from the dependencies of the democracies and have included Luxemburg only where its customs union with Belgium made separation impossible. I have excluded other allies from both sides but have included mandated territory on either side. I have included the Philippines among dependencies of the United States since they will remain for several years under American sovereignty. The figures are all taken or computed from data contained in official League of Nations publications.

Table 1 gives details of population and area. It shows that the fifteen have a total self-governing population of 280,000,000. In view of the number of their citizens dwelling in their dependencies or abroad it seems fair to put the total number of these democrats at roundly 300,000,000,— especially since it would need only the addition of a democracy or two to surpass this figure. When dependencies are included the man-power of the fifteen democracies swells to more than 900,000,000. The population of Japan, Germany and Italy aggregates only 189,000,000, and when dependencies are added their combined man-power is 260,000,000,—less than a third of that of the democracies. In land-power the superiority of the democracies is even greater, nearly 62,000,000 square kilometers against nearly 6,000,000, or ten times. The population and area of Soviet Russia and of Latin America are also given to assist those who would add them to one group or the other.

Table 2 measures the world power of our fifteen in 30 essentials. It

TABLE I

POPULATION AND AREA (END OF 1936)

Country and Group	Population without Dependencies (thousands)	Population with Dependencies (thousands)	Area (Sq. Km.) with Dependencies (thousands)
DEMOCRACIES:			
United States..........	128,840	144,505	9,694
United Kingdom.......	47,187	505,528	14,299
France...............	41,910	112,358	11,558
Canada..............	11,080	11,080	9,543
Netherlands..........	8,557	75,135	2,085
Belgium.............	8,331	21,898	2,471
Australia.............	6,807	7,758	7,936
Sweden.............	6,267	6,267	448
Switzerland..........	4,174	4,174	41
Denmark............	3,736	3,779	347
Finland.............	3,603	3,603	388
Ireland.............	2,954	2,954	70
Norway.............	2,894	2,895	389
Union of South Africa...	1,944 [1]	10,060	2,058
New Zealand..........	1,585	1,659	272
Totals..............	279,869	913,653	61,599
AUTOCRACIES:			
Japan...............	70,500	136,678 [2]	1,984 [2]
Germany [3]............	75,347	75,347	555
Italy................	42,677	51,497 [4]	3,329 [4]
Totals..............	188,524	263,522	5,868
Soviet Russia..........	175,500	175,500	21,176
Latin America........	127,540	127,540	20,479

[1] White population.
[2] Including Manchukuo.
[3] Including Austria and the Sudetens.
[4] Including Ethiopia.
Source: League of Nations *Statistical Yearbook*, 1937.

gives in per cent their joint share of the world total of each, that of the three autocracies combined (including Manchukuo, Ethiopia and Austria), that of Soviet Russia, and that of the rest of the world. In all but six of these essentials the fifteen have more than half of the world total—and in most things one does not need to have half the supply to control the world, divided as it is. In four of the six,—artificial silk, land area, population, and wheat production,—the fifteen have more than 40 per cent of the world total. In the other two, potash and raw silk, the fifteen have 25 per cent of the first and more important.

The combined power of the fifteen democracies stands out the more when compared to that of the three aggressively autocratic countries. The latter have more than 50 per cent of only two of the 30—potash, which Germany controls, and raw silk, which Japan almost monopolizes. They have together more than 20 per cent of only five of the 30 essentials. Where in 23 of the 30 the fifteen have more than 60 per cent control in half the 30 the three have less than 8 per cent control.

The deeper one goes into this table, the more overwhelming appears the position of the fifteen and the feebler that of the only countries from which the democracies now fear war. It is precisely in the things that are most essential whether to modern civilization or to war that the fifteen are most powerful and the autocracies weakest. The democracies produce more than 95 per cent of the world's rubber and nickel, the autocracies none. The autocracies have

less than 1 per cent of the oil, and cotton,
less than 2 per cent of the tin, natural phosphates and wool,
less than 3 per cent of the known gold reserves,
less than 4 per cent of the gold production,
less than 5 per cent of the world's area,
less than 8 per cent of the ground nuts, iron ore, copper ore, lead ore and motor car production,
less than 11 per cent of the air traffic.

In all these 16 things except area the fifteen democracies have more than 60 per cent of the world total, and in all but cotton and lead they produce in their own territory more than 65 per cent of the world total, with high ratings in motor cars, gold reserves, ground nuts and tin. They also have more than 63 per cent of the world's trade, electricity and coal, and more than 70 per cent of the butter, merchant shipping, wood pulp and sulphur.

The fifteen democracies, in short, are shown by this table to be in a position to control overwhelmingly the world's most essential raw materials—minerals, fuels, textiles, chemicals, foodstuffs—its manufacturing resources in such things as steel and wood pulp, its transportation resources in such

TABLE 2
THIRTY MEASURES OF WORLD POWER

Measure	15 Democracies	Three Autocracies	Soviet Russia	Remaining Countries
	Per Cent of World Total in 1937			
Nickel production*	95.8	0.0	3.0	1.2
Rubber production	95.2	0.0	0.0	4.8
Motorcar production	90.2	6.3	3.1	0.4
Ground nuts production*	90.0	5.0	0.0	5.0
Gold reserves (known)	89.6	2.9	1.6	5.9
Sulphur production	82.2	15.5	0.0	2.3
Wood pulp production*	76.2	17.0	3.2	3.6
Iron ore—(m.c.)*	72.7	6.9	12.7	7.7
Tin production (m.c.)	72.2	1.1	0.0	26.7
Gold production	72.2	3.9	16.8	7.1
Butter production*	71.2	16.2	5.6	7.0
Merchant ship tonnage	70.1	17.5	1.9	10.5
Air traffic (miles flown)*	66.7	10.8	14.4	8.1
Petroleum production	66.0	0.3	10.0	23.7
Copper production (m.c.)*	65.0	6.7	4.8	23.5
Foreign trade (value)	65.0	18.0	1.1	15.9
Coal production	65.0	18.8	9.4	6.8
Raw cotton production	64.7	0.6	10.0	24.7
Natural phosphates production*	64.2	1.5	29.3	5.0
Electricity production*	63.1	19.0	7.9	10.0
Wool production*	63.0	1.8	5.2	30.0
Lead production (m.c.)*	61.6	7.6	3.3	27.5
Steel production	60.6	21.4	13.1	4.9
Aluminum production (smelter)	56.3	34.1	9.1	0.5
Silk, artificial, production	47.7	48.4	1.3	2.6
Area	46.3	4.4	16.0	33.3
Population	43.1	12.3	8.3	36.3
Wheat production	42.6	11.6	23.3	22.5
Potash production*	25.2	63.6	6.0	5.2
Silk, raw, production*	0.4	86.6	3.1	9.9

* 1936, figures for 1937 too incomplete.
(m.c.) Mineral content of ore.
This table is computed from data in League of Nations *Statistical Yearbook*, 1938. For other explanations see text.

things as ships and motor cars and airplanes, its commerce in general.
One can extend the table's list of essentials but this will not change the
picture of decisive world power in the hands of fifteen democracies, it will
only emphasize it.

One can emphasize it perhaps better by pointing out two things. First,
even the figures in the table underestimate the power of the democracies,
because (a) the citizens of the fifteen own or control a substantial share
of the raw materials, factories and means of transportation in the rest
of the world, and (b), the figure fifteen understates the number of
democracies in the world and leaves out of account many other countries
who would stand with the democracies in the event of attack by the
autocracies. Second, even if one lumps Soviet Russia with Germany, Japan
and Italy, the four together have more than one-third of only eight of the
30 essentials (raw silk, potash, artificial silk, steel, wheat and aluminum),
and less than one-fourth of 21 of the 30—including only 3 per cent of
rubber, tin and nickel.

Table 3 shows the relative financial power of democracy and autocracy,
as indicated by the banked wealth of the fifteen and of the three, dependencies excluded from both sides. It shows that each democratic citizen averages nearly five times more money in the bank than each autocratic
subject, and that the banked wealth of the fifteen is more than seven
times that of the three. Excepting the special case of France—that wealthy
people which is habituated to keeping its savings in the sock or in bonds
or abroad rather than in the home bank—the per capita banked wealth
in each democracy is greater than the highest per capita rating among
the autocracies. With the exception of Finland, Belgium, and Holland, it
is more than twice as great.

Table 4 throws more detailed light on the buying, selling and trading
power of the fifteen democracies and the three autocracies, dependencies
again excluded.

The figures for the fifteen are divided into three groups, the three great
democracies, the eight small European democracies and the four British
overseas democracies, to allow their comparative trading importance to
be seen. This brings out the fact that the trade of the three great democracies alone is more than twice as important to the world as that of the
three great autocracies, which is barely greater than that of the eight small
European democracies.

Per capita the democratic citizen is two and a half times more important to the world as a market than is the autocratic subject and twice
as important as a source of supply. The trading power per capita of democracy is more than twice and absolutely it is nearly four times greater
than that of autocracy.

TABLE 3

DEPOSITS IN COMMERCIAL AND SAVINGS BANKS

1937

Country and Group (Dependencies excluded)	Total Deposits (In millions of dollars)	Per Capita
FIFTEEN DEMOCRACIES:		
United States..................	$59,000	$458
United Kingdom...............	19,678	417
France [1].....................	3,290	78
Switzerland...................	3,267	783
Canada.......................	2,835	256
Australia.....................	2,190	322
Sweden [2]....................	2,035	325
Netherlands..................	1,165	136
Belgium......................	1,106	133
Denmark.....................	975	261
Ireland [3]...................	900	305
Union of South Africa..........	743	382
Norway......................	609	210
New Zealand..................	570	359
Finland......................	340	94
Totals....................	98,703	360
THREE AUTOCRACIES:		
Germany [4]...................	6,788	94
Japan........................	4,606	65
Italy.........................	2,727	64
Totals....................	14,121	76

Computed in devaluated dollars from data in League of Nations *Monetary Review,* 1938.

[1] 1936 commercial bank deposits. The misleadingly low per capita figure for the French, who are famed for thrift, is partly due to French habits of keeping money outside banks and, recently, France. French deposits, for example, are partly responsible for Switzerland's high per capita figure.

[2] 1936 savings deposits.

[3] 1935 savings deposits.

[4] The exchange problem presented by the artificial character of the reichsmarks and the variety of other marks has been solved by exchanging reichsmarks into dollars at an estimated depreciation of one third. Most other currencies have depreciated more than this and the mark has been estimated high so as to be conservative. Austrian deposits have been included at the official exchange rate for the schilling.

TABLE 4

BUYING, SELLING AND TRADING POWER

(In thousands of "old gold" dollars, 1937)

Country and Group (Dependencies excluded)	Imports	Exports	Total Trade
GREAT DEMOCRACIES:			
United Kingdom.............	$2,787	$1,523	$4,310
United States................	1,779	1,946	3,725
France.....................	1,003	565	1,568
Totals..................	5,569	4,034	9,603
SMALL EUROPEAN DEMOCRACIES:			
Belgium.....................	546	508	1,054
Netherlands.................	504	373	877
Sweden.....................	318	300	618
Switzerland.................	244	174	418
Denmark....................	214	201	415
Norway.....................	187	119	306
Finland.....................	118	121	239
Ireland.....................	127	65	192
Totals..................	2,258	1,861	4,119
OVERSEAS DEMOCRACIES:			
Canada.....................	479	665	1,144
Union of South Africa........	311	363	674
Australia...................	293	343	636
New Zealand................	131	155	286
Totals..................	1,214	1,526	2,740
TOTALS, 15 DEMOCRACIES.......	9,041	7,421	16,462
THREE AUTOCRACIES:			
Germany...................	1,299	1,406	2,705
Japan......................	634	532	1,166
Italy.......................	430	324	754
Totals..................	2,363	2,262	4,625

Source: League of Nations *World Trade Review*, 1937.

Table 5 indicates the existing armed power of the democracies and of the Triangle, dependencies included. All figures on existing armaments are bound to be very faulty, and for more reasons than those touched on in the notes attached to this table. Much has been said of the secret armament of Germany, but there is really secret armament everywhere. While Germany has been feverishly preparing, the others have been, too. Bluffing, concealing, lying to fool adversaries into thinking that one is stronger or weaker than one really is—this has always been so elementary a principle of military strategy that all armaments figures need always to be regarded skeptically.

The figures in Table 5 have been drawn where possible from the *Armaments Yearbook* of the League of Nations as giving with all their faults the most authoritative picture of relative strength.

Britain's dominating position in the pre-war world was based on a navy equal to that of the two next strongest powers put together. Table 5 shows that to attain this two power standard as regards the only countries that threaten war, and to attain it not only on the sea but on the land and air sides, the fifteen democracies, once united, would need to disarm instead of arm.

Yet Table 5 reflects only dimly the real war power of these democracies as compared to that of the Triangle, for it omits potential power. To get a true picture one needs to consider this table in connection with the other tables, especially Table 2 which shows the overwhelming superiority of the democracies in war essentials. The autocracies are like poker players who make a strong impression by putting most of their money on the table, while their opponents (the democracies) put only their small change on it and keep the rest in their pockets.

These tables suggest that the fifteen have more than enough power to form a sound nucleus world government. They suggest, indeed, that the fifteen have so much power that the problem of ending the present chaos and organizing the world is nothing more nor less than a problem in organizing these few democracies. It appears from these tables that it is unfair to blame the depression on the Mussolinis and Hitlers; their countries weigh too little in the economic balance. The economic, financial and monetary world war we have been suffering appears from these tables to have originated and continued among these fifteen democracies, for they control the world in raw materials, manufacturing, transportation, finance and trade. The only creditors able to cause the runs on the schilling, mark, pound, dollar, French franc, Swiss franc and guilder were the dollar, pound, franc and guilder nationals. They are clearly the only ones responsible for the lack of stable money. It would seem evident that to end once for all world monetary insecurity and economic war there is

Table 5

ARMED POWER

Group and Country (Colonies included)	National Defense Expenditure in Millions 1937–1938	Navy Tons Built and Building 1937	Air Force, Number of Planes (2) 1937	Army Effectives (3) 1937
DEMOCRACIES:				
Britain and India....	$1,458.3	1,354,865	4,000*	689,600
United States.......	993.2	1,378,595	3,150*	405,200
France.............	598.5 [4]	639,182	5,000*	733,300
Belgium............	48.4	—	210	85,900
Sweden............	46.3	82,378	330*	36,200
Netherlands........	41.3	67,882	500*	66,300
Canada............	35.5	5,424	183	54,600
Australia...........	33.1	42,360	32	29,800
Switzerland........	24.5	—	330*	180,000
Finland............	20.1	9,620	180*	39,700
Denmark...........	11.2	12,360	150*	12,300
Norway............	10.4	29,687	220*	14,200
Union of S. Africa...	8.5	800	38	15,700
Ireland............	7.9	—	16	17,200
New Zealand.......	5.0	16,745	28	9,700
Totals............	3,342.6	3,639,898	14,369	2,389,700
AUTOCRACIES:				
Germany [1].........	405.7	311,980	2,700*	232,600 [5]
Japan.............	349.8	916,933	3,800*	528,600 [6]
Italy..............	540.0	547,108	3,000	550,000
Totals..........	1,295.5	1,776,021	8,500	1,311,200

Later figures: The latest authoritative Great Power figures, obtained in December, 1938, from a high source, raise British expenditure to $1,620,200,000, French to $805,400,000, Italian to $712,000,000, Japanese to $1,035,600,000 (including Chinese war), and German to $4,400,000,000 (including construction of war factories, airfields, reserves of arms and munitions); British fleet to 1,758,000, French to 643,489, Japanese to 1,194,260, and Italian to 862,174; British army effectives to 850,000, German to 750,000, Italian to 724,630, and Japanese to 1,230,000 (but this last is not peacetime establishment).

The same source increases British warplane figure to 6,200, German to 9,900 and Italian to 4,710; it cuts the American figure to 2,176, the French to 2,212, and Japanese to 3,130. (Excluding training planes and those it deems obsolete.) Its figures give a misleadingly strong picture of autocratic air power because it necessarily omits needed only agreement among our fifteen to quit fighting each other and to organize law and order among themselves.

The tables tell throughout the same story. It is democracy that brings the individual not only freedom in its narrower political sense, but wealth

---

the potential and defensive advantages of the democracies. Potentially, for example, the United States is far stronger in aviation than Germany. This is true for fliers as well as building power for Germany has a much lower per capita figure for automobiles and a much higher one for ox or cow drawn vehicles than America, France, Britain, or the United States. Moreover, one must count in on the defensive side anti-aircraft guns, etc., as well as planes, whereas for offense first-line planes alone count, and even enormous superiority in them has not proved decisive in the Spanish and Sino-Japanese wars.

The latest figures, in short, do not change the underlying picture of relative strength which the table gives when one keeps in mind the potential power of the democracies, the tremendous superiority in smashing power needed at the outset for successful aggression, and the fact that there is no question of anything but defense by the democracies.

The following notes refer to the figures in the table, which I have not amended since it is based on the latest official source that can be cited.

General note: Unless otherwise noted, all figures are taken or computed from the *Armaments Yearbook*, 1937, of the League of Nations (referred to here as *A. Y.*) and are the latest given there, if they are not—as is usually true—for the year mentioned at the head of each column.

(1) Germany. Since Germany gives no official figures except for the navy, the other figures are estimates. I estimated the war expenditure figure had increased since 1934 (the latest official one) at the rate at least that Japan's had increased in that period in yen. The resulting figure makes German expenditure about equal to that of France. I reached the estimate for German war planes by taking the mean between official French and Russian estimates. The army estimate is taken from *A. Y.* 1936.

(2) War planes. Since the figure from Germany was based on French and Russian estimates (see note 1), the figures for the countries marked (*) were taken from a comparable German source, *Jahrbuch der Deutschen Luftwaffe*, 1938. It gives figures later than those in *A. Y.* and all of the same date. The others are drawn from *A. Y.*

(3) Army effectives. In all countries reserves and naval effectives (except marine corps) have been excluded and air and colonial forces included. The military systems vary so much that it is practically impossible to obtain comparable figures. The aim here has been to keep the general picture from being too out of proportion on any side. In all countries on a volunteer basis forces, such as the National Guard in the United States, the Territorial Army in the United Kingdom, the militia in Canada, etc., have been included. In all countries on a militia or short-term conscription basis such as Switzerland, Denmark, Holland, etc., the figure includes the number of men doing military service, regardless of the number of days done. In countries on a long-term conscription basis, such as France, Italy, Japan, etc., the figure given represents the number of permanent and conscript troops in service.

(4) This figure is a mean between maximum and minimum figures.

(5) Peacetime establishment, 1935, latest normal figure in *A. Y.*

(6) Peacetime establishment, '34-35, latest normal figure in *A. Y.*

and power; it is autocracy that blights. It is democracy that is curiously under-estimated even by those whom it has most benefited; it is autocracy that is wildly over-rated.

These figures should dispose of the theory that what ails the world is the power of the dictatorships. They make the talk of fascism's triumph and democracy's decadence seem ridiculous. The seat of an inferiority complex is in the mind; the best doctor can not cure it if he starts by diagnosing it as ulcer of the stomach, and he risks killing the patient by his needless operations. It can not be safer to keep treating the body democratic for pernicious anemia, whether with old-fashioned drugs or new patent medicines, when all that ails it is a trifling lack of mental and muscular coordination that can be remedied with a little common sense and practice.

The facts are: Fifteen democracies together practically own this earth, and do not know it. Each of these democracies was made to secure precisely the same object, the freedom of man, and they all forget it. These democracies have no one but themselves to blame for their difficulties and to fear for their freedom, and they do not see the beam for the mote.

United, these fifteen are (within human limits) almighty on this planet. They are united in holding dear the Rights of Man, but not in maintaining them throughout the land of the free. They are united in practising the principle that in union of free men there are freedom and peace and prosperity as well as strength. But they do not practise it beyond their borders even with each other to preserve it against those who sacrifice the freedom of man to the freedom of his government. United, these fifteen democracies become impregnable, secure beyond danger of attack, and the world is made safe for individual freedom and saved from further economic and monetary warfare. But they are not united. There and nowhere else is the rub.

Disunion among these democracies is the source of their ills, and of the world's. The problem of organizing world government is the problem of organizing government among only a few democracies.

THE TWO ESSENTIALS

A right result at this time will be worth more to the world than ten times the men.—Lincoln, *Message to Congress*, July 4, 1861.

Why the figure fifteen? Why not a few less, a few more? There is nothing hard and fast, nothing mystic in my choice of fifteen. I came upon this number originally in 1933. The widespread assumption then of the weakness of democracy ran counter to my own observations and I decided to make a study of the relative power of the democracies and the autocracies. To be conservative I limited the democracies to fifteen whose inclusion promised to be non-controversial. The results of this study, which were published at the time and which have been brought down to date in the preceding sections of this chapter, led me to study why these democracies did not unite and how they could best unite, and thus led to this book.

This should make evident that I attach no decisive importance to the figure, fifteen. There are only two points with regard to the nucleus (aside from the manner in which it is organized) that seem essential to me. One is that it should be composed of between twelve and twenty of the most experienced or otherwise best qualified democracies. The other is that the nucleus should make quite clear from the start that the restriction in the number of founders is intended only to make possible and hasten the organization of effective world government, that other states accepting this democratic government will be admitted to it by a simple majority vote—as with the admission of new states in the United States—and that universal world government by peaceful growth is the ultimate aim.

TWELVE TO TWENTY FOUNDERS

You must realize that when Stanley Baldwin said the other day in the House of Commons that the Rhine is now the frontier, he may not have been speaking in terms of military organization at all. He may have been speaking in terms of political, civil and economic ideals. All that is left of organized Liberty is west of the Rhine—the Scandinavian countries, Holland, Belgium, France, Switzerland, Great Britain, Canada and the United States. Therefore our responsibility is tremendous.—Nicholas Murray Butler addressing the American Club of Paris, June 20, 1935.

FEWER THAN FIFTEEN?

Some may think it better or easier to begin with the English-speaking world, or a British-American-French combination, but I believe both have serious disadvantages. Among the grave defects of a single language are these: It gives the nucleus an offensive air of exclusivity. It tends to falsify and limit the basic democratic principles of equality and freedom, to alarm the old and powerful democracies it excludes, and to encourage hostile combinations. It deprives the nucleus of the great advantage of strength so overwhelming from the start that no possible combination can come near it. It is, moreover, badly balanced internally: The over-

seas contribution to its citizenry would be about 145,000,000 against 49,000,-
000 from the British Isles, or three to one; the American element would
have nearly twice the voting strength in it of the British Commonwealth.
Neither can be expected to accept such a combination without misgivings,
if only because it exposes the Americans to the dangers of a precarious
foothold on the edge of a powerful and possibly offended European
continent, while it exposes the British to absorption. An English-speaking
union calls on its members, particularly in England and the United States,
to make much more direct and therefore greater sacrifices of pride than
does organization on a broader base. It allows the British opposition to
exploit everything as a sacrifice to the Americans, and vice versa, with
freedom rather than pride and prejudice the thing most liable to be
sacrificed by both in the end.

The value of a common language for the purposes of organizing inter-
state government has been over-rated, I think, and the value of common
political principle under-rated. I attach much more importance to the
latter, particularly at the start. Surely it is easier to maintain effective
democratic government among peoples of common political principle but
different languages (consider the experiences in Switzerland, Canada,
Union of South Africa), than among people of the same language but
of opposing political principles (consider the American war for independence, the American Civil War, the Spanish Civil War).

Many of the objections to an English-speaking union are reduced by
bringing in the French, but they are not reduced enough. From the French
viewpoint such a nucleus is ill-balanced and unfavorable to freedom of
language, tradition, etc.; it means four English-speaking votes for one
French. The questions of pride and prestige remain vexatious when organization is confined to three great historical peoples. If one can not in
the name of freedom and equality unite Americans and British and fail
to invite the French, one can not fail to invite too the Dutch and Belgians and Swiss and Scandinavians who have contributed so much to freedom and equality and have shown so long how dear they hold democracy.
If one could morally justify their exclusion at the start, there would be
no material advantage or political wisdom in it.

The material contribution the small European democracies bring has
already been shown. On the political side they make several contributions. They make the nucleus better balanced: The voting population
would be 130,000,000 in Europe, 150,000,000 overseas. These smaller
democracies bring the advantages of variety at the start without the
disadvantages of too much of it. Thus, the fifteen are divided practically
into only two racial stocks, Germanic and Latin, two religions, Protestant
and Catholic, five major language groups, English, French, Scandinavian,

Dutch, Finnish,—and most educated people among the latter three already know some English or French.

To each of the last four language groups the presence in the nucleus of the other three would be a strong safeguard against an undue domination of English, while to the English-speaking peoples the existence in the nucleus of these other languages would be a standing guarantee against hysteria sweeping through it and against the centralization of government they abhor. For official purposes in the few fields where the nucleus would govern one could limit languages to English and French as the League does. The League's experience has brought out many advantages, especially for the deliberative functions so essential to democracy, in having two official languages.

The presence of the small European democracies in the nucleus would be a standing token both to those inside and outside it that this government was genuinely based on the principle of freedom and equality for all men—not simply for men of one race or one language. That I consider to be of high political value.

To hold together solidly three great stones it often helps to take some small stones to fill the holes. An example of the beneficial effect gained in inter-state organization by the mere addition of small countries to big ones may be seen in the fact that whereas the Four Power Pact had to be drafted in four languages, Germany and Italy were able to accept English and French as the only languages in the Fifty-seven Power League. If the small European and overseas democracies did not exist it would almost be necessary to invent them for the purpose of bringing the Americans, British and French to swallow false pride in a constitutional convention, compromise and adjust their differences, and agree on a definite detailed constitution. It is not, however, essential that the nucleus include every one of these small democracies. If a few of them balk at coming in, the nucleus could be formed without them as the American Union was constituted without Rhode Island. If a few should seek to drive as dangerous a bargain as did South Carolina and Georgia in the American Constitutional Convention—where they refused to allow free trade to be established in the Union until they were guaranteed continuance of the African slave traffic for twenty years—it would seem wiser to go ahead without them. It would be preferable, however, to include them all, if reasonably possible. That brings us back to the figure, fifteen.

MORE THAN FIFTEEN?

Why not go on and include more than fifteen? We have already seen that the line must be drawn somewhere but why not add four or five or one or two democracies such as Czechoslovakia and at least one Latin American Republic? Twenty is not too many for the nucleus constituent assembly, if they draft this constitution by simple majority vote as the American States drafted theirs. There would seem to be no decisive objection to the fifteen raising the number of founders to twenty by inviting whatever democracies they agreed it was wise to add, and requiring only, say, three great power ratifications for the constitution the assembly drafted to go into effect. I have preferred to draw the line at fifteen at this stage mainly because of these considerations:

Once the generous minimum needed for a sound nucleus is reached at fifteen, the addition of other democracies may still be desirable. Since such additions are not necessary, however, one should lean backward to avoid slowing or endangering the organization of government by including elements liable in any way to rouse controversy or other difficulty.

Even if one keeps to the fifteen, the inclusion of Finland, for example, may be attacked on the ground that it would give the nucleus a common frontier with Soviet Russia, and this might cause other democracies to hesitate to join in organizing the nucleus through fear of being drawn into too close contact with the communist state. I do not share such fears, but I am concerned with the danger of their existence among others making the foundation of world government harder. Should there rise serious reason to believe that inclusion of Finland in the nucleus would delay its organization it seems to me that it would then be in the interests of the Finns as much as any one to let Finland wait till the others had actually established the nucleus. The Finns need not fear being left out thereafter, and they do need to fear failure to create this government.

What has been said regarding Finland applies only more strongly to the Spanish and Czechoslovak republics. Their great services to democracy and their magnificent struggle for it against terrifying odds make me desire keenly to include them in the nucleus. I have nonetheless omitted them because it seemed to me wiser and more in their interests as well as ours to leave this question to be decided by the prevailing opinion among the other democracies after they have accepted the idea that a nucleus should be formed. I hope I am wrong but I fear that for me to include in it either or both of these republics would make many consider their inclusion essential to my proposal that a nucleus of democracies be organized and cause them to oppose it from fear of being drawn immediately into war by Spain or Czechoslovakia. It seems to me that no democracies stand to gain more than these do from anything that hastens the formation of a nucleus of democracies, and that none stand to lose more than they from anything, however well-intentioned, that keeps any such nucleus from being formed, or delays its formation.

As for the inclusion of one or two Latin American republics, the main difficulty I see is that this might be found offensive to other Latin American states and might lead inevitably to the inclusion of so many as to bring the number of founders beyond the maximum of twenty and cause much needless argument and delay in the constituent assembly.

WHAT OF SOVIET RUSSIA?

At the moment when mines are being laid to blow up the organization in which were fixed the great hopes of our generation, . . . when, by no accidental coincidence, decisions are being taken outside the League which recall to us the international transactions of pre-war days, . . . when there is being drawn up a further list of sacrifices to the god of aggression and . . . nothing succeeds like aggression,—at such a moment, every State must define its moral responsibility before its contemporaries and before history.—Maxim Litvinoff, U. R. S. S. Foreign Commissar, addressing the League of Nations Assembly, Sept. 21, 1938.

There remains the peculiarly controversial case of the Union of Socialist Soviet Republics. The mere fact that many democrats would class it among the dictatorships and that many other democrats regard it as an advanced type of industrial democracy suffices, it seems to me, to prove the practical wisdom of not including it in the nucleus but at the same time being careful not to push it into the arms of the absolutists.

Certainly Soviet Russia's political theory and practice differ radically from that of Japan in admitting no divine right monarch, and from that of Germany and Italy in denying the nation's supremacy over man. These three countries make the accident of birth the all important thing in politics, and Soviet Russia shares the democratic abhorrence of this theory that makes men bow down before blind, arbitrary force outside them. Far from contesting the democratic principle that power over men should not descend forever by accident of birth within a family or a nation or a race, communism like socialism seeks to apply this theory particularly in the field of economic power. It shares the democratic theory that all men are created equal.

It is democratic again in seeking to apply this theory to those to whom it is most applicable, those to whom it is now least applied. Nazi Germany holds all Germans to be equal, but not all men; it holds those born Germans superior to others, particularly to those born with any Jewish blood. Soviet Russia draws no national, race, color or sex line; where it discriminates among men it is always because of things they have acquired, such as ideas or property, and never, in principle, because of the accident of birth.

I deplore the Soviet departures from democratic equality but I condemn them less than legal discrimination based on factors which men cannot change or escape no matter what they do. Men can always change their minds, their views on politics or economics, and free men frequently do; they can acquire and lose property, the poor among them can become conservatives and the sons of the rich can turn communist. But one can not possibly change the color of his skin or the race of his grandfather; to exclude men from equality on such grounds is to put them in a hopeless position, it is to punish them not for doing but for being; it is stupid, cruel, and the very antithesis of democracy.

Democrats can not quarrel with Soviet Russia because of its use of collective machinery. Democracy itself introduced collective machinery into politics; this machinery's extension to other fields can not be necessarily undemocratic. What democrats can not admit, however, is that the extension of collective machinery to economic fields must be necessarily and always through state ownership and administration, as Soviet Russia seems to believe. But if the democrat must object to the communist tendency to extend—particularly through the state—collectivist machinery simply for its own sake, he must object equally to the same tendency in capitalist society to maintain willy-nilly the method of private enterprise, whether or not it is promoting individual freedom. Neither is common sense, both are fetish worship.

It is a profound mistake to identify democracy necessarily or entirely with either capitalist or socialist society, with either the method of individual or of collective enterprise. There is room for both these methods in democracy. Individual enterprise in certain times and fields best serves individual freedom. In other times and fields this end of democracy requires collective action, and in still others, a combination of the two methods. Democracy requires society to be so organized that it is free to choose between or combine these methods peacefully at any time and in any field.

It is here that Soviet Russia unquestionably falls short of democracy. Democracy not only allows mankind to choose freely between capitalism and collectivism, but it includes marxist governments, parties and press as well as *laissez faire* governments, parties and press. Soviet Russia allows no such choice and no such freedom in its territory, even under its new and more democratic constitution. Is this Soviet policy one of temporary expediency or one of permanent principle? If it is the former, Soviet Russia must be classed with the immature democracies. If it is the latter, Soviet Russia must be classed among the absolutists, for its real end then is not to serve individual freedom and equality but merely to preserve and strengthen one form of the state, and a form that makes the state all-powerful in everything.

The practice of the marxist theory in Russia, it may be added, has necessarily been influenced by the fact that the Russians have always been accustomed to absolutism and bureaucracy. One can no more expect them to rid themselves of their past in a few years than fascists can hope by revolution to end quickly democracy in the United States or in any other people long habituated to individual freedom. Allowance made for popular habit and training, even the practice of marxist theory in Russia has undoubtedly so far marked a substantial *net* advance for democracy over conditions there before.

It is true that before Hitler and Mussolini began attacking democracy, the communists were attacking it, though their attacks seemed often due to their confusing the *laissez-faire* economic theory with democracy. They often talk still as if the marxist theory inevitably harnessed the individual to the collectivity rather than the collectivity to the individual, as the democratic theory does. We need more time to answer definitely whether Soviet departures from the basic principles of democracy have been matters of expediency or principle.

All we need to note for the present is that whereas basic Nazi political theory is incompatible with democracy—if only because it flatly and aggressively rejects for purely racial reasons democracy's root principle, *all men are created equal,*—basic marxist political theory may easily be compatible with democracy, however much it (like capitalism in Germany, Japan and Italy) may also be made to serve the ends of absolutism.

UNIVERSALITY THE ULTIMATE GOAL

Freedom of thought, freedom of speech, freedom of association, are the ideals which inspire progress not only in the continents of America and Australia, but also in the countries of Asia.—Harold Butler, Director, International Labor Organization, 1938, Report.

We come to the second essential, that no limit whatever be placed on the power of growth of this nucleus, that its constitution make explicitly clear that it is meant to grow peacefully into universal government. If it is in the interest of the freedom of the individuals of fifteen countries to unite, it can not be in their interest to bar themselves in advance for any reason whatsoever from uniting with other men whenever it seems wise to them to do so, and when these others desire it too. Any exclusivity would run counter to the freedom for which the government would be made and would fatally turn against the nucleus those excluded and thus, at best, expose it to unnecessary dangers.

An easier way of safeguarding the new government could hardly be devised than provision for unlimited expansion backed up by definite pledge that it aimed to attain universality peacefully. This simple clause would serve the nucleus far better than doubling its army. It would soothe in an honorable way the pride of those democracies which were left out of the nucleus at the start, and thus make it easier to keep the original nucleus down to a small number. Assurance that democracies later admitted would enjoy absolute equality, that—as in the United States—no distinction whatever would be drawn between them and the founders, would be proof that questions of pride had not determined the choice of founders. Certainly Americans born in Missouri or Montana or even naturalized feel no less pride in being Americans than do those born in Virginia or New York.

In this connection it can not be stressed too much that this government is to be created not so much by democratic states as by the individuals in them. Though many states must be left out of the nucleus, nothing prevents individuals anywhere from helping found it. In the founding of the United States there was room for such Englishmen as Tom Paine, such Frenchmen as Lafayette, such Germans as von Steuben, such Poles as Kosciusko. Their fellow nationals still take pride in their contribution to the United States. Men like Paine and Lafayette contributed more to the American Union than did some of its founder states. In the work of establishing a nucleus world government there will be similar room for individuals of this calibre from no matter what outside nation. I am confident there will be Germans, Italians, Japanese and other individuals from states outside the nucleus who will contribute more to its foundation than will a good many citizens of the founder democracies.

Provision for unlimited growth would, then, help to establish world government both by enabling its constitution to be made by a minimum of states and by encouraging individual democrats in all outside states to give the movement their whole-hearted aid. It would also serve, once the nucleus was established, to strengthen enormously its powerful natural position. By rousing hope of membership, it would draw the immature democracies still more closely to the nucleus. It would keep them from falling, through despair or offended pride, into the hands of the absolutists. It would encourage them to practise and not merely profess democracy at home, for that would be the surest way for them to attain the great advantages which membership would bring.

The admission of new members from time to time would help this world government to remain a powerful stimulus to democracy everywhere; it would need no propaganda bureau. Would not the establishment of genuine freedom of the press in, say, Soviet Russia, be hastened by the wish to join this world organization?

The provision for ultimate universality on the basis of equality among all the citizens would be particularly useful in removing the danger which absolute militarism in Italy, Japan and Germany now holds for democracy. This provision would enlist within these countries all the active force that can be needed to replace their present regimes with democracy. Up to a few years ago the democratic movement in all these countries was much stronger than in many immature democracies; it succumbed sooner to absolutism because it was more exposed. The repressive measures taken by the absolutists in Italy since the Matteotti assassination in 1924, in Japan since the Manchukuo adventure in 1931, in Germany since only 1933, make it impossible to say how strong the democratic element within these countries is today. These measures themselves are, however, proof enough that the autocrats governing these countries—with all their secret information regarding public or, rather, private opinion in them—remain afraid of their democrats.

Since the autocrats are already afraid of their own people overthrowing them, how much more will they fear the democratic movement from within once the German, Japanese and Italian democrats know that only by overthrowing their autocracies can they gain the equality, freedom, security and other advantages membership in this world government would bring? Would this situation encourage the autocrats to go to war in the hope of thus saving themselves? Nothing would speed their downfall faster than such an attempt to escape it. Even were their people solidly united under them, such a war against the democracies would still be utterly hopeless. An autocrat who to divert his people from revolution arms them for a clearly hopeless war is simply arming revolution.

COOPERATION MEANWHILE WITH NON-MEMBERS

The policy of the nucleus toward non-members pending their admission should be whatever policy would best advance the freedom of its citizens. The nucleus could cooperate with the other nations through the League of Nations or diplomatic channels. Inheriting all the voting and veto power its members now have in the League, it would have as strong and safe a position there as the United States now has in the Pan American conferences. By the admission of new members it would gradually absorb the League until that institution disappeared. What the nucleus should do to aid Spain, Czechoslovakia and China, and whether the nucleus should make the Covenant and Peace Pact its Monroe Doctrine, its warn-

ing to absolutism to keep hands off the immature democracies, are among
the questions that the people of the nucleus need not decide until they
have organized themselves. Then they will find that—thanks to their
having organized themselves strongly—they have greatly simplified these
questions and made them much easier to solve without resort to arms.

Every consideration would urge them to be a good neighbor to all. No
one will deny this as regards the weaker outside countries that would be
awaiting admission. Can any democrat deny it as regards the others?

I see no reason for hostility between the nucleus and Soviet Russia
and many reasons why both should be good neighbors. Hostility by the
nucleus to Soviet Russia would mean making what is now a hollow Triangle
a solid one, and greatly increasing the strength of autocracy. Hostility
by Soviet Russia to the nucleus would mean putting Soviet Russia at the
mercy of its only aggressive enemies. I would favor admitting Soviet
Russia to the nucleus as soon as it guaranteed freedom of the press and
the other Rights of Man to the minimum degree common to the peoples
in the nucleus. A world government whose principle of freedom not
only allows but encourages the United States to retain its republic and
Great Britain its monarchy could not refuse Russia its soviet. For Russia
to try to promote freedom in its territory by communist experiments
is no worse than Sweden trying to do the same by socialist experiments,
or others by capitalist experiments—once Russia guarantees her capitalist
and other opposition the same freedom to express and advance their
views peacefully as the capitalist democracies guarantee their opposition.

Nor is there reason for the nucleus to adopt a hostile policy toward
such autocracies as Japan, Germany and Italy. To think of this nucleus
as a sort of democratic Holy Alliance is to misunderstand it completely.
Where despots joined in the Holy Alliance to restore absolutism abroad
the democracies would unite to preserve their freedom at home from
despotism. For absolutists to unite suffices neither to overthrow democracy nor even to preserve absolutism; they must, because of absolutism's
nature, still depend on force, the force by which the Holy Alliance sought
its end. To endanger absolutism the free, however, need but unite. Three
million free Americans, by merely establishing their small distant Union
in an absolutist world, started a movement that since then has swept
despots from thrones and established republics all over the world. Why
then should a colossal nucleus of nearly 300,000,000 free men need to raise
a finger against the few feeble autocracies left? It needs but exist for
democracy to flourish and autocracy to fade.

It was not because the old democracies were united and strong that
the Italians and the Germans lost their freedom. It was because the free
had weakened freedom by their divisions, their disunion, their economic

war. Had a strong government of the democracies been created in 1919 instead of the League of Nations there would never have been a Fascist or a Nazi state, and probably democracy would rule Japan today. When, and only when, this world democratic government is created may one look forward confidently to the end of absolutism among the German, Italian and Japanese peoples. They have sacrificed their liberties because they were deluded—partly by their sufferings from the effects of disunion among the democracies—into thinking that the only kind of equality possible is equality on the mystic nation-to-nation basis, and that sacrifice of their personal freedom and self-government is the price of their individual self-respect. When this world democratic government is founded they will know that only by first establishing their rights as men can they gain the kind of equality that really counts with them as with everyone—equality on a man-to-man basis with the freest men and women on earth. I do not expect to see the Germans, Italians and Japanese among the last peoples added to the nucleus. I expect to see them prove themselves worthy to be among the first.

CHAPTER VI

How to Organize the Democracies

All men are created equal.—Declaration of Independence.

That only holds men together which aggregates all in a living principle.—Whitman.

A frequent recurrence to fundamental principles . . . (is) absolutely necessary to preserve the blessings of liberty, and keep a government free.—Pennsylvania's Declaration of the Rights of Man, 1776.

PLAN OF CHAPTER

We examine afresh in this chapter the basic principles of all inter-state government in order to solve our next problem: How shall world government be organized among the few democracies with which it must begin? Basically there are only two ways of organizing inter-state government—the league way and the union way—and we must choose between them.

We have already examined the League of Nations enough to see that this particular application of the league method offers no solution and that we must approach the whole problem anew, both as regards the states to be organized and the method of organizing them. Having now narrowed the problem down to one of organizing a few democracies prudence requires us to re-examine more thoroughly the league method to learn whether this problem could possibly be solved by any type of league or could be solved only by union.

To this end this chapter analyzes the two methods first from the standpoint of their fundamental principles, leaving it to the next chapter to consider the application of these principles to the problem of organizing our democracies. First, that is, we examine the principles of all government to learn the essential characteristics of these two methods and the basic difference between all leagues and all unions. We trace this to their difference in unit. Then, in the next chapter, we apply the two opposing principles and units to the problem at hand by subjecting the league and the union methods each to three tests.

WHY THE CHOICE IS BETWEEN TWO UNITS

*To understand political power right, and derive it from its original, we must consider what state all men are naturally in, and that is a state . . . of equality.—*Locke.

*Nationality does not aim either at liberty or prosperity, both of which it sacrifices to the imperative necessity of making the nation the mould and measure of the State.—*Acton.

*The essence of our system of democracy . . . has been the freedom of the individual as against the tyranny of government, and equality of rights among individuals. The essential test of man's security in that freedom and in that equality lies ultimately in the underlying conception of his relation to his government. Does that government exist for him as was announced in our Declaration of Independence? Can the individual man standing on his own right make secure his freedom by means of free speech, free discussion, a free press, and in the last resort by the invocation of the aid of an independent judiciary? Or, on the other hand, do all his rights come from his government and does his security depend solely upon the privileges which that government sees fit to grant him? These are the two essential conceptions of individual rights which have been fighting in this world during the past thousand years. They met on the battle front in the recent war and the issue was decided in favor of our system. We shall not reverse that decision.—*Henry L. Stimson, *Democracy and Nationalism in Europe,* 1934.

Many who agree that our problem is to organize inter-state government among a few democracies are likely to assume as a matter of course that these must be organized as a league. This is partly because it requires some effort to get rid of the habits of mind formed during all the years in which the problem was seen as one of organizing the whole world at once, and to see that narrowing the problem down to a few democracies makes union become possible. The mere fact that the League of Nations exists leads many to conclude that despite its faults the only practical thing is to build on it some way or other. Others are not yet convinced that the League's failure results from the league system and ascribe it to minor defects or to men lacking the will to apply the Covenant. Then there is the widespread belief that the principle of national sovereignty is now so deeply rooted that it is hopeless to go against it. For such reasons all thinking on the problem of world organization still seems to center on the league method.

I too began this way. When it dawned on me that the problem was to organize not the world but a few democracies I first thought that they should form a league. No doubt such a league would be better than the League of Nations. The longer I have studied the problem both in practice and in theory, however, the more I have come to believe that a league at best offers no solution to it and that the only possible solution is union.

To explain why, I shall try first, before turning to the more practical aspects with which I am mainly concerned, to simplify theory on a complicated question whose difficulties are evidenced and, I fear, augmented by the monumental literature already devoted to it. I am afraid I may be misunderstood or found naive or shallow by the more academic of the experts in this field, but I run this risk in the hope of making some important points clearer to the mass they bewilder with their technical terms or fail to reach.

Every science has its units, though political science seems to neglect them. One rarely finds political organization analyzed according to its unit or hears the term, *unit,* used in constitutional discussions. Yet government, whether state or inter-state, has to be government of some unit, by some unit, for some unit. Since in all human organization, whether political, economic, or other, men must be taken either singly or plurally, that is, as individuals or as subordinate parts or cells of an organized body, there would seem to be, in the constitutional field that concerns us, only two basic units, Man and the State.

In solving the problem of what the relations of man to man shall be by organizing themselves as a body politic, men raise a new problem: What shall be the relation between each of them and the whole of them, between the individual and the collective or "plural man,"—Hobbes's "great Leviathan called a commonwealth or State which is but an artificial Man,"—of which he forms a part and helps create?* This question, which usually rises so gradually as to pass unperceived and to be solved at first unconsciously, has the importance for political organization that a continental divide has on the course a raindrop will take on reaching earth.

* To simplify matters and for other practical reasons I confine the discussion of this problem of the relation between individual and collective man to the more generally accepted political terms for the latter unit. Those who would organize men by economic groups according to the work they do, or by any other system,—in the Ottoman Empire men were organized according to religious belief,—instead of organizing them as they are now politically organized, that is, according to where they live or were born, need only substitute for State or Nation whatever term for and type of organized collective man they prefer. The underlying principle that there can be only two units, men taken singly as one or plurally as one, and the problem of their relations is what concerns us here and they remain basically the same whatever may be the collective unit or its name. Those who still think I stick too much to the 18th century are referred to Chap. X, last section.

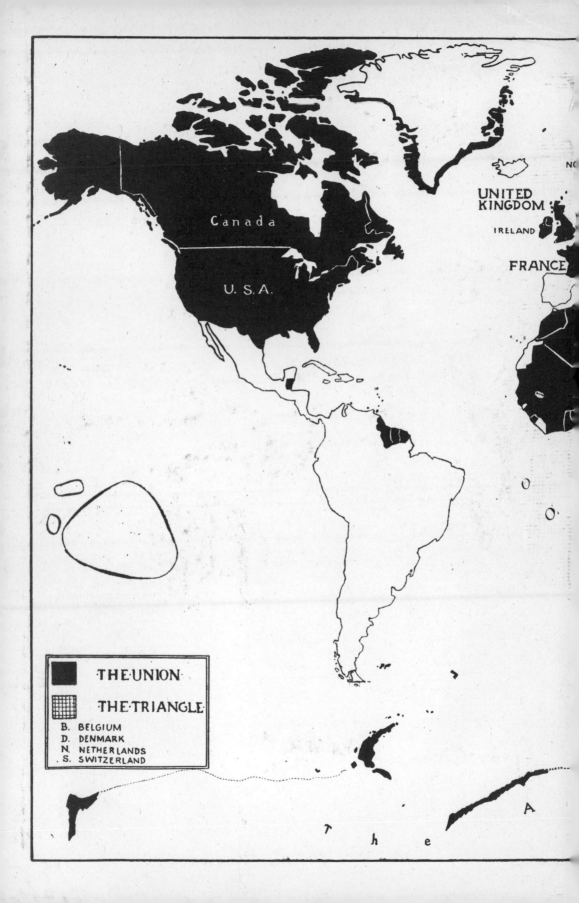

UNITED
KINGDOM

IRELAND

FRANCE

Canada

U.S.A.

THE·UNION

THE·TRIANGLE

B. BELGIUM
D. DENMARK
N. NETHERLANDS
S. SWITZERLAND

A

The

However imperceptible it may be, the point where a continent divides into two opposing slopes suffices, though two raindrops fall only an inch apart on either side, to send each inevitably to oceans worlds apart. So it is with our political problem. Just as the divide has only two basic slopes, and these are hidden amid those running every direction in the labyrinth of mountains around it, there are basically only two answers to this question of the relations between man and the state.

Either one must consider man as a cell in the body politic, a means to an end, the state supreme and the individual subordinate to it. Or one must consider man as himself the entity and the state as his tool, a means to his ends, the individual as supreme and the state as subordinate. Compromises between the two extremes are, of course, possible, but in the last analysis men in organizing government must either allow themselves to be taken plurally as parts of something greater and organized with the organization as unit and end, or they must take themselves singly and organize on the basis that they themselves constitute the equal units and the equal ends of their organization.

The solution that relegates the individual to the role of cell is a mystic one. Its indivisible unit, the body politic, is, as Hobbes admitted, an imaginary body. Unlike individuals it has no flesh, no blood, and can neither live nor die in the common sense of the words. Men can pretend to endow the state with their own attributes, they can work themselves into believing their own make-believe. They can not change themselves from an organic whole into an organic cell, least of all into the cell of so abstract a body as the body politic. The individual remains indivisible, individual, and the body politic is always dividual.

The solution that would create the state in the image of man out of men tends to carry its false and mystic analogy to the point of reducing men as far as possible to cells with specialized hereditary functions. It leads to governing power over all the people being given to a special class or person as absolutely as power over the body is given to the head. It reaches its ultimate expression when some one man, whether Louis XIV or Adolph Hitler, declares, "I am the State." This is the absolutist conception.

The opposite conception has nothing mystic about it. It centers in the tangible fact that individual man is a living, indivisible, independent entity, that he has blood not ink in his veins, that he can enjoy life and suffer death, that he has deep within him a longing to be more independent, to be freer from everything that hems him in and holds him down, and to live his own life, and that his most vital interest and dearest possession is himself. This conception gives majesty not to the state but to Man. It treats the state as only an instrument made by man for his own benefit

as he has made houses, weapons, tools,—a great instrument, but still an instrument. It sees nothing intrinsically more sacred in a method of government than in a method of transportation. It judges each according to the service it renders the living individual,—and that depends on the conditions in which he must live, for as the automobile is better for men than the horse where there are roads, the horse is better where no roads exist.

Men of this second conception do not refuse, simply because a mechanism is a political one, to scrap it in favor of a better one. Their attitude toward the existing form of the state is at bottom the attitude of men toward the existing form of any instrument for doing what they want, one determined less by gratitude for past service to them than by their present and future needs and desires. They dismiss as contrary to observe fact and common sense the theory that men of one family or class are born to rule and others to obey. They delegate but never alienate their governing power; they carefully safeguard their right to re-delegate it; they employ men to serve them in politics as in anything else. This conception of politics, in short, begins with the plainest facts, proceeds by reason, sticks to the ground; it keeps its emotion and its awe for Man. It is the democratic conception.

The question, which shall be the unit, man or the state, is then a basic question in political organization. That becomes clearer when we pass from the general to the particular field that concerns us, inter-state government among democracies.

In a union by our definition each man counts for one; it follows that in a union the states with more men count for more than the less populous ones: Union is based on the principle of equality for men rather than for states. In a league each state counts for one; therefore the citizen of the least populated state counts for more than the citizen of the most populated one: There is equality for states but not for men. A union organizes inter-state government of, by and for the people of each state as individual men and women; a league organizes government of, by and for the states as states, as individual bodies politic made up of men and women as cells.

We must choose between these two units; we cannot have both supreme. Many, it is true, think that union or federal governments use equally man and the state as units because they usually balance equal representation of men in one legislative house with equal state representation in the other. This, however, does not make the states units in our sense, units whereof, whereby and wherefor the union is made. What union does is to divide not government between two units but the fields or powers of government between union state and member state, both of which it or-

ganizes with the same unit, man. In it men govern their local concerns through the state and their inter-state concerns through the union, but both governments have the same relations to the men concerned—they are both made of individuals, by individuals, for individuals.

Equal state representation in one union house does not upset this for what it provides is not representation of the state government, as in a league, but representation of the people in the state,—a very important difference. It is made to preserve the basic division between the powers of the state and union governments. It safeguards the people of each state against the union government invading the field left to the state government, just as the popular house in a union safeguards the people of the whole union against the state governments invading the union's field. Both are checks made by the people against the centralizing tendency of all government, the former checking centralization in the union government and the latter checking it in the state governments.

HOW THE UNIT SHAPES THE END

We must organize inter-state government, then, either with man or the state as unit, and the importance of this choice will be still clearer when we understand how our choice of unit determines the real end toward which our government will be directed. At first it may seem that it is the end for which we organize government that determines our choice of unit. That was long my own belief, but it assumes that men act more logically than they do. We should no doubt always proceed by first deciding clearly what we want to get and then deciding how best to get it. But usually we start with a very vague idea of what we want, and often our thought is so confused that we end by finding that our expressed aim is not at all the one we really want. In practice we can set out to organize government for the sake of ourselves but defeat our end by choosing the wrong unit, whereas by choosing the right unit we shall willy nilly achieve this end, however confused we may be about it.

Clearly the real end which the democracies had in mind when they organized the League of Nations was to organize world government for the sake of the individual: They sought to make the world safe for democracy. But this did not suffice to make them choose the democratic unit. From confusion due to various causes they chose instead the opposite unit and organized a league of states.

When we take the state as unit we are led into taking the state as sacrosanct. When we organize a government of states we are bound to have its laws bear on them as units, for if they bear directly on the citizen regardless of his state government the state is not the unit and the citi-

zen is. Our government must therefore govern state government, not individual men. Our choice of the state as unit obliges us also to provide
that our inter-state government shall be by these state governments for
if we provide inter-state government directly by the people in the states
then the states can not be equals, for the more populous will have more
representatives than the less populous. In order to have this government
of and by states, we are bound to provide government for the sake of these
states, to preserve their integrity, equality, independence, sovereignty.
That is precisely what we were led to do in the League of Nations by
our choice of unit, and we have not been making the world safer for
democracy.

Our choice of unit has led us instead into trying to make it safer for
national sovereignty first of all, and we have succeeded only in making it
safer for absolutism. Instead of making government for men we have organized men for the sake of government. We have turned our democracies
into houses divided each against itself, governing inside by the democratic
unit and governing outside by the absolutist unit. The two will not mix,
and the unit taken in the broader field tends to become supreme in the
smaller field. And so each of the democracies has been driven, since they
organized as a league, into strengthening the state against its citizens in
order to strengthen it against other states, into centralizing more and
more power in each national government. By confusion and frustration
we have been led to the rampant nationalism we are suffering and to the
dogma of the divine right of the nation which Hitler preaches. Practising
absolutism toward others has led us into practising absolutism toward
ourselves. Not our will nor our desire but the unit we chose has shaped
our course and end.

Conversely, we may aim to organize inter-state government for the
sake of the member states, but if this time we choose man for unit we
shall again defeat our end. Whatever our express purpose, the fact that
we organize government of men inevitably undermines the position of the
member states as states and strengthens the position of their citizens as
individuals. It is as hard to promote absolutism in states by organizing
inter-state government with the democratic unit as to promote democracy
among them by organizing them on the absolutist basis. In each case it
is the unit chosen in the broader field, no matter why or how, wittingly
or unwittingly, that shapes the course of government in both fields.

Where the League of Nations illustrates the one case, the American
Union illustrates the other. Though none of the drafters of its Constitution favored absolutism, many of them sought by it to check democracy.
Even the strongest champion of democracy among them, George Mason,
"admitted [Madison noted] that we had been too democratic." Most of

the drafters seemed from what they said, more concerned with safeguarding the rights and powers either of the state governments or of the central government than with strengthening the powers of the citizens. The unit they chose, however, was man. True, this was hidden in such confusion that they called the result the United States instead of the United Americans, and it took a civil war and Lincoln to make indisputably clear that they had constituted not government of, by and for the states but government of the people, by the people, for the people. Yet when we analyze the Constitution we shall see how thoroughly they took man for their unit, and when we study the history of the American experiment we shall see how immediately, continuously and tremendously this unit has worked to promote democracy not only in America but everywhere.

NATION—THE MODERN JANUS

Much of our confusion now roots in our two-faced use of *nation* to mean both people and state, and in the tendency to use the former to mean race, too. The way democracy has developed has contributed heavily to this ambiguity. Democracy grew first in one existing state and then in another. By replacing royal sovereignty in an existing state with popular or national sovereignty it seemed to make nation and state one. According to democratic theory the nation (in the sense of a people) made the nation (in the sense of a state) to preserve the freedom of the nation (in the sense of a people). The nation seemed thus both means and end, though in reality the nation-state or nation-unit was the means and the nation-people, the individuals in it, was the end.

In his far-sighted essay, *Nationality,* that great liberator of the mind, Lord Acton, pointed out in 1862 that the theory of nationalism had already come to cover two opposing ideas which he called the theory of unity and the theory of liberty. The latter is our democratic or individualist conception of the nation, the former the Fascist or Nazi or absolutist conception of it. For my part, I would limit the term *nationalism* to this absolutist conception for, as Acton feared, it usually means this today. To free ourselves from our present confusion, to distinguish between the great good and the great evil that the nation can do us and our individual liberty, and to keep the good while avoiding the evil, we can not do better than re-read what Acton wrote prophetically of nationalism when this theory began creating modern Italy and Germany. Here are the more important passages, taken from his illuminating *History of Freedom:**

* *History of Freedom,* p. 288 ff., Macmillan, London.

In one case, nationality is founded on the perpetual supremacy of the collective will, of which the unity of the nation is the necessary condition, to which every other influence must defer, and against which no obligation enjoys authority, and all resistance is tyrannical. The nation is here an ideal unit founded on the race, in defiance of the modifying action of external causes, of tradition, and of existing rights. It overrules the rights and wishes of the inhabitants, absorbing their divergent interests in a fictitious unity. . . .

While the theory of unity makes the nation a source of despotism and revolution, the theory of liberty regards it as a bulwark of self-government, and the foremost limit to the excessive power of the State. Private rights, which are sacrificed to the unity, are preserved by the union of nations.

No power can so efficiently resist the tendencies of centralization, of corruption, and of absolutism, as that community which is the vastest that can be included in a State, which imposes on its members a consistent similarity of character, interest, and opinion, and which arrests the action of the sovereign by the influence of a divided patriotism.

The presence of different nations under the same sovereignty is similar in its effect to the independence of the Church in the State. It provides against the servility which flourishes under the shadow of a single authority, by balancing interests, multiplying associations, and giving to the subject the restraint and support of a combined opinion. In the same way it promotes independence by forming definite groups of public opinion, and by affording a real source and centre of political sentiments, and of notions of duty not derived from the sovereign will.

Liberty provokes diversity, and diversity preserves liberty by supplying the means of organization. All those portions of law which govern the relations of men with each other, and regulate social life, are the varying result of national custom and the creation of private society. In these things, therefore, the several nations will differ from each other; for they themselves have produced them, and they do not owe them to the State which rules them all. This diversity in the same State is a firm barrier against the intrusion of the government beyond the political sphere which is common to all into the social department which escapes legislation and is ruled by spontaneous laws.

This sort of interference is characteristic of an absolute government. . . .

The combination of several nations in one State is as necessary a condition of civilized life as the combination of men in society. Inferior races are raised by living in political union with races intellectually superior. Exhausted and decaying nations are revived by the contact of a younger vitality. Nations in which the elements of organization and the capacity for government have been lost, either through the demoralizing influence

of despotism, or the disintegrating action of democracy, are restored and educated anew under the discipline of a stronger and less corrupted race.

This fertilizing and regenerating process can only be obtained by living under one government. It is in the cauldron of the State that the fusion takes place by which the vigor, the knowledge, and the capacity of one portion of mankind may be communicated to another. Where political and national boundaries coincide, society ceases to advance, and nations relapse into a condition corresponding to that of men who renounce intercourse with their fellow men. . . .

Those [States] in which no mixture of races has occurred are imperfect; and those in which its effects have disappeared are decrepit. A State which is incompetent to satisfy different races condemns itself; a State which labors to neutralize, to absorb, or to expel them, destroys its own vitality; a State which does not include them is destitute of the chief basis of self-government. The theory of nationality, therefore, is a retrograde step in history. . . .

It is a chimera. The settlement at which it aims is impossible. . . .

It must contribute, therefore, to obtain that which in theory it condemns —the liberty of different nationalities as members of one sovereign community. . . .

Nationality is more advanced than socialism, because it is a more arbitrary system. The social theory endeavors to provide for the existence of the individual beneath the terrible burdens which modern society keeps upon labor. It is not merely a development of the notion of equality, but a refuge from real misery and starvation. However false the solution, it was a reasonable demand that the poor should be saved from destruction; and if the freedom of the State was sacrificed to the safety of the individual, the more immediate object was, at least in theory, attained.

But nationality does not aim either at liberty or prosperity, both of which it sacrifices to the imperative necessity of making the nation the mould and measure of the State. Its course will be marked with material as well as moral ruin, in order that a new invention may prevail over the works of God and the interests of mankind. There is no principle of change, no phase of political speculation conceivable, more comprehensive, more subversive, or more arbitrary than this. It is a confutation of democracy, because it sets limits to the exercise of the popular will, and substitutes for it a higher principle. It prevents not only the division, but the extension of the State, and forbids to terminate war by conquest, and to obtain a security for peace. Thus, after surrendering the individual to the collective will, the revolutionary system makes the collective will subject to conditions that are independent of it, and rejects all law, only to be controlled by an accident.

Mussolini and Hitler, by carrying the theory of nationalism to its logical absurdities, have made clearer now how right Acton was and is.

It was not this that Mazzini and Cavour saw in nationalism; they preached national unity in the interest of individual freedom, the rights of nations as a means to the Rights of Man. So, too, did the French, British, and Americans from whom they drew their theory. But, as we have seen so strikingly in Czechoslovakia,—where the democratic theory of the rights of nations has been used to strengthen the declared foe of democracy and deprive three million Germans of their rights as men, while endangering those of seven million Czechs—all the liberal fathers of nationalism were unwittingly fathering, too, the absolutism of Hitler and Mussolini. These liberals with their interchangeable use of *nation* to mean a sovereign democratic people and a sovereign state led men insensibly into assuming that the people, or nation, is a unit as natural and human and living as man himself. Thinking of domestic affairs, they used *nation* to mean ten million heads working freely together to make each one freer, and then, thinking of external affairs, they used *nation* in the next breath as if these individuals had melted or should melt into one composite head ten million times greater,—and as usual the conception in the greater or supreme field grew supreme. With this tendency to personify there slipped in the inevitable tendency to glorify and then deify this giant champion of individual freedom and complete the myth. Mysticism too abhors a vacuum.

Considering how far the most advanced democracies have gone in this direction it is not surprising that the peoples who got from them their democratic and their national theory together and who looked to them vainly for leadership should have gone still further astray. It was only to be expected that these peoples who had no long background of sturdy, rational individualism to brake the centralizing tendency, whose background had been formed instead by long sufferance of absolutism, and who had only recently thrown off divine-right rulers, should fall a prey to the mystical absolute nationalism of the Mussolinis and Hitlers.

But the great danger now to our freedom and theirs does not lie in their mistakes, it lies in the confusion among the older democracies. It is only our own nationalism, not theirs, that can prevent our union. Indeed, the nationalism of Hitler and Mussolini is doing much to drive the democracies back to their senses, and to force them to apply to each other their own democratic principles. It is for us of the older democracies to take the lead in undoing the damage we have done by failing to think things through, failing to read long ago Lord Acton's handwriting on the wall.

It is for us first of all to remember that *nation* and *state* are bloodless

words and that the millions of us men and women they represent are living individuals—not mystic symbols, legalistic abstractions, composite photographs. We know our millions form together a unit only in desiring the freedom to have our own individual opinion about everything and to tell it to the world, to be our different selves and live our own lives. We know we never grouped ourselves into a nation and instituted government to melt down our differences into uniformity. We know we made the nation only as a step toward making the world safe for the enjoyment of these individual liberties and individual differences. We know now that the next step we need to make toward this end is to unite ourselves in a world democracy. It is for us who know better to do better, and cease blaming others for our ills.

·   ·   ·   ·   ·   ·   ·

Mussolini is always right.—Benito Mussolini.

·   ·   ·   ·   ·   ·   ·

You are nothing, your nation is everything.—Adolph Hitler.

·   ·   ·   ·   ·   ·   ·

Too solid to be overthrown? The livery stable business never seemed more solid than the day the first garage opened.

·   ·   ·   ·   ·   ·

Reduce power diplomatics to mathematics and its falsity leaps out for it would have us believe that we over them are greater than we beside them, that $\dfrac{A}{B}$ is greater than AB, and that 2 times 2 makes less than $\dfrac{2}{2}$ or 1.

CHAPTER VII

League or Union? Three Tests

Man is not the enemy of man but through the medium of a false system of Government.—Paine.

The fatal tendency of mankind to leave off thinking about a thing when it is no longer doubtful is the cause of half their errors.—Mill.

We may now turn from these general considerations to more particular reasons why we must organize our democracies as a union instead of a league, to the reasons why leagues are undemocratic and unions democratic, why leagues can not work and unions can, why leagues can not be trusted to enforce law and unions can. In other words, we shall now submit our choice to the super-state test, the practical test and the acid test, exposed respectively in these questions:

Is it democratic? Can it work? Can it be trusted? We thus find the basic reason (1) why leagues at best encourage autocracy and the super-state while unions make for democracy and tend to lessen the state's power over the individual and increase his power over it; (2) why leagues at best can not reach agreement in useful time while unions can; and (3) why unions, but never leagues, can be relied on to enforce their laws and eliminate inter-state war.

1. THE SUPER-STATE TEST

Centralization is a word which is unendingly repeated nowadays and which practically no one seeks to define.—De Tocqueville.*

WHY LEAGUES ARE UNDEMOCRATIC

Suppose we organize our democracies as a league. This league would have obvious advantages over the League of Nations. Yet because it was a league this organization of democracies would be a perversion of democracy. Its equality would still be the equality of states. It would accord

* See his penetrating discussion of this subject which opens with these words in the penultimate section of Chap. VI, Vol. I, *Democracy in America*.

one vote each to 4,000,000 Swiss, 40,000,000 French, 130,000,000 Americans,—flouting the most elementary democratic principle to this extreme degree for the sake of the state. It would require for any important action unanimous agreement among its state members; democracy proceeds by majority agreement among men. In it 4,000,000 Swiss would not only count for as much as 130,000,000 Americans but they could block action on which all the other democracies in the league were agreed—4,000,000 could thwart nearly 300,000,000. If all this is not a perversion of democracy, what is?

Even were all our democracies equal in population, to organize them as a league would still be to encourage dictatorship among them. A league of democracies must necessarily favor its least democratic member for the same reasons that a league of all kinds of governments tends (though not so much, of course, as does anarchy) to give undue advantage to dictatorship. A league by giving an equal vote to the government of each nation in it allows the government least responsible and responsive to its people to manœuvre best.

The more democratic a people is the more it respects the minority and requires a government to explain policies to the people before committing them, and the more important the issue the more vigilant is its public opinion. But the more these conditions obtain the more handicapped the government is in defending the interests of its citizens in a league. The league system thus places a premium on whatever strengthens the government as regards its own people and a penalty on whatever strengthens the citizen's power to restrain his government. This premium and this penalty operate incessantly with accumulating force.

Their action is powerfully accelerated by the fact that, in forming the league on the basis of the state and for its preservation as an independent unit, the citizens tacitly admit that not their individual but their collective liberty is their supreme end. To advance their individual interests the league must produce agreements, but a government cannot obtain important agreement in the league without sacrificing some of its own independence, the very thing it entered the league to preserve.

Where in a democracy patriotism calls on all good citizens to defend the inalienable rights of the individual, in a league it calls on them to sacrifice their own rights in order to strengthen the government and preserve the state. National solidarity thus replaces respect of the minority or individual as the ideal. The idea spreads that the salvation of all the nation depends on a party, having once gained power, maintaining its power by suppressing all other parties and all freedom of speech and press so that the government may be stable and strong in its dealing

with the rest of mankind; and the race is on toward the totalitarian state. Those who want the proof of experience need only look about them.

WHY UNIONS ARE DEMOCRATIC

It is not on these grounds, however, that the League of Nations has usually been attacked as undemocratic. The great cry against it has been that it involves sacrificing a member democracy's freedom, independence, sovereignty, that it forms a super-state. This cry is invariably raised against every proposal for inter-state government, whether league or union, and it has been raised even more loudly against the latter. Partly because of this democracies in their attempts at organisation have always turned first toward the league system as the lesser evil, as seeming to require less sacrifice of freedom, and have rejected the union system at first as being the super-state *par excellence.*

Where Senator Borah urged against the League of Nations that it would sacrifice the national sovereignty of the American Union, Patrick Henry opposed the Constitution of the American Union as sacrificing the state rights of Virginia. Whether the reference is to national sovereignty or to state's rights, the critics mean that the inter-state government involves sacrifice of the citizen's individual freedom, rights, sovereignty. Even the backers of inter-state organization usually seem to accept this view; they concede the sacrifice but plead that it is needed for the general good.

This reflects profound confusion over what occurs when democratic government, whether national or inter-state, is formed. We have already noted how this confusion rises partly from the assumption that the freedom of the state and the freedom of its citizens are necessarily identical. It also rises from the assumption that the organization of democratic government involves "sacrifice" of rights by the citizens.

"Sacrifice" is a most misleading word for what we do with our rights when we organize democratic government; the operation is really one of safeguarding or investing these individual rights.

When we hand over money to a bank to have it keep a heirloom in safe deposit for us we do not say we are sacrificing the money and the heirloom for the good of the bank. We say we are safeguarding our heirloom and paying for the service. When we hand over money to a corporation in order to gain more money through ownership of its stock we do not say we are sacrificing our money for the good of the corporation. We say we are investing it for ourselves. Even if we lose we do not call the operation a sacrifice; we call it a bad investment. We sacrifice our money only when we hand it over with no prayer or hope or intention of gaining thereby.

No more in politics than in business can we get something for nothing. To keep our freedom and to get more of it we must give freedom. It would not seem to need proving that individuals have always needed to give some of their liberty to the state in order to secure the rest of it; every free people has always admitted this.

Nor would it seem to need proving that united action by men, such as the organization or maintenance of government, involves some loss of freedom or power by each individual unit in it, and yet may result in a net gain in freedom or power by each. Where a government is made of, by and for the people every citizen, as Lincoln was fond of saying, is an equal sovereign, and national sovereignty would seem to be composed of the sovereignty its citizens have given it to secure better the rest of their individual sovereignty. *In a democracy a state's rights can only be the rights its citizens have individually invested in it.* All this is so evident that when men form a democratic government they say that they make the government for the sake of their own freedom. It is, in fact, because this is so clear that they tend to identify their individual freedom with the freedom of their state, and are thus led into the great mistake of assuming that any loss of the nation's sovereignty is necessarily a loss to them.

They forget that for the individual citizen to gain rights the state must lose rights, just as a bank must reduce its charges if the heirloom is to be guarded more cheaply, or a corporation must not merely pile up power in the form of surplus if stockholders are to get dividends on their investment in it. If, for example, the citizen is to gain the right to buy and sell freely in a larger market, his state must lose the right to levy a tariff or interfere with this trade.

When a democratic state's rights over its citizens are increasing more than are their rights one of two things would seem to be happening. Either it is retaining too much of the power gained through its formation—like the corporation that piles up an unreasonably huge undivided surplus— or it is running at a loss and requiring the citizens to throw good money after bad, to hand over to it more and more rights in order to keep the rest. This last would seem to be the case when citizens are required to give their government in the form of taxes more and more of the individual freedom that money represents and yet remain despite the state's increasing armed power more and more exposed to losing even their lives in war.

The object of democratic government is to provide increasing return in individual freedom to the citizens for decreasing investment of their freedom,—for example, more individual security for less taxation and military servitude. Consequently, loss of rights by a government, far from

being a thing necessarily to be avoided or deplored, is a thing to be sought whenever the rights of the citizens are thereby really increased.

INVESTING IN UNION

When democracies form a union what really happens is this: The citizens of each withdraw certain powers they had invested in their national state and reinvest them or part of them in the union state. The operation involves loss of power by their national states but no loss of power by the citizens of any of them. At most they give the union state no more rights than they gave the national state, they simply shift certain rights from one to another.

The reason why there is no loss but merely a shift is that the citizens base their union government on the same equal unit that each of their national government is based on, namely, individual man. Each man consequently remains in precisely the same relation to the new government as to the old. When 10 men unite on this basis each equals 1. When 10 men thus unite with 90 or with nine groups of 10 each of the 100 men still equals 1 for all political purposes. If a democracy of 100,000,000 men thus unites with others of, say, 5,000,000 and 10,000,000 and 50,000,000, each of the 165,000,000 citizens of the union still equals what he did before, 1.

It is different when democracies league together. When 100,000,000 men league with 50,000,000 they lose power as regard the field of government they transfer to the league, for whereas each formerly had the power of 1 over policy in this field they now have only the power of one-half since the league weights 50,000,000 and 100,000,000 alike. Because it thus shifts the unit in shifting the field of government a league entails loss of power to the citizens of all but the least populous of the democracies in it.

As for the common illusion that citizens also lose when democracies unite, two things contribute to it: (A) One of the possible relations of one unit to 10 units is 1/10th, and of 1 to 100,000,000 units, 1/100,000,000th, and so the greater the number the less important each man appears to be. (B) Since 100,000,000 is more than 10, and 10 is more than 1, the greater the number of citizens the more important the state appears to become. But the action of a democracy, whatever its population, is determined in final test by 1, any 1 of the citizens, for it is determined by a majority and 1 can make a majority. If 10 men are divided 5 to 5 and 1 changes sides he carries with him the power of all 10 for he makes a majority of 6 to 4. Raise the number of voters to 100,000,000 and the majority that determines action is not 60,000,000 to 40,000,000 but 50,000,001 to 49,999,999. No matter what the population of a democratic state or union the citizen's

relation to the government and his power to decide its action remain precisely the same.

Far from losing, the citizen gains power by union. While his power to decide action remains unchanged the power of the union whose action he decides becomes much greater as the population increases. Again, if a man must depend on himself alone for his security he must be on guard 24 hours daily. When he unites with five other men democratically for mutual security he needs stand guard only four hours. He gets 24 hours security for an investment of four hours. He gets six times more freedom, six times more defensive power. The more men with whom he unites the more freedom and power he has for less investment of them. In union therefore the progression from 1 to 1/10th to 1/100,000,000th is a progression downward, not in power and freedom for the citizen, but in the amount of it he needs to invest in government, and the progression from 1 to 10 to 100,000,000 is a progression upward, not in the absolute power of the state over the citizens, but in the power it places at the service of each.

When the citizens of several democracies form a union they create a new state but, as we have said, this creates no new rights or powers for the state as State. If they have invested a total of, say, 15 rights in each national government and they shift five of these rights to the union and leave the others untouched the total rights of Government remain precisely what they were, 15. The citizens divide them between two governments instead of centering them in one but lose none of their own power over government.

On the contrary they gain power in another way and Government loses power as regards the citizen. By dividing the rights of Government between two governments the citizen leaves each of them incomplete. The national state loses supreme right to the union state but the latter is not the complete State the former was, for the union's supreme right is limited by all the rights that remain reserved entirely to its member states. By this division and by the fact that both governments equally and independently originate in him the citizen gains the power of balancing two governments to his own advantage, of shifting rights or appealing from one to the other as circumstances may suggest. The citizen of a complete national state has no such check-and-balance power over Government. He is in the exposed position of one with all his eggs in one basket, all his investments in one company.

How union extends the individual's effective freedom from the State,— whether the national, the union, or the foreign state,—may be seen by considering the state rights that he completely transfers to the union. These usually are:

1. The right to grant citizenship.
2. The right to make war and peace, to deal by force or treaty with foreign states.
3. The right to regulate inter-state and foreign trade.
4. The right to control the value of money.
5. The right to control postal and other means of communication.

(The union also has the right to tax individuals and enforce its laws on individuals, but these rights are not transferred to it from the national state, for the latter retains these rights equally; these are really enabling rights required by both governments to govern effectively in their fields and they are inherent in democracy's choice of individual man as the unit of government.)

Now, when the citizens of, say, fifteen democracies withdraw from each of them the above five rights and reinvest these in a union they create within the much larger area of their common state the conditions which had prevailed in each of its component parts, namely, one citizenship, one defense force, one free trade area, one money, one stamp. While leaving each citizen legally where he was as regards the outside world in these five respects they greatly reduce the area of that outside world by removing from it fourteen sovereign states. In reducing fifteen state sovereignties to one in these fields they reduce enormously the amount of actual interference from the State suffered by the inhabitants of this whole area—and, it is worth noting, by the outside world, too. Without taking any right from any citizen of any state anywhere on earth they thus free each citizen to exercise his existing rights on a far greater scale—in fourteen states which before gave these rights to their citizens, but not to him.

TODAY'S SUPER-STATE: THE NATION

The term *super-state* must be read in terms of power of the state, and since this can be understood in several ways *super-state* can easily be misunderstood. This term can really have terror for democrats only when it means greater power for the State over the citizens. When it merely means greater power for the democratic state over their foes, whether Nature, chaos, or aggressive absolutist states, they must welcome the super-state for then it means more power for each democrat and the achieving generally of what democracy seeks.

Yet such is their confusion that many shy at any inter-state organization simply because it must necessarily be greater in size than any member. They assume this means greater governmental power over themselves as if territory meant tyranny. Now tyranny is tyranny, whatever the

geographic scale on which it is practised, but the wider this scale the less intolerable men generally seem to find the same degree of tyranny. The states that gave us the word *tyrant* were among the smallest, not the largest, in antiquity. The tyranny that seems to irritate men most is petty personal tyranny. Though tyranny in a great state may sometimes be petty, the tyranny of a small state must be petty. Given equally autocratic states, tyranny will usually be worst in the smallest for the petty tyrant is more dangerously exposed from without and within, and his tyranny will be more personal for more men. Given equally free institutions, the greater group will normally provide the greater freedom for the individual.

It is sometimes claimed that the citizens of the small Euopean democracies are freer from the danger of war than those of the large democracies. But can this really be attributed to their smallness? As autocracy has been growing in Europe the small democracies have been losing their feeling of security. If autocracy should gain the upper hand over Britain and France where would these small democracies be left? They never knew security until the great democracies rose; if size makes the super-state they would seem to owe their security to these super-states. Let those who argue that there is some inherent democratic virtue in the tiny and some inherent danger in the big consider where individual freedom would be now if there were no democracies larger than the smallest of the cantons that united to make such a *super-state* as Switzerland.

No, it is not size that the individual really fears in the state, but power over himself, interference with his liberties, meddling in his life. He resents his travel being vexed by more and more frontiers and frontier restrictions, his savings wiped out by monetary magic, his market cut off by a tariff, his source of supply ended by a quota. He resents having higher taxes to pay, being forced to depend increasingly on the state, having to turn to its soup-line to live, being exposed to more military service. He resents, in short, being afflicted with more and more government. It is the snooper state, the trooper state, that men really fear when they shy at the epithet, *super-state,* and that super-state today is the nation-state.

Nationalism has shown that it can even eliminate many of the normal advantages of size and, by pitting such great democracies as the American, British and French against each other, raise governmental meddling to monumental proportions and armaments to appalling figures. Nationalism has proved in Germany how far it can outdo the absolutism of the past. And the nation-state has only begun in recent years to show itself, we have only hints of what it has in store.*

Bureaucracy and centralization and taxes growing, growing, growing;

* This entire section was written in 1934.

the state's power over the citizen reaching out, reaching in, reaching all round him, taking livelihood first, money next and freedom all the time until it troops him off to war,—if the nation-state everywhere today is not the super-state what super-state then need be feared?

The dustbins clogged with superfluous government and unnecessary generals, the war clouds gone, tariffs down and taxes trifling, the individual freed to roam and trade in half the world, needing neither to carry passport or change money, the security and freedom of each extended in every way and magnified a hundredfold and the same equal opportunity assured each whether born in the largest or smallest nation in the union—it is union of the free that ends the snooper trooper super-state.

2. THE PRACTICAL TEST

It may perhaps be asked, what need there is of reasoning or proof to illustrate a position which is not either controverted or doubted; to which the understandings and feelings of all classes of men assent, and which in substance is admitted by the opponents as well as by the friends of the new Constitution? . . . But the usefulness of the concession . . . is destroyed by a strenuous opposition to a remedy, upon the only principles that can give it a chance of success. . . . This renders a full display of the principal defects of the confederation necessary, in order to show, that the evils we experience do not proceed from minute or partial imperfections, but from fundamental errors in the structure of the building, which cannot be amended, otherwise than by an alteration in the first principles and main pillars of the fabric.—Hamilton in The Federalist, XV.

WHY LEAGUES CAN NOT WORK

We come to the practical test of everything: Will it work, can it work? Men have shown time and again that they prefer undemocratic, even tyrannical government to ineffective, futile government; indeed, it is to escape this latter that they turn to dictatorship. There would seem no need to prove, after all the evidence of history (of which Geneva's record is only the last chapter), that leagues do not work, can not work. Yet though there is widespread agreement that leagues have not worked there is still widespread faith that the league system can work.

The failure of the early league of the Thirteen American States which Hamilton laid bare in *The Federalist* along with the failures of all the leagues before it did not keep any one, least of all the American Union, from seeking to organize the world as a league. It was not the league character of the Wilsonian institution that kept the United States from

entering it; the irreconcilables sought to make it, not a union, but more of a league. Their opposition implied faith that the league system would work if only rightly made or applied. The fact that all proposals for reform of the League of Nations have left the basic league principles untouched also implies faith in this system. This faith in the Geneva League itself is still avowed explicitly by many whose words have weight.

In the Geneva Assemblies in 1936, in the written replies to the inquiry they instituted into the problem of Covenant reform, in the records of the committee set up to deal with this subject and in subsequent discussions of it in the Council and Assembly, one can find the views of statesmen who personally participated in the League's Ethiopian test. Many of them had similar firsthand and confidential knowledge of the League's functioning in the Manchurian test and in the Disarmament and Economic conferences. Not one of them blamed the league system itself for the League's failures. Instead, nearly all these experts blame everything but the Covenant for Geneva's record and declare that the basic league system is sound and needs no great change.

This view was summed up strikingly by Earl de la Warr when, in the midst of the Sudeten crisis and at the lowest point Geneva has reached, he told the League Assembly, Sept. 16, 1938: "If there is one thing on which I would expect complete unanimity in the Assembly it is that there is nothing essentially wrong with the Covenant." It would seem evident that the unworkability of leagues has still to be demonstrated.

Some of the reasons why the League of Nations has not worked and can not work have already been noted, but not all of these apply to a smaller league of democracies. I would show now that even such a league is unworkable because its unit is the state. We shall first consider generally why a league can not act in time, and then, more specifically, why its enforcement machinery is unsound and untrustworthy.

WHY LEAGUES CAN NOT ACT IN TIME

Our civilization, we have seen, requires constant and rapid political adjustment to be made to meet change. The league system does not allow this adjusting to be done in time. The speed with which an inter-state organization can act depends much more on its unit than on the number of units it contains, whether states or men. Because the state is its unit even a league of fifteen democracies can act only through its state governments, by unanimity on important matters, and subject to ratification. All this makes for delay.

Because each state must act in a league through its state government, public opinion must be strong enough in each state to move the whole

government before important league action is possible. Because public opinion can not act directly on league delegates but only indirectly through the governments that name them, and because the delegates do not de-pend directly on the voters, much more pressure is needed to get action in a league than in a union.

Moreover, public opinion in a union can exert pressure directly over the whole union area, and a majority leader always risks seeing the minority leader carry the fight into his own district and defeat him. But a league divides its public opinion into state compartments, and the dele-gate of one sovereign government can not go campaigning in another state to have its sovereign government thrown out or its delegate changed.

Again, since a league holds the state sacrosanct and is formed to pre-serve the state, the first concern of each state government in it must be state not league affairs. Normally each state government will owe its elec-tion to its policy on internal, not league questions, and it is bound to devote most attention to them and treat league affairs as secondary, until perhaps they smell to heaven.

Even could a league avoid the difficulty of having to act through gov-ernment delegates, its action would remain slow and doubtful because of the unanimity rule. At best it is extremely hard to get unanimous agree-ment on any important matter, far harder than to get a majority to agree. It requires a different technique, and a degree of tact, understanding, and persuasive power that Geneva experience shows is extremely rare even among the world's ablest and most experienced politicians and statesmen. A league delegate must persuade not only his fellow delegates to the point where they will persuade the governments behind them to change their instructions, but he must often also persuade his home opinion at the same time, or keep it persuaded. He must also persuade the public opinion behind each of the delegates opposing him. And, since under the rules of national sovereignty every state must seek to win, the delegate of, say, the United States must publicly prove to the American people that they win by his policy while taking care to avoid thereby convincing, say, the French or British, that they will lose. For they will then disown the dele-gates who accepted this policy and the victory will be empty.

The worse the emergency the more swiftly there must be action, but the more a league then requires unanimity for action and the harder it is to get unanimity, if only because action then involves especial risk, and more risk or profit to some than to other states.

The units of a league, unlike those of a union, are not mobile but rigidly fixed to earth. Voters in a union being men can move from one region to another if political controversy gets too dangerous for them, but the voters in a league being states can not change neighbors. Consequently

the men who decide how the state's vote is to be cast must not only consider the issue on its general merits but ponder even more how their vote is liable to affect their relations with a neighbor, especially a more powerful neighbor. All this makes for hesitation, vacillation, inaction; and makes the difficulty of getting unanimity grow with the importance of the issue.

WHY LEAGUES CAN NOT ESCAPE THE UNANIMITY RULE

There seems no escaping the unanimity rule in important matters so long as the unit of organization is the state. The choice of this unit means that the supreme object of government is the preservation of the state's sovereignty. One must then admit that each state government is more competent than any outside government to decide what is essential for its own sovereignty.

The latest and best example of how impossible it is for a league to escape the unanimity rule was given by the League of Nations in September, 1938, when Europe seemed on the verge of war. The votes of Poland and Hungary then defeated—and one veto would have sufficed to defeat —an Anglo-French proposal to re-interpret the Covenant's unanimity rule so that the veto of one or both parties in a conflict could no longer prevent the Council from adopting measures to preserve peace.

An organization that gives each state one vote and lets the majority of states rule the minority is repugnant both to democracies and autocracies. It lets a minority of men over-ride the majority. That defeats democracy even more than does the unanimity rule, for though the latter allows a minority to block the majority, it does not let any minority take positive control. As for the absolutists, majority rule in a league puts other states or the league above their state, and that is incompatible with the absolutist principle that nothing can be higher than the state.

The unanimity rule may save the absolutist, but not the democrat. Absolutism thrives on disorder and chaos, whether caused by action or inaction. Democracy needs law and order to survive, it can not get them without practical governmental means of timely action, and the unanimity rule allows it no such means. For it saves individual freedom from bad law only to expose it to the danger of no law, or law so weak and ambiguous that it can not be relied on, or law made too late to do any good.

Then there is the difficulty of ratification. To get the agreement needed for action in a league one must persuade not only all the delegates but the governments behind them, and, in democracies, the legislative authority too. After one has persuaded a delegate his government may drop him, or after he has persuaded his government it may be overthrown— perhaps on this very issue, perhaps on something quite unrelated to it.

Even if the delegate remains at the league he may be unable to persuade the new government. While the league statesman is bringing one government in line another may break loose—for time is passing and conditions changing. When all sorts of delicate adjustments have made agreement finally seem possible, conditions may have changed so that this delicate balance has to be readjusted to meet new facts: One must start this heart-breaking work again. If the treaty does reach signature it must then be ratified by all the governments whose unanimity was practically required in negotiating it, and this may take years. The failure of only one or a few states to ratify their delegate's signature has crippled or killed many a treaty.

None of this is theory, it is all the history of the League of Nations, of the League of Friendship among the Thirteen American States, of the international conference method. Consider how slowly the League moved in the Manchurian and Ethiopian conflicts, how many governments changed during the Disarmament Conference, how conditions changed. And military disarmament is fairly simple compared to economic disarmament. Military armament is, after all, the monopoly of each government. Some very temporary and extremely restricted armament limitation agreements can be reached with great effort by this method. But economic affairs are the monopoly of only one government. The simplest tariff agreement arouses in every country a multitude of conflicting private interests. Despite all the pressure for agreement no economic treaty of any importance has yet been achieved by the league or conference method.

WHY UNIONS CAN ACT SWIFTLY

Because it takes man for unit a union can put any important proposal directly before all its principals simultaneously, as in an election or plebiscite. Even if a league could assemble in conference the whole executive and legislative branches of each government instead of a small delegation, it would not be equalling the direct action possible in a union. It would still be dealing with agents, not with the sources of power, the men and women, the citizens, who elect the state executives and legislatures.

When a union proceeds indirectly, through agents or representatives of its units, it can still act more rapidly and easily than a league. Where in a league no agent ever represents more than one unit, in a union every agent must represent many units, his power is always delegated to him by several hundred or thousand of the union's units. A league inevitably makes the delegate a puppet depending on the instructions of his government; a union inevitably keeps its representatives from being rigidly tied

to instructions and makes them freer to respond quickly to new facts or arguments.

The representative in a union may be advised by different units in his district to do this or that on a given issue; the advice may be contradictory; he must use his own judgment and strike a balance between the conflicting instructions he thus gets—and guess what all the silent units in his district want him to do. Presumably he will try to follow the wishes of the majority of units in his district, but he is free to decide (under penalty of being defeated at the next election) what these wishes are. He is free, too, to vote against the wishes of the articulate majority in his district, presumably in the belief that the inarticulate are with him or that time will justify him or that he can persuade a majority at the next election that he was right. The delegate to a league cannot possibly do this; he would be recalled and replaced at once by his government.

The representative in a union is the more responsive to demands for action because the opposition in the legislature can always enter his constituency and help his opponents there defeat him. Far from being able to count, as can the league delegate, on local patriotism defending him against such an outside campaign, he often stands or falls with his own union-wide party.

The representatives in a union, representing as each does only a majority or plurality of units in his district, must act by majority instead of unanimity. Since the nature of a union's unit makes their number so great that it is impossible for each unit to have a veto, the agent of these units can not claim this right after his principals have renounced it. The American presidential veto is not to be confused with this; it is accorded to the president not because he is one unit in the union but because he is the only representative of all the units together. Even so his veto is not absolute, as is that of any league unit.

Because a union acts by majority it can act much more quickly than a league. The league system slows action not only because it discourages many by making action different but also because it makes others fear that once done an action may be hard to undo. Union encourages the doubtful to act because of the facility of repeal.

Once there is agreement in a union to act, action can follow at once. There is no need in it to wait for its units to ratify the decision of their agents; the vote of these representatives suffices for law to take effect. Here again union has a tremendous advantage over a league.

Finally, the greater the emergency in a union the greater is the popular pressure for action—that is, the greater is the pressure of the units on their agents—and the faster the union machinery moves. The difficulty and danger in a union is that it can and may act too swiftly or even be

stampeded in a moment of hysteria. Where the problem in a league is to get up enough steam to turn the wheels, in a union it is to control the speed, to arrange safety valves, governors, brakes, such as the American Union has in the powers reserved to the people and the states, the two-house Congress, the presidential veto, the Supreme Court, and the time required to amend the Constitution.

The United States has often shown how a union can rush action in an emergency when the prime psychological and material need is for action, and how when the emergency has thus been overcome the hasty, ill-considered, or dangerous elements in this action can be eliminated. Neither the Supreme Court nor any of the brakes in the American Union kept the NRA from being put into force at the height of emergency and maintained until there was more complaint against the measure's effects than against its cause. It was when, and only when, this point was reached that the Court invalidated the NRA, reminding the people in effect that they could not continue along certain NRA lines unless they adopted these policies not hastily but with the deliberation which amendment of the Constitution requires.

How much more swiftly a union can move than a league even in its slowest gear may be seen by another example. The slowest procedure in the American Union is that required for amending the Constitution and there is much complaint that it is too cumbersome. Yet in less than 15 years the American people not only amended the Constitution to prohibit alcoholic beverages but amended it again to undo this prohibition. In that period the League of Nations obtained no action whatever as regards even armament reduction, despite the tremendous public demand for it.

3. THE ACID TEST

The important truth . . . is that a sovereignty over sovereigns, a government over governments, a legislation for communities, as contra-distinguished from individuals, as it is a solecism in theory so in practice it is subversive of the order and the ends of civil polity, by substituting violence in place of law, or the destructive coercion of the sword in place of the mild and salutary coercion of the magistracy.
—Hamilton in *The Federalist, XX.*

It may be, if we are to see these things correctly, we must look at them in a longer perspective than is possible tonight. It may be that . . . when the time comes to assess the attempt to make collective security operative this unhappy, this tragic [Ethiopian] War, and the lessons derived from it will be found to have played an important part in establishing lasting

peace.—Anthony Eden defending his League policy in the House of Commons, April 6, 1936.

WHY LEAGUES CAN NOT ENFORCE LAW

It is not enough for a government to be able to make laws in time, it must also be able to insure their effective execution. This brings us to the core of the problem of political organization, whether state or inter-state, the acid test of any government. Law depends on confidence that it will be executed. No system of political law has yet gained that confidence without providing for execution of law by force against those who refuse to accept it.

The Thirteen American States produced in their first attempt at inter-state government the "new and unexampled phenomenon," Hamilton wrote in *The Federalist*, "of a government destitute even of the shadow of constitutional power to enforce the execution of its own laws." He added:

There was a time when we were told that breaches by the States of the regulations of the federal authority were not to be expected; that a sense of common interest would preside over the conduct of the respective members. . . . This language, at the present day, would appear as wild as a great part of what we now hear from the same quarter will be thought when we shall have received further lessons from that best oracle of wisdom, experience. . . . Why has government been instituted at all? Because the passions of men will not conform to the dictates of reason and justice, without constraint. Has it been found that bodies of men act with more rectitude or greater disinterestedness than individuals? The contrary of this has been inferred by all accurate observers.

This lack of coercive power more than any other one factor led to the breakdown of the American Confederation and the establishment of the present Union. We need merely refer to this experiment those who today tell us the League of Nations would succeed if only all its powers of coercion were removed.

To be sound any government or system of law must be built to meet the danger of an attempt being made to upset it, and to meet it in a way inspiring confidence that its law-enforcing machinery can and will overwhelm the lawbreaker. To do this the system must be designed to give the greatest possible guarantees that the more dangerous the violation is the stronger the position of the law-enforcer will be and the weaker the position of the lawbreaker.

Nowhere is the question of the unit in government more important than here. If the unit is the state, then the law can be enforced only by states against states; if the unit is man, the law can be enforced only by men against individual men. To quote Hamilton again, the "penalty, whatever it may be, can only be inflicted in two ways—by the agency of the courts and ministers of justice or by military force; by the coercion of the magistracy or by the coercion of arms. The first kind can evidently apply only to men; the last kind must of necessity be employed against bodies politic or communities or States." Every national law system bears on men as individuals, and we are all so accustomed to this that when we organize a league which bears instead on the state we tend to continue thinking of its functioning in terms of our national experience, as if the change in unit made no serious difference. The fact is that it makes all the difference in the world. The whole effect of taking the state as unit is to weaken the law-enforcing machinery and strengthen the position of the lawbreaker. Here are some of the reasons why:

Suppose we form a league of democracies and one of them, say with a population of 20,000,000, elects by 60 per cent majority a government that proceeds to violate its league obligations. If the league law is to be enforced, it must be enforced against a group so powerful and well organized as to give the enforcer pause. This group is not simply 12,000,000 strong, as it may seem at first glance, but 20,000,000 strong because its government has control of the state's whole war power and because the league law must be enforced against the state as a unit. Whether the coercion is by war, blockade, or non-military sanctions, it can not possibly be restricted to the 12,000,000, it must punish just as much the 8,000,000 who presumably sought to prevent the violation. This fact, on top of the patriotic ideology responsible for the democracies having organized a league instead of a union, must encourage the 8,000,000 to join the 12,000,000 in resisting the law.

Here we have the essential unsoundness of the enforcement machinery of a league. This system begins by making sure that its weakest lawbreaker will be far stronger than any gang or mob of men—the strongest lawbreaker that a union faces—for a league lawbreaker must be at least an organized nation of men. Then the league system proceeds to strengthen its lawbreaker by itself outraging justice. Worse, it is incapable of sparing the innocent when it would punish the guilty. Still worse, it is bound to punish the innocent common people more than the responsible leaders. Its blockade strikes the ruler only by starving the half-starved into revolt, its bullets kill few statesmen. While it is putting the whole nation behind the offending government,

this stupidity and injustice is demoralizing and weakening those upon whom it must depend to coerce the offender. For such reasons I predicted early in the Ethiopian war* that "the results of these sanctions are bound to be slow," and recalled, "It is always easier to keep a people united under outside pressure than when outside applying that pressure." To remember that Ethiopian experience is to see how serious is this defect in a league.

WHEN LAWBREAKERS ARE IMMORTAL

Again, the league system requires enforcement by immortals against immortals. Its unit is the nation, and nations are immortal, compared to individual men. Because of this a league in coercing a state of 20,-000,000 population must really coerce a state that is more than 20,000,000 strong, for the state disposes of all the power past generations have stored in it and is fortified by its generations to come, by its aspirations for and obligations to them.

What is more, to enforce law one must find the offender guilty. It is one thing for the immortal state to brand as a criminal one of its millions of mortals, and quite another for a few mortal statesmen to attach the stigma of guilt to an immortal nation. It is an appalling blunder, a monstrous thing, inherently indefensible.

"I do not know the method of drawing up an indictment against a whole people," Burke declared in his plea for conciliation with America. "I cannot insult and ridicule the feelings of millions of my fellow-creatures . . . I hope I am not ripe to pass sentence on the gravest public bodies, entrusted with magistracies of great authority and dignity and charged with the safety of their fellow-citizens, upon the very same title that I am. I really think that for wise men this is not judicious; for sober men, not decent; for minds tinctured with humanity, not mild and merciful."

All this would be true even were a nation mortal, and the fact that a people does not die makes Burke's statement only truer. What could be worse folly than to encourage men (as a league does by its subordination of individuals to their state) to put their pride in their nation, to identify their individual self-respect with their nation's status in the world—and to condemn then their nation as criminal? This system which visits on the children the sins of the fathers seems designed to rouse and maintain a spirit of bitter resistance to league law both among the fathers and the children; it strikes at what every self-re-

* *The New York Times*, Oct. 20, 1935. See also despatch Nov. 24, 1935.

specting individual must hold dear, the name he inherits, has made for himself, and would pass on. The effect of Geneva's verdict against the Italian government in uniting Italians behind that government, stimulating them to sacrifice and invent, spurring them in the field and at home to much greater effort than most people expected, should suffice to show how any system that would enforce law against immortal nations tends to defeat itself. It should be evident, too, that to attach war guilt to a people, as at Versailles, without even doing it by a league's process of law does not make matters better.

There remain the after-effects. Whether a league fails or succeeds in coercing its guilty nation, the condemned people is not likely to rest until it has forced its judges to recant, to absolve even the guilty among it in order to save their innocent compatriots, dead, living and unborn. One cannot better organize enduring bad blood, feud on a colossal scale, than by trying to establish peace and justice, law and order, through the coercive machinery of a league.

To make matters worse, a league's unit is not only immortal but immobile. An individual man who has been found guilty can hope to escape the disgrace by moving elsewhere, changing his name, beginning anew, or his family can. Not so the nation. It is fixed. The individual Englishman can change from one condition of life to another and another but the English as a national unit must face the world forever as an island. The Italians as a nation cannot escape from the problem Gibraltar and Suez pose, though the farmer whose gates to the highway are similarly held by another can always, at worst, move away. The immobility of a league's units breeds and nourishes unnecessary conflict and makes its enforcement machinery stiff and rigid. It also makes it harder for the nations that must adjoin forever the accused nation to condemn it, or for it to accept such disgrace from its neighbors.

The neighboring nations must remember, too, that condemning the accused endangers them more than other league members; on the neighbors falls the main burden of coercion in a league, their trade suffers most from economic sanctions, and they are the most exposed to the acts of desperation or vengeance of the condemned. These neighbors may be as weak compared to the lawbreaker as Switzerland and Austria compared to Italy, may have no material interest in enforcing the law against this particular offense, may hope to profit considerably from not enforcing it. Their failure to enforce the law may strengthen the offender as greatly as did the action of Switzerland and Austria in keeping open Italy's communications with Germany. This shows how the immobility of a league's units undermines its power to enforce law.

WHERE TRIAL PRECEDES ARREST

The procedure a league is bound to follow tends to make its law enforcement hesitating and untrustworthy. People often talk as if the League of Nations could enforce the law in about the same way their own government does. The difference in unit, however, makes the procedure of the two radically and inevitably different. One can lock up a man pending trial, but not a nation—one can not imprison a nation at all. When a policeman sees a man, knife in hand, creeping up behind another man he doesn't stop to consider whether perhaps no crime but only a practical joke is intended. He doesn't wait till the blow falls, the blood spurts, the victim appeals to him. He jumps in at once and arrests the man on suspicion. When the Italian government openly prepared for nine months to invade Ethiopia and the League of Nations did nothing to stop it except try to reconcile the two, many criticized the League for not acting like a policeman. But one can not arrest a nation on suspicion.

Even had a league the force to do this it would lack the will. The policeman does not need to consider whether public opinion will approve his intervention. But coercion in a league means war or risk of war, and the more democratic the members of a league are the less they will like to resort to coercion without first making sure that public opinion is behind them. One can get few if any peoples—let alone all members of a league—to agree suddenly to risk war on mere suspicion of aggression. To move public opinion to that degree one must arrange that the crime, if committed, will seem as flagrant and black as possible. To do this one must convince the public first of all that all means of peacefully preventing the crime have been exhausted.

If, as in the case of Italy, the suspected government not only protests its peaceful intentions but agrees to arbitrate the dispute, what can a league do but take it at its word? If the league does not, it itself spoils the possibility of conciliation, assures the suspected government stronger support at home and sacrifices the league's chances of rousing public opinion among its members to support coercion. It thus strengthens the potential offender while weakening the enforcer.

If the league does take the suspected government at its word, shows the utmost trust in its good faith, leans backward to be just and patient, then if the crime is committed it appears the more heinous and may possibly rouse enough indignation to make effective coercion possible. But this means waiting till the crime has been committed. It also means making eventual reconciliation and peace among these immortal im-

mobile nations all the harder by making the crime and stigma worse. It means that the league is really a partner in the crimes it would repress, responsible for their being worse than they would have been otherwise. What must one say of a system of law whose possibility of repressing crime depends on its success in making crime worse?

[Since the rest of this chapter was written (in 1934-36), we have seen in the Sudeten crisis in September, 1938, how all this applies only to a more dangerous degree when, as in the old diplomatic machinery, the unit for international relations remains the state but the action takes place outside a league's regular processes of law. Then to get the law-abiding peoples to resist flagrant treaty violation one must fly to Berchtesgaden and Godesberg, help the aggressor force the victim to surrender, and by all manner of manoeuvres and pathetic appeals contrive to make aggression at once cataclysmic in its consequences and trifling in its cause. And then one must bring mankind to the brink of world war and keep it trembling there for weeks, not to get justice done but merely to defer a worse crime by strengthening the criminal. How much law and order can we expect to get by such methods, and for how long?]

Moreover, what law and order would any nation enjoy if the police could not arrest even a flagrant offender before they had convicted him in court? Yet this is just what any league must do. The diplomatic machinery must convict him overwhelmingly in the opinion of the world, and achieve this without a regular trial, as in the preceding example.

After the Italian government had invaded Ethiopia and while war was going on the League's Council and then its Assembly met, heard Italy's defense, and decided that the Italian government had resorted to war in violation of the Covenant. Only then could the League begin action against the aggression. Yet how can any organization of sovereign states allow even its highest-ranking official to act against an aggressor as the lowest-ranking policeman does? How can Sovereign States let him use their armed force against a state before they have formally agreed in each given case to such grave and dangerous action? In a league the trial must come *before*, not after, the arrest; and the action a league takes after the trial is not to punish the offender as many assume but only to stop the crime continuing or prevent the criminal from succeeding in his plan.

For seven months after the Italian aggression was condemned the crime continued—if it can be said yet to have ceased. One can murder a man in a minute but one can not keep on murdering him for months. Nor can one take all year, or even all day, to arrest a man; the policeman needs only a minute. But one can keep on committing for years

any crime in a league calendar. These considerations may help make clear how ordinary conceptions of law are thrown out of gear when we change the unit from man to the state, and how this change complicates the problem of enforcement.

THE FALLACY OF BLOODLESS SANCTIONS

One effect of all this is to force a league to begin its enforcement gently and slowly, to turn then to stronger measures, and to encourage the aggressor thereby to commit worse crimes. But many have traced Geneva's failure to coerce Italy to the fact it did not begin by applying at once all of Article Sixteen's sanctions, as that article requires. But many countries that agreed to the verdict against Italy which made Article Sixteen applicable did so only because they understood beforehand that only the milder sanctions would be applied. It proved impossible, in fact, to get even all these mild sanctions applied by Switzerland, and other less strategically important countries.

At best every nation is very strongly and naturally reluctant to agree to participate in the wholesale bloodshed which any decision to apply military sanctions risks involving. This reluctance is made all the stronger by the hopes of success that non-military measures seem to hold. On paper one can make an attractive case for such measures. One can argue—as was argued in the Italian test—that sufficient agreement can be obtained on economic sanctions to make sure that the aggressor will be brought down eventually without the coercers themselves shedding any blood, that all they need do is sit by coolly and patiently and keep the screws on. It was also argued in the Italian test that the aggressor, seeing that there is such wide agreement against him and that it is bound to ruin him in the end, will not wait till his ruin is consummated but will give up long before. One can thus reach the conclusion that though these sanctions seem slow their effect will really be swift.

To the kind of men who are bound to predominate in a league such reasoning is the more persuasive because such men have a pronounced professional weakness for the theory that it is best always to begin mildly. The argument is that if one then wins one wins at least risk and cost, and if one fails one can still win by turning to stronger and stronger measures, whereas by applying the strongest measures at the outset one sacrifices the possibility of winning cheaply, and if one fails nothing more is left to do.

This argument, however, is never likely to work out in a league better or differently than in the Italian test. A case can be made for

gradually increasing pressure, and also for staking all on a bold policy, —and the merits of this aggressive policy are naturally bound to appeal most to the aggressive-minded, and therefore to the aggressor, just as the merits of passive action appeal most to the pacific. Where desire to win by economic sanctions leads the coercers to see all the possibilities of victory through the aggressor reading the handwriting on the wall, the same process of wishful thinking leads the aggressor to concentrate on all the possibilities of nullifying these sanctions by economies, inventions, quick military triumph, etc. He becomes too engrossed in all this to see the handwriting on the wall, let alone surrender to it. The result is that the crime of war for which the league has condemned the aggressor continues to be perpetrated week in, week out, the league appears to be doing nothing effective even to stop the crime or aid the victim, public opinion is outraged by the spectacle, it demands that the killing be stopped and refuses to keep coolly and patiently content with slow-moving sanctions in the face of continued slaughter. The cry for something more effective is soon bound to rise, just as the demand for the oil sanction rose soon after the other sanctions were applied to Italy.

But what is the effect of the threat of stronger measures that thus rises? It encourages the victim of aggression to continue an otherwise hopeless war, and it encourages the aggressor to redouble his attack and resort to more frightful warfare—just as Italy turned to poison gas as Geneva turned toward the oil embargo—in the hope of winning the war before the sanction takes effect.

"The main hope for any slow-moving instrument to be effective," I wrote when sanctions went into force against Italy,* "lies in the one against whom it is aimed foreseeing his inevitable disaster and renouncing the hopeless struggle. There seems no reason to doubt that sanctions, continued long enough, would ruin Italy. But if this is encouraging Rome to stay in the League and keep exploring possibilities of compromise in Paris and London, it also is serving to speed Italian efforts to conquer Ethiopia before Italy is too weakened by sanctions. Is a method which shortens war by lengthening the casualty list effective?"

JUDGE, SHERIFF, CRIMINAL,—ALL IN ONE

These examples by no means exhaust the difficulties and absurdities into which a league falls through having the state as its unit. Another result is that each member of a league is at once judge, juryman, and sheriff. Worse, as I helped point out when the Italian government, while

* *The New York Times,* Nov. 24, 1935.

undergoing sanctions, took part in the League's hearing on Germany's violation of the Locarno treaty, the league system "allows a nation to fill simultaneously the roles of condemned lawbreaker in one case and judge and sheriff in another." This weakness, the dispatch continued, was "exemplified by the first international meeting to be held in the new League palace, that of the Locarno powers on the afternoon of April 10, 1936. In it the Foreign Ministers of Britain and France, who that very morning had debated before the Committee of Thirteen in the old League building what to do about Italy, whom the Council found guilty of committing the worst crime in the League's calendar, debated with Italy what to do about Germany, whom the Council, with Italy as one of the judges, found guilty of committing its next worst crime.

"This situation results from the fact, underlying all the League's main weaknesses, that it, unlike any other system of government, takes for its operating unit not an individual mortal but an immortal collectivity of mortals called a nation which has the further peculiarity of being geographically fixed," I then wrote.

"Possibly the reason that no remedies yet touch this is that it is impossible to shift the League's law-making and law-enforcing unit to an ordinary mortal without scrapping the objective for which the League was formed. This objective, contrary to the general assumption, is primarily not peace but the preservation of the integrity and independence of these existing national units."*

This may help make clear why a league can have no effective central or executive authority. There can be no sheriff in a community where every man is equally sheriff. The example should make clearer, too, why projects to endow a league with a permanent league police force for the coercion of members are doomed to failure. It is not the international character of such a force that makes it impossible—look at the French Foreign Legion—but the fact that a league army's real unit is not man but the nation.

It results that when a league does decide to enforce its law it must then improvise its instrument, whether non-military or military. It "must at the last minute organize an army out of a mob of armies of sovereigns so jealous of their sovereignty that they are unable to organize a league force beforehand."† We have already noted why a league can not provide even the advance military planning needed for confidence in its enforcement machinery. For similar reasons it can not make concrete advance plans to enforce its law by non-military means.

* *The New York Times*, Apr. 19, 1936.
† *The New York Times*, Dec. 29, 1935.

Even if it could do this, and even if it did succeed in organizing an army to coerce a member, it would still face the difficulty of forcing its members to coerce the aggressor. Article Sixteen of the Covenant provides measures against the member that resorts to war, but the Covenant provides no means to compel members to apply these measures. It provides no sanctions, that is, for violators of Article Sixteen itself, and if it did how could they be enforced? A state that has no desire to coerce a particular state may profess to be applying sanctions and yet leave open a hundred loopholes whose existence could only be proved if the league had inspectors everywhere. To attempt to coerce a member that flatly refuses to apply a sanction means giving the aggressor an ally, strengthening him and adding to the burden on the coercers. Whatever a league's law may be on this point, the members who refuse to help coerce seem likely in practice to escape their obligation with the impunity that Austria, Hungary and Switzerland enjoyed in the Italian test.

Worse still, the possibility of successful coercion by a league is in inverse ratio to the need. As Geneva's experience shows, a league may succeed in minor conflicts, but the stronger the lawbreaker and the worse the crime, the less a league is likely to succeed. Yet we organize government more to protect us against the greater than the lesser dangers.

RESULT: NO LEAGUE CAN BE TRUSTED

The result is that a league can not inspire confidence among its law-abiding members nor respect and fear among the aggressively inclined. This encourages its members to arm, and whether they arm for defense or aggression they make matters worse by putting the enforcement problem on a still more enormous scale. The aggressive are encouraged to gamble by the lack of confidence members show in a league when they steadily increase their armaments. Whether the gambler wins or loses the cost and risk are tremendous. Even if he loses the success of the league is offset by the appalling heritage it leaves. Six months before Geneva's sanctions failed in May, 1936, I wrote:

If Ethiopia succumbs to aggression, can league members condone this better after they have put millions into sanctions for the sake of upholding the law? If Italy collapses, will that not leave a pretty problem? However essential it may be to frustrate Mussolini's methods, is frustrating them enough to cure what caused them?

What poisonous use will future Italian demagogues make of the sanctions, considering the use made of war debts in the United States and

of war guilt in Germany? Meanwhile . . . what else is going to be
happening? Consider how remote now seem the problems which were
worrying the world six months ago and it is possible to make a better
guess regarding how the present will look in May.

The public, which earlier despaired too hastily of the League and
now overrates its achievement, will know better then how complicated
this whole problem is. It will be only human if it then blames the
League. . . .

The fault lies much deeper in the League machinery, . . . so built as
to be inevitably too weak and too slow to prevent war, and then too slow
and too rough in stopping it to assure peace with justice.*

Since no league, no matter how strong its paper guarantees to enforce its laws, can possibly remove the fatal defects inherent in itself,
it can not possibly succeed in getting its members to trust it enough
to disarm and avoid chaos. As long as the state must depend, in a vital
emergency, on its own arms it must also protect strategic industries and
prepare against blockade by artificially maintaining its agricultural production. So long as it must do this it can not afford to renounce control
over such essential weapons as its currency and trade. Practically, there
is no more possibility of monetary stability or free trade than there is
of disarmament, security, or peace in any inter-state government requiring coercion of states. Through and through the league system is untrustworthy.

WHY UNIONS CAN ENFORCE LAW

To be sound, a system of law, we have said, must be built to meet
the danger of some attempt being made to upset it, and to meet it in
a way inspiring confidence that its law-enforcing machinery can and
will overwhelm the lawbreaker. To do this it must be devised to give
the greatest guarantees that the more dangerous the violation the stronger
the position of the law-enforcer will be and the weaker that of the lawbreaker.

A union pins any violation of its law on the weakest possible political unit, a single mortal, and arrays against him the organized cen-
tralized power of millions of these units—the union state. Suppose we
have fifteen democracies of 20,000,000 population each. If they league
together the theoretical ratio of law-enforcing power to law-defying power
is at best 280,000,000 to 20,000,000, or 14 to 1. If they unite the ratio
is 299,999,999 to 1. This shows how overwhelmingly the change of unit

* *The New York Times*, Nov. 17, 1935.

from state to man weakens the lawbreaker and strengthens the law-enforcer.

For law (whether treaty or statute) to be broken some individual man has to break it. A union by pinning the responsibility for the violation on this individual and on him alone tends to deprive him of all support. Members of his family or gang may help him, but they are not to be compared in power with a government which controls the force of an organized nation and can appeal to patriotic sentiments to justify its treaty violation. Union law does not by its very operation drive the innocent to support the lawbreaker as does league law; instead it tends to isolate him even from those most likely to support him. His family seldom resists his arrest.

No group, not even the family, is stigmatized legally in a union by the guilt of one member, let alone punished simply because of relation to him. The criminal's family may suffer some social disgrace, but the family can move away, change its name, begin afresh. Or it may find protection in the fact that many other unrelated men have the same family name. A union's units are so numerous and their names descend in such fashion that the unit whose name is unique is a rare exception, and many names less common than Jones and Smith are common enough to be protective. The name of each nation in a league is unique, and so there is no escape from that name and any blot on it stands out more, lasts longer, and is harder to bear.

There have been many celebrated murderers, but how often is one of their descendants identified as one—as, say, the grandson of Dr. So-and-so who was executed for poisoning a patient? The children of criminals often attract attention during trials, but how long does it last? They are soon mercifully lost or forgotten among the millions of men.

In a union there is, then, no enduring disgrace attached to the group to which a lawbreaker belongs, nothing to entangle all its members willy-nilly in the crime and turn them, as in a league, against the law in order to right this injustice or save their self-respect. By its condemnation a union, unlike a league, does not inevitably turn against it even the condemned criminal, for, unlike an "aggressor nation," he can hope to live down the stain on his name, change it if it is uncommon, move away.

The union system, moreover, gives those it arrests as lawbreakers much stronger guarantees of justice and much greater hope for acquittal than does a league. It is therefore easier for the innocent to accept arrest unresistingly. As for the guilty, it is noteworthy that a union's guarantees to each individual that its overwhelming power will not be used unjustly against him helps to weaken him at the critical time when he is about to break the law or is breaking it. The Bill of Rights serves

to isolate the criminal and deprive him of misplaced sympathy by assuring all other men that their combined power will not be used wrongly against the weakest man, that the innocent individual will not be punished, that punishment will fall on the guilty or on no one.

These guarantees to the individual together with the individual's inherent weakness, mortality and mobility allow a union to act against offenders much more quickly than can a league. They allow it to stop crime in the bud, to arrest on *prima facie* evidence of criminal intent. The number and weakness of its units not only permit but require a union to have the powerful central authority a league can not possibly have —and to maintain law and order normally with a tiny fraction of the power at its disposal. It can have, say, one policeman to 1,000 potential lawbreakers and yet be able in an emergency quickly to outnumber or outpower the lawbreaker. The nature of a union's unit, moreover, permits and requires specialized functions for the enforcement of law —this union unit being a soldier, that union unit a policeman, another a judge, another a juryman, still another a prosecutor. It thereby escapes the grotesque absurdity into which a league is led by its unit; in a union no condemned criminal can judge for it the crimes of others while continuing his own.

The union system of law enforcement does not work perfectly. Sometimes the guilty escape, sometimes the innocent are punished, sometimes the union may even suffer revolt, civil war. But its principle is sound and the system does work well: it insures general respect for and enforcement of law by insuring that at the critical moment—the moment when the law is flagrantly broken—the enforcer will be at his strongest and the violator will be at his weakest. And it does this in direct ratio to the importance of the violation. It does insure the citizen more security against burglary than petty theft, and still greater security against murder than against burglary, and still greater security against war than against murder.

HOW UNION ELIMINATES INTER-STATE WAR

It may be objected that the enforcement of law against thieves and murderers is normally left to each state in a union and that such examples do not apply to conflicts between states in the union or between one or more states and the union itself. The examples were used, however, to illustrate the idea of varying degree of crime and security. Moreover, whatever may be the division between a union and a member state as regards the laws to be enforced, each enforces law by the same basic method, for the unit is the same. Consequently, whatever may be

the range of crimes in the union code the union system does assure
the citizen more security against its major than its minor crimes.

It is true that in a union as in a league conflicts may rise between member states in their corporate capacity and between them and the union.
A union may refer such disputes to its supreme court, but refusal to
accept the court's decision faces it with a league's problem of enforcing
law against a state. There remain, however, great differences in favor
of union.

In a league such conflicts and problems are the only ones possible;
in a union they are abnormal. The state's position in a union differs
radically, as we have seen, from its position in a league. The transfer to
the union of some of the state's most important rights (which it most
jealously retains in a league) tends to remove many of the worst sources
of dispute and war among states. It leaves the state no longer an economic entity, the regulation of its trade with other states inside and
outside the union is transferred to the union government which enforces
its inter-state commerce laws not against the states but against individuals in them. Above all, the fact that its citizens have transferred
from state to union the power to make war and peace eliminates the chief
danger of inter-state disputes resulting in war. The state government
loses not only its motives for war, but also the means of waging it
successfully.

The knife edge is removed from disputes between states in a union because the citizens of each state are also citizens of the union, have the
same control over both, and inevitably rate higher the citizenship that
opens the wider field to them, lets them move freely from state to state,
and gives them their standing in the world. When a man is equally sovereign in two governments, as he is in a union, disputes between these
two agents of his tend to make him an arbiter instead of a partisan.
A man can be at war with himself, of course, and this can lead him
to commit suicide, but men organize government to save them from
murder, not suicide, and to gain over each other some of the control
they have over themselves.

History is even more reassuring than reason in these regards. For example there were many disputes—including eleven territorial ones—among
the Thirteen American States during their league period. War threatened
to result from some of these disputes and this danger was one of the
reasons that led them to shift from league to union. All these disputes
lost in explosiveness after union, none of them threatened war thereafter.
Supreme Court decisions settled them without the theoretical danger of
a state defying the Court ever actually arising. Since this liquidation of
the disputes inherited from the league and colonial periods, disputes be-

tween states have lost in importance. There are few Americans today
who can recall offhand what states and what issues were involved in any
inter-state disputes before the Supreme Court, least of all the latest. That
shows how popular interest in inter-state disputes dies out in a union.
The way Americans still remember the Supreme Court's distant decision
concerning one of the humblest among them, Dred Scott, shows how a
union centers interest instead in cases that directly affect the freedom
of the individual.

There is no example in the history of the American Union of a state
refusing to accept the Court's decision in an inter-state dispute or seriously
threatening to use force against another state. A state that contemplated
such action in the American Union could not gamble on being left to fight
it out with the other state as could Italy with Ethiopia and Japan with
China in the League of Nations. Each state government knows that
should it resort to force it would change its conflict from one with another state to one with the government of the United States, which is required by the Constitution to "protect each of them against invasion"
and "domestic violence," which has enough armed power at hand to overwhelm at once the strongest single state and which can draw immediately,
directly and without limit on the Union's whole potential power. The
Union, moreover, can aim its coercive power at the Governor and other
responsible members of such a state government as individual offenders.
It can act against them personally on the ground that they and not the
people are to blame and that as American citizens who are waging war
against the Union they are committing treason.

The only memorable conflicts in American Union history in which states
figured as parties were both, significantly, conflicts not with other states,
as in the American league period, but with the Union government. There
was South Carolina's nullification of the Tariff Act; President Jackson's
blunt warning that he would uphold the Union law with force against
such treason* sufficed to maintain the law. Then there was the attempt

* See Jackson's *Proclamation to the People of South Carolina,* "The dictates of a
high duty oblige me solemnly to announce that you can not succeed. The laws of
the United States must be executed. I have no discretionary power on the subject;
my duty is emphatically pronounced in the Constitution. Those who told you that you
might peaceably prevent their execution deceived you; they could not have been deceived themselves. They know that a forcible opposition could alone prevent the
execution of the laws, and they know that such opposition must be repelled. Disunion
by armed force is *treason.* Are you really to incur its guilt? If you are, on the heads
of the instigators of the act be the dreadful consequences; on their heads be the
dishonor, but on yours may fall the punishment. On your unhappy State will inevitably fall all the evils of the conflict you force upon the Government of your
country." In this Proclamation Jackson also declared: "The Constitution of the
United States, then, forms a *government,* not a league."

of the eleven Southern States to secede which the Union overcame by force in the Civil War.

This last, however, was not, strictly speaking, a test of the Union's ability to enforce its laws but a test of its ability to maintain itself. The fact that the American Union has suffered one civil war in 150 years cannot be held against the union system, for secession and civil war can occur and have more often occurred in other systems of government. The American Civil War must be cited, if at all, in favor of the union system. It shows what tremendous resistance that system can successfully overcome. What is more important, it shows too how swiftly, completely and solidly a union can make peace, even in the exceptional case where it must use its coercive power against a state instead of an individual.

Theory and practice which alike condemn a league alike attest the fact that a union works. Both testify that this system is trustworthy, sound. We can not go right if we organize our democracies as a league; if we go wrong in organizing them as a union of ourselves we shall be the first to fail with union.

. . . .

Any system that defies reason and defies accident is anti-Man.

. . . . . .

Too small a cause for so great a consequence?
The motorcar that climbs the Alps in a driving rain can be stopped in the desert by one drop of water in its electrical heart.

. . . . . .

In the story told in these pages I can point to no time which appears so fraught with disaster to the human race as a whole as the present, the moment at which I am bringing this book to a close. . . . We have now reached a stage in the growth of civilization which cannot go further, and is doomed to go back, until we discover the means of passing from the national to the international state. . . . Human nature has made immeasurable strides since our Lord showed in His own person how divine it can be. But it cannot advance further till men learn to think of the scheme of human relations which He conceived as one to be brought from the realm of dreams to the earth in which they live, to be made incarnate in the flesh and blood of a living society. That is the world situation, as I see it, today:
—Lionel Curtis, closing in 1936 his monumental "Attempt to Show How the Past [from ancient times on through] has Led to the Present Position in World Affairs," in his work, *"The Commonwealth of God."*

. . . . . .

Many people ask why we are abolishing the German States. I can only answer: "I do not know why we are doing this. I only know that I must do it. You lose the past and gain the future."—Adolph Hitler, speaking at Munich, Jan. 27, 1936 (as reported in *The Times*, London).

The League, in my view, has reached the stage that the United States reached when the Articles of Confederation proved much too loose to set up an effective common life . . . That was what led to the framing of the Constitution of the United States . . . I am sure there are millions in my country who are ripe for such a policy and I am sure also that throughout Europe and the world there would be a great response to such a lead.

We have now reached a stage in human affairs where we must either set out deliberately to build up a World Commonwealth, or suffer the collapse of civilization in another and infinitely more frightful world war.

World government based on democracy, social justice and racial equality is not only a noble ideal. It has become a stark necessity. Those who share that conviction must have the courage of their conviction that the future belongs to us and that it is we who must take the lead in order to save peace and lay the foundations of a new civilization.—Herbert Morrison, British Labor M. P., addressing the Geneva Institute of International Relations, Aug. 21, 1936.

CHAPTER VIII

How the Union Remedies Our Ills

The effort for disunion produces the existing difficulty.—Lincoln, *Message to Congress*, Dec. 3, 1861.

We can turn now to the major ills that are afflicting our world and defeating our best doctors and see how the Union remedies them. We shall then see better what Union means and what we get from it, how much for how little.

MILITARY DISARMAMENT AND SECURITY

Our democracies have devoted nearly twenty years of patient effort to this problem. It has been tackled from apparently every angle: By all the nations together and by small groups of them; piecemeal, by this or that arm or this or that region, or as a whole on a universal scale; by secret diplomatic channels and by public League debate; security first and disarmament afterward and *vice versa*—by every way within the limits of national sovereignty. The problem remains. The progress that seemed at times to have been made has always proved illusory. There are more security pacts than ever and less secure peace. Only the World War knew heavier armaments than today, and its lead is falling every hour everywhere on earth. The efforts to solve the armaments-security problem have proved only that it cannot be solved under the league or national sovereignty system.

When the fifteen democracies unite in abandoning this system for Union what happens to this problem? A two-power standard in all arms provides more armed security than any nation now dreams of enjoying. Merely by establishing the Union and only by it can democracies be mathematically certain of gaining reduction in armaments while at least doubling their armed security.

Armament, however, is only one measure of power. Our Union, we have seen, would be even more powerful in other respects. It would enjoy almost monopoly world control of such war essentials as rubber, nickel, iron, oil, gold and credit. This, with the invulnerability from surprise attack its decentralized strength would confer and the prestige its cen-

tralized general staff and its swiftly effective Union government would give, would enable it to reduce its armaments safely below the two-power standard. The Union would have nothing to fear from most of the peoples left outside at the start; it could count on their support even before they entered it. Except for police work the Union's only need to keep armaments at all would be as a temporary precaution against the militant absolutist powers—Japan, Germany and Italy. Even a much tighter alliance among the three than seems likely to be made would be no more formidable to the Union than an alliance of, say, Mexico, Venezuela, and Italy would be to the United States.

If one can imagine Russia preferring to join with its present enemies, Japan and Germany, rather than to live on peaceful terms with the Union, it still needs considerable imagination to see real substance in an alliance of such bedfellows. And when one has imagined things as black as possible, he has imagined no real immediate danger to the Union. The figures already given show enough of the basic weakness of such a four-power combination to reassure all but the congenitally fearful. Moreover, the mere attempt to form such an alliance would make the heavily armed states of central Europe fearful of becoming its first victims and throw them all the more on the side of the Union. Those who are reassured for the present but fear a dangerous alliance might develop in twenty or thirty years can cancel their fears by imagining too how much the Union would be developing and expanding during this time.

Practical men, and even dreamers and nightmarers with fairly well-balanced imaginations, will find when they study the world in which our Union would exist that there is no reasonable conceivable combination that would dare contemplate attacking it. The reasonable probability is that all the aggressive dictatorships would soon be overthrown one after another from within because of the powerful stimulus the creation of the Union would give their peoples to revolt, regain their freedom and enter the Union. With each revolution the Union's security would rise and its need of armaments fall.

All this can be done without a disarmament conference or treaty. If the Union desired to speed the process of disarmament by a treaty it would be in a much better position to obtain agreement than the democracies are today. But there would be no real need for such a treaty. For all practical purposes, the simple act of Union by the democracies would suffice to end the whole armaments danger and problem, provide security for all the democracies and make every people on earth more secure from war than it is now. The present disunion among the democracies exposes no one more to war than the Germans, Italians and Japanese. Even they

can have no security for their lives until they see their rulers faced
with a democratic Union too mighty for them to attack.

The failure of the Disarmament Conference has left us with another
problem. It has left us with world and national economy based on a
quickening rhythm of armament-making, and with unemployment growing nonetheless. How can this arming be ended or even slowed now without plunging the world into acute depression, and through it into civil
and international war? Some believe that the only way to avoid depression
is to let war quicken this productive rhythm still more. No doubt war
is one of the things that can do this: It is the final burst of speed to
which arms racing logically leads, but it can not solve our problem. It
merely ends the race later and in worse conditions. If we can not stop
arms racing now without dangerous depression, we shall not, by stopping
it after a war, suffer its consequences less.

The only hopeful way of stopping the arms race without dangerously
upsetting world and national economy is to stop it in a way that greatly
stimulates confidence in peace and strongly encourages production. Nothing is more opposed to depression than well-founded optimism, nor is
there surer cure for fear than confidence,—and what can cause such
buoyant optimism and confidence as the establishment of the Union?

To solve this problem without war we need a substitute for war that
will equal war's power in speeding production and absorbing idle men
while doing it healthily instead of unhealthily. World war is no half-
measure, its substitute can not be one. It can be nothing less than our
world Union.

ECONOMIC DISARMAMENT

We come to the second great problem of the day. If economic disarmament is not the first of our problems, as Secretary Hull maintains, it
would seem to be the hardest. Production and trade, unlike armaments
and money, are not the monopoly of any democratic government. They
are instead in the hands of tens of millions of individuals, operating alone
or through great collectivities called corporations. When democracy deals
as a unit with democracy in this field where not the state but the individual is in fact the governing unit its negotiations are unimaginably
complicated by the multiplicity of conflicting and connecting independent
interests involved. Mixed with these are strategic considerations arising
from the failure to settle the military disarmament-security problem.
The result is again failure, and the failure induces in turn a trend to make
production and trade as much a weapon of the state as the army is.
Whatever may be the merits of managed economy the danger of managing it as a weapon is clear enough. It is no less evident that making trade

more a thing of war than it is already will not solve the problem of economic disarmament.

Union is not, like a league, an improved means for solving this problem; here again it is itself the solution. There is no other way than Union to solve this problem, if only because Union alone allows this tangle of private property interests to be tackled by its own common denominator, the individual. Where under the best of leagues trade barriers remain and any reduction in them is not only temporary but precarious, exposed to the sudden exercise by any nation of its sovereign right to denounce them because of a national emergency, these barriers vanish completely and forever when states form a union.

Since these democracies do two-thirds of the world's trade, mostly among themselves, their abolition of trade barriers among themselves would solve the economic disarmament problem not only for themselves but practically for all the world. It is highly important to keep in mind that the trading power of the democracies as regards the rest of the world is even greater, much greater, than their armed power. No serious foreign trade problem would remain for the Union and no outside country could withstand the bargaining power of this rich market with its monopoly control of essential raw materials. The Union would not need tariffs to protect any industries as strategic or subsidies to agriculture as preparation for a blockade. Because of its great reduction of armament and governmental expense it would need a tariff for revenue much less than any democracy now.

Here again the Union of only fifteen democracies provides a base big enough to solve practically the whole world problem. Even before more countries entered the Union its influence would inevitably tend, powerfully, pervasively, to free trade and restore prosperity everywhere on earth. If one considers how much poorer the rest of the world would be if the principle of union did not give it now the rich market it enjoys in the United States, one can understand better how much the non-democratic world suffers now from the barriers dividing the democratic market. One may temporarily increase the prosperity of some at the expense of others as all the nations are now trying to do, but one can never long make any nation more prosperous by impoverishing the rest of the world. And one can not possibly add to the wealth of some nations all that our Union does without making all mankind the richer.

MONETARY STABILIZATION

With managed money currency has become like armaments and tariffs a weapon of the state. It is the swiftest, most sweeping and high-powered, the clumsiest, blindest, and most incalculable of the economic weapons

in the arsenal of the state. It acts as a tariff on all imports—except that it brings the government no revenue—combined with a subsidy to all exports. When one resorts to ordinary tariffs or subsidies one can choose the commodities to which they apply, and vary the degree, but monetary depreciation like rain falls alike on rich and poor, ocean and desert, and like rain it falls most generously where in fact it is needed least.

Other nations may meet this tariff-subsidy by depreciating their currency too and restoring equilibrium, but they thereby render that equilibrium more precarious and give every trader less reason to trust in it, and more reason to fear that some nation will use its sovereign right suddenly to lower the value of its money and thereby change profit into loss on goods in transit or under contract. At best the uncertainties of managed money remain to harass trade and burden government,—and not least by stimulating gold production. It seems harder to see the stupidity of seeking recovery by managing the measures of value than by shortening the yardstick to 30 inches, or "managing" any other measure. Yet few weapons seem more intrinsically unmanageable than money.

It is not strange that the problem of monetary stabilization has grown worse under managed nationalism and has given birth to such costly nonsense about silver and gold and paper and internal price levels and deflation, inflation, reflation, and such hen-or-egg debates as that over which comes first, monetary stabilization or tariff reduction. It would be strange, however, for this monetary problem to be solved enduringly without the world economic problem, the world armaments-security problem and, above all, the world government problem, being solved at the same time.

We have already seen how insoluble the monetary problem is so long as the great democracies remain sovereign. We have also seen that the stability of the gold standard before the war was based really on Britain's predominance, and that to restore that stability we must restore its essential basis—a single responsible government overwhelmingly powerful in the economic world, a single budget and a single gold reserve. We can restore that basis by the Union of the democracies and only by their Union, for no other combination is strong enough.

The money of the Union would be stabler than any that men have ever known and the stablest that is now humanly possible. Businessmen everywhere want a stable money in which to make their contracts for future deliveries, particularly in international trade. There can be no doubt that in every country outside the Union they would at once tend to use the Union's money for all such transactions, even more than non-British traders used the pound before the war for international business between them. The Union, in short, would not need to spread round the world to establish a world money, it would need only to be created.

COMMUNICATIONS

For years the world has been struggling to unify and standardize and simplify transit regulations through the cumbersome machinery of diplomacy and the League. One needs only compare the situation in this whole field within the American Union to that still obtaining in the much smaller area occupied by the democracies of the United Kingdom, France, Belgium, Holland and Switzerland to understand what a difference union makes.

It makes the greatest difference with aviation. The essential difficulty civil aviation presents to sovereign states is that it lends itself so swiftly and dangerously to war that a prudent government must remain always more or less on its guard against the aviation of any powerful neighbor, however friendly. So long as the neighbor's government is sovereign there can be no real guarantee that it will not suddenly use its air power as an instrument of national policy. No state in the American Union and no canton in Switzerland, however, has the slightest anxiety about aircraft from neighboring states or cantons; in these two areas the people think of aviation in terms of the whole union, not of the states within it. They escape the wasteful, dangerous competition between democracies in subsidies to civil air lines intended to maintain and strengthen their respective air arms.

Union of the democracies, by bringing half the world into one air union, would allow civil aviation to spread its wings at last and really fly. One can safely predict that in the Union's first ten years aviation would develop beyond the dreams of men today. It would profit not merely from removal of artificial barriers but from the positive stimulus it would receive from the great intensification of trade and travel resulting from the Union. It would profit, too, from the huge funds made available by the elimination of the present waste on arms and unnecessary government.

What has been said of aviation applies only in different degree to all other forms of communication. To mention but a few points, the Union would leave the problem of a tunnel under the English channel no more of a problem than is a tunnel under the Hudson river. It would reduce the North Atlantic to the status of Lake Michigan and bring three-fourths of the world's merchant marine under a common law. No more at sea than in the air could any outside country stand the competition of this Union. It would inevitably set the standard for all the world, and its control of all important means of communication would grow more and more complete as it spread.

It would also speed communications and make them cheaper. It would free us and all the world from all the financial, red tape, or other obstacles to postal, telegraphic, telephonic, wireless, cable, or radio communications which rise not from such natural factors as distance but from such artificial factors as national sovereignty among the democracies. Since it is possible for a German in New York to communicate by letter with a Japanese in San Francisco for three cents, it ought not to cost more for an American in New York to communicate with an Englishman in London. There is no service to our freedom in continuing a system whereby the believer in free speech in Lyons must pay to send a letter to the believer in free speech in Geneva three times what he pays to send it to the believer in free speech in more distant Cherbourg. Nor is there any service to our freedom in maintaining all the sovereignty barriers to communication among the free by motor car, railway, ship and airplane.

The amount of unnecessary vexation and bother and waste of time and financial imposition we now suffer in the great field of the communications of men and of their thoughts and things will make our children pity us. With all the improvement the Union would bring in the speed, safety, simplicity, comfort and cheapness of all communications, the world would truly become the workshop and the playground of the individual. More than anything else the development of all means of communications has made the organization of world government urgent, and its organization would develop these communications more than anything else.

MEN, JOBS, TAXES, GOVERNMENT

I have left to the last the problem of our persons because it runs through all the other problems, too. Disarmament, security, trade, money, communication,—these are really important to us because of the way they affect our persons. They are really problems in the freeing of our individual selves which have been handled separately here only for reasons of expediency and habit. Nationalism has habituated us to considering these things as separate problems of the state, and not as what they are— mere facets of our basic problem, that of gaining more and more freedom of every kind for our individual selves. The other facets we may more conveniently lump together here as the problem of our persons. A few examples may suffice.

There are all the disabilities, burdens and hindrances we suffer in our persons simply for the sake of maintaining our fifteen national sovereignties. There are passports, visas, quotas, "permits" to live. The citizen of one democracy founded on the principle of no taxation without representation is not only taxed without right of vote, if his business requires him to

reside in another democracy devoted to this principle, but he is often obliged to pay taxes to both governments and disqualified from voting in either. Could we get rid of such anomalies while keeping national sovereignty, we still could not keep it and stay rid of them. Union rids us of them all for good.

There is the unemployment problem. It has been growing increasingly formidable in our generation. The momentary improvements achieved here and there and now and then are insignificant when measured by the cost and effort they have required and the time they have endured. Consider, for instance, all our democracies did in one year, 1934, to solve the unemployment problem. They spent billions on public works, on priming the pump in many ways to induce private employment, on doling out relief, on paying more in insurance benefits than they could collect in premiums. They spent further billions on monetary magic, quotas, tariffs, subsidies, and other contraptions to protect the worker and keep the factory going by lowering prices below cost to the foreigner and raising them proportionately to the citizen,—by, that is, combining hidden donation abroad with hidden taxation at home. They discriminated against the citizens of other democracies who sought work among them. They ran the risks of centralizing government, of increasing the authority of the state, of making the mass of men more dependent on the state, all to give men a chance to work and keep alive. They created all sorts of new governmental commissions and boards and bureaux. They investigated, legislated, pontificated. They made codes by hundreds and their workers went on strike by thousands. They inflated here and deflated there. They did about everything except unite. And the number of unemployed among the fifteen which totalled about 15,900,000 when 1934 began totalled 15,500,000 when 1934 ended. Thereafter, it is true, they got the total down considerably—but only by jumping from the frying pan of unemployment into the fire of armaments racing and only for a year or two, for since 1937 their unemployment has been rising again.

The Union promises to reduce unemployment to where it would be no grave problem, where it could be handled like other predictable accidents through normal insurance methods. The Union would do this by freeing trade, stabilizing money, lowering costs, reducing armaments, guaranteeing political security, eliminating the war danger, diverting into healthy channels the billions now being wasted, cheapening and speeding communications and making the worker and his product far more mobile, restoring confidence and opening vast new enterprises. If the problem of unemployment cannot be solved along these lines it would seem indeed insoluble.

Then there is the pressing problem of reducing taxes, economizing on

government, avoiding centralization's danger of dictatorship. Under national sovereignty taxation and governmental powers have been growing everywhere like weeds. Only the Union seriously tackles the problem of how the democracies are to recover from the taxation and borrowing and bureaucracy and unnecessary government with which the various nationalist recovery measures have afflicted them. With the creation of the Union would vanish not merely the costly governmental excrescences that have mushroomed up since the depression but also an almost unbelievable amount of unnecessary government that has endured so long that men seem calloused to it. The Union would not only end duplication and dangerously wasteful competition (as in war departments and foreign offices) but would eliminate the *raison d'être* of all sorts of governmental departments, boards, commissions, administrations, bureaux and services now devouring taxes in each democracy without serving the freedom of their citizens half so well as would their disappearance through union.

The fifteen democracies now maintain not only fifteen foreign ministries but hundreds of ambassadors and ministers and thousands of minor diplomats and consuls. Their Union's Department of Foreign Affairs would need less than fifty ambassadors and ministers and only a few hundred minor diplomats and consuls. Incidentally it would eliminate entirely the most expensive embassies the democracies now maintain, those at Washington, London, and Paris. The saving this would bring is suggested by the fact the British Ambassador at Paris receives a much greater salary than the British Prime Minister himself, and the American Ambassador to Belgium receives more than the Secretary of State.

When one begins thus to go into the details of what the Union means, one begins to understand why the departments of the Union government, far from being larger than their counterparts in the greatest democracies today, would, from sheer lack of governing to do, be much smaller and less expensive. The saving would be further increased by the dropping from the public payroll of all the taxation and customs officials whom this economizing on government would render unnecessary. Each of the present budgets of the democracies could be reduced astonishingly by the Union,— unless the Union led them to develop enormously their social, educational and health work, their fight against the real enemies of man: poverty, ignorance, disease and death.

DYING TOGETHER OR LIVING TOGETHER?

Thus does the Union remedy simultaneously our armament, security, tariff, quota, monetary, budgetary, communication, unemployment, taxation, centralization and governmental ills, and the list is not complete.

It cannot be completed. The evil done by nationalism is too extensive, too all-pervading.

Time and again statesmen and experts have declared that all our major world ills are inextricably inter-related. To tackle any of these ills separately is to learn this quickly, but to tackle the bewildering tangle all together has seemed even more discouraging. Yet the Union by striking at their common political source undoes them all at once. What else but the Union promises half so great a boon?

The non-unionist is left facing two dilemmas. If he solves some but not all of these problems the remainder will upset his solutions. How long will monetary "stabilization" last without economic disarmament or political security? On the other hand, could all or any of the major world problems be solved without the Union the problem of organizing effective world government would remain to upset such solution. If a miracle led us all to abolish armaments and trade barriers, stabilize money, guarantee every democracy against invasion and dictatorship, it would not be enough; we would need to have a continuing miracle to keep all this from vanishing next day like a dream. Or we would need to organize our relations well enough to keep our money stable, our arms down, our freedom secure and meet the problems that our miracle left or made.

Only by dying together can we escape this problem of living together, of organizing world government. We have already seen that to organize it we must take either man or the state as unit, we must organize either a league or a union. We have seen, too, why a league cannot possibly solve our problems by its mere creation, nor provide the government we require to keep solved any problem it may solve. By the Union alone can we hope to solve our insolubles all together and at the same time give ourselves the government we must have to keep them solved and meet the new problems that their solution brings.

. . . .

With the passage of time, it becomes more and more clear that no fundamental, durable recovery can be hoped for unless and until a general stabilization at least of the leading currencies has been brought about.—Leon Fraser in his 1935 Report as President of the Bank for International Settlements.

. . . .

Our Creator the Great Ruler never intended that man should engage in any such work as the destruction of human life. There are many who have

*perished in the direction you are now facing, and these lords have come
to induce you to join them so that the shedding of human blood might
cease and the Good Tidings of Peace and Power might prevail.*—Traditional narrative of the founding of the Confederacy of the Five Nations, or
Iroquois Indians.

.   .   .   .

*War or battle, as a thing very beastly (and yet no kind of beasts so much
use it as man) they do detest and abhor . . . And therefore . . . they
never go to battle, but either in defence of their own country, or to drive
out of their friends' land the enemies that have invaded it: or by their
power to deliver from the yoke and bondage of tyranny, some people that
be therewith oppressed . . .*

*They be not only sorry, but also ashamed, to achieve the victory with
bloodshed; counting it great folly to buy precious wares too dear . . .*

*If any prince stir up war against them, intending to invade their land,
they meet him incontinent out of their own borders with great power and
strength. For they never lightly make war in their own country.*—More,
Utopia, II-10, 1516.

CHAPTER IX

Isolation of the Germ

I have no other purpose than to place truth before my eyes . . . and to draw the world away from its old heathenish superstitions.—Leeuwenhoek, discoverer of the microbe world.

It is only when a man or beast has tuberculosis that I can find these bacilli. In healthy animals I never find them.—Robert Koch.

Science has shown that the only sure way to overcome disease is to isolate the germ. It has shown too, by then eliminating the germ, that the effects of a germ can ramify far and that what seems to be a complicated condition of the body or a series of separate ills in it can be cured by the simple act of removing a microscopic germ. Though political science does not have guinea pigs to experiment with, those with remedies for ills of the body politic need to give what proof they can that they have really isolated the germ.

This book holds that the major ills of the world today originate in the assumption among the democrats that their own freedom requires them to organize the relations among the democracies with their state instead of themselves for unit, on the absolutist principle of nationalism instead of the democratic principle of individualism. For clarity we can name the germ, *absolute nationalism,* and the serum that eliminates it, *unionism.* We may now prove isolation of the germ by showing that injection of absolute nationalism in healthy political organism will give them the disease the democracies now suffer, and that injection of unionism will cure it.

Among the states composing the afflicted area there are two which are themselves composed of many states: the United States with forty-eight and Switzerland with twenty-two. Neither of these groups of democracies has the ills of our world group of fifteen. Switzerland, that is, is afflicted with such things as quotas only in its relations with other states; the Swiss cantons are not afflicted with quotas in their relations with each other. The citizens of each American state suffer as citizens of the United States from the armaments disease ravaging the fifteen democracies but they are free from it in their relations with the citizens of the other forty-seven American states. *If all the world should sink except the area oc-*

*cupied either by these forty-eight states or by the twenty-two cantons their
citizens would no longer suffer from ineffective government, armaments
racing, fear of war, trade barriers, monetary instability; all mankind would
then be free of these ills.*

One may therefore consider the states within the American and the
Swiss areas to be healthy organism, and consider as diseased organism the
fifteen democracies.

Inject now into the people of each of these forty-eight states and twenty-
two cantons the virus, *absolute nationalism.* Let the people of New York
and of New Jersey, or of Zurich and of Geneva, think and act toward
each other in terms of the state instead of the citizen precisely as Americans and Swiss now do toward each other or toward the British or French.
Let their relations be infected with the same confusion that makes anarchy
of those of the fifteen: Let them too identify the freedom of the citizen
with the freedom of his state, the rights of man with rights of nations,
the equality of man with the equality of states. Let them ground their
relations on the state instead of man as unit. Let the citizens of each
of the forty-eight and of each of the twenty-two democracies seek their
individual freedom in establishing seventy national sovereignties where
there now are two, and in guarding these seventy sovereignties as jealously
as the fifteen democratic people guard theirs today. Who needs human
guinea pigs to know that the seventy healthy organisms would then at
once suffer the ills of the fifteen?

Consider more closely the effects of injecting the virus, *absolute nationalism,* into either the forty-eight or the twenty-two. They must then have
not merely forty-eight (or twenty-two) flags where now they have one,
but forty-eight (or twenty-two) armed forces, forty-eight (or twenty-two)
currencies to keep stable by equalization funds, forty-eight (or twenty-
two) national industries, farming classes, internal price levels and standards of living to protect by tariffs, quotas, subsidies, currency, depreciation,—all for the sake of the one thing left them in common: The Rights
of Man.

The citizen of the sovereign republic of New York, when he crosses the
Hudson to the sovereign republic of New Jersey, must then not merely
stop to have his baggage searched and his money changed. He must first
have a passport and a visa—for the republic of New Jersey seeks to
protect its workers from the immigration peril that cheap Harlem labor
forms. To cross this line in his automobile he must first get a customs
paper for that and stop at the frontier to get it stamped. To send a
letter, he must pay double postage.

What of the freedom of the individual to do as he pleases with the
money he earns? The same 125,000,000 men must then pay enough taxes

to maintain not one but forty-eight national governments, foreign departments, diplomatic and consular services, customs and immigration services, armies, airforces, and navies. What would it cost New York to protect its precious corridor to the sea against Connecticut and New Jersey making an alliance against it with the support of Pennsylvania? How big an air fleet would New York need to keep off bombers then? How many Holland tunnels would it need to dig—not under the river for commerce and pleasure but in Manhattan's rock for shelter in war time? What would it cost New Yorkers to seek safety in invading and annexing New Jersey— and thus coming face to face with powerful Pennsylvania?

This injection of nationalism causes the people of the forty-eight or the twenty-two to sacrifice their liberty and prosperity in other ways too. It involves them in all sorts of costly and dangerous political, economic and financial quarrels,—quarrels that centre in mad, maddening, mystic questions of the ratio of one sovereign people to another. By identifying a man's self-respect with what he imagines is the standing of his state in the world this nationalistic virus turns into a curse even the sense of dignity that freedom gives a man.

We see how the ills of the fifteen can be produced at will among the healthy forty-eight or twenty-two injecting in them the same nationalism. Suppose we now inject into the fifteen our serum, *unionism*. Suppose the Americans, British, French, Australians, Belgians, Canadians, Danes, Dutch, Finns, Irish, New Zealanders, Norwegians, South Africans, Swedes, and Swiss all begin to think and act toward each other in terms of men and no longer in terms of nations. Suppose that by some miracle we could inject simultaneously into these fifteen peoples, as doctors can inject serum into patients, the simple idea that their freedom required their union instead of their national independence. We can turn gain by this one costless priceless change all they are now vainly struggling to gain by deepening their dugouts the higher they fly. Does any one need human guinea pigs to believe that the injection of this serum would effectively cure the fifteen of all those ills they now suffer from which the forty-eight and the twenty-two are free?

For those who demand more proof of isolation of the germ more proof is available. We do not need to confine ourselves to imagining what would happen if the American states or Swiss cantons became infected with the idea that individual freedom required their separation instead of their union, nor what would happen if the people of the fifteen democracies should get the idea that their individual freedom required their union instead of their national independence. We can turn to laboratory record. American history provides an exceptionally clear and complete account of what happens to the same people when infected with the germ of *absolute*

nationalism and then when treated with our *unionism.* In doing this book, I have carefully studied the record of this American experiment and written a fresh analysis of it,—but that is another book. While the American experiment seems from the scientific viewpoint the best for general study, every democracy is to some extent the result of a similar experiment. The citizen of each democracy can turn for proof to the history he knows best.

Let each ponder where he would be now had not his forebears "sacrificed" to a union the sovereignty of the sub-division he now inhabits. Let him reckon all that he must lose for that sub-division to gain the right to levy tariffs, coin money, issue stamps, raise an army, fly a flag and stain the map. Let him think where he would be could it count only on those living in it to defend his rights as a man. Let each do his own book on his own case. There is no better way for us each to know how much freedom each would gain by making his sovereign union a sub-division of our Union now.

·   ·   ·   ·   ·   ·

One of the early things men did was to make water run up, but because it took them long to learn what they had done they have had only 150 years of the Steam Age.

·   ·   ·   ·   ·   ·

Our true State, this state that is already beginning, this state to which every man owes his utmost political effort, must be now this nascent Federal World State to which human necessities point . . . Nationalism as a God must follow the tribal gods to limbo. Our true nationality is mankind.— H. G. Wells, Outline of History.

·   ·   ·   ·   ·   ·

*A dark modern world faces wars between conflicting economic and political fanaticisms in which are intertwined race hatreds. To bring it home, it is as if within the territorial limits of the United States, forty-eight nations with forty-eight forms of government, forty-eight customs barriers, forty-eight languages and forty-eight eternal and different verities, were spending their time and their substance in a frenzy of effort to make themselves strong enough to conquer their neighbors or strong enough to defend themselves against their neighbors.—*President Franklin D. Roosevelt, Aug. 14, 1936.

CHAPTER X

The Union

Let us discard all these things and unite as one people throughout the land . . . declaring that all men are created equal.—Lincoln, *Reply to Douglas,* Chicago.

The work of practical organization to which this is a prelude excludes no loyal help or good will . . . It is the guarantee of all against all the forms of disunion that lead to chaos, anarchy and war. The road is henceforth open before us and nothing shall stop our collective march.

. . . Equally attentive neither to disappoint the expectation of the peoples nor to compromise our chances of success, we must go methodically forward step by step with clear-sighted and firm decision and without ever forgetting our sense of what is possible or ever turning either from the final goal we seek.—Aristide Briand, addressing the Commission of Enquiry for European Union, Jan. 16, 1931.

PLAN OF CHAPTER AND TWO THINGS TO NOTE

The battle of freedom is to be fought out on principle.—Lincoln in his *"Lost Speech."*

A difference in degree grown large enough becomes a difference in kind. —Underwood.

Once we agree that our democracies must organize as a union, the next problem is one of practical application of the unionist principle to this particular case: How far to apply it and how, first a question of degree and then one of method. Before answering these two questions with a concrete application of the union principle, we need to note two things.

First, we should keep in mind during this whole discussion of practical application that it is subordinate to the question of principle and is to be regarded as illustrative of the concrete working of a hard and fixed principle rather than as forming a hard and fixed plan. This book is concerned above all with showing why we democrats of the world must organize our inter-state government with ourselves instead of our states as the equal units, and it discusses the application of this principle mainly to promote this end. This book aims to explain and defend the key principle of union

175

rather than to insist on any concrete plan for union. When our democracies have agreed to turn to the union principle there will remain plenty of time for the practical problem to hold first place. To accord it even equal importance now risks obscuring clarity on the essential and dissipating in secondary disputes on method what common will for union we do develop. There seems no use debating how to bridge the Tiber before the Rubicon is crossed.

Secondly, we should keep in mind during the coming discussion that any application of the union principle to our problem in inter-state government differs radically from all previous applications of it because this time it is applied on a world scale and provides world control. The democracies to be united this time are so powerful that their Union would be all powerful and would be the first democratic state that from birth would dwarf all the rest of the world. Unless this be remembered, reasoning about our Union on the basis of the experiences of existing unions may mislead. Every existing union or democracy bears in its political thought and constitution the scars of revolutionary experiment, uphill struggle, one against a world. This has left a feeling of inferiority against which we need to guard.

To understand what union means today and what it can bring us in freedom we must create it in our imaginations, we must think in terms of the world in which our Union will exist, rather than in terms of the past and present worlds to which we are accustomed. We must never lose sight of the essential fact that the conditions in which the strongest of the seven great powers exist today are not the conditions in which our Union would exist. Its mere creation changes fundamentally the world situation and therefore the problems we face.

Our Union will be *the* great power, not one of the great powers. It will tower above all the rest of the world as the United States now does in the Americas. At the outset its population will be nearly twice that of China, its gold reserve and shipping tonnage about double that of the United States and the United Kingdom respectively, its area thrice that of Russia, its navy thrice that of the United Kingdom or the United States, its air force four times that of France. Its problems in the foreign field will be greatly simplified by the ratio between its strength in each domain and that of the strongest outside power or practical combination of them.

HOW FAR SHALL WE UNITE?

The economic, the financial, the political problems of the building of the United States, I repeat, . . . are precisely the economic, the financial, the political problems of today, and those of today can only be solved by the

*application of precisely the same principles that the American people then
used to solve them under the leadership of Washington and Hamilton.*—
Nicholas Murray Butler, addressing the American Club of Paris, June 20,
1935.

To what degree should the democracies in organizing inter-state government apply the union principle or government of the people, by the people,
for the people?

Government of the people: Here the principle must be fully applied:
The inter-state government where it governs at all must govern people,
never states. It must have the power to maintain itself by taxing all the
people of the Union and its revenue must not depend in any way on the
governments of member states. It must have the power to raise and rule
directly the armed forces of the Union and be entirely independent of the
state governments in this field, too. Whatever laws it makes must never
bear on the member states as states but only on all the inhabitants of the
Union as individuals. It must have its own independent machinery for
enforcing these Union laws throughout the Union. Insofar as it governs
it must, in short, govern the people, the whole population divided as
individuals, not as states.

"Insofar as it governs"—that brings another question. The union principle, we have seen, requires the fields of government to be divided between
the Union and member states. Just which shall be the fields where the
Union shall govern the people and which those where the nation shall
govern them is, of course, a great and abiding federal problem. The answer
depends on which government, Union or National, will best promote in
any given field at any given time the object for which both were made,
namely, the freedom in every sense of the individual. We shall therefore
consider this question later when we reach the third point, *government for
the people.*

Government by the people: Here again no exception to the union principle must be allowed in favor of the National government, but some exceptions may well be allowed in favor of the nations as peoples. That is, all
the organs of the Union government, legislative, executive, judicial, and
the machinery for amending the Union constitution, must be based directly
on the people. Their National government must have nothing to do with
these organs. But the Union government does not need to be based entirely
on the population with the individual taken as equal unit; it can be based
partly on the population divided by nations. It must however be based
predominantly on the former, as, for example, in the American Union.
How the balance between the two should be struck is one of several questions in constitutional mechanism raised by the principle of government

by the people; these will be discussed when we reach the problem of method. We are now concerned only with the problem of how far principle is to be applied. The exceptions from the principle of the equality of man in favor of some representation of the people as nations are made in order to prevent the Union government from encroaching on the fields reserved to the National governments,—in other words, to prevent the Union itself nullifying the principle of government by the people as regards the National governments. Consequently the rule should be to allow these exceptions to the degree necessary to assure this object.

Government for the people: This must be fully applied. The constitution should make explicitly clear that the Union is made for the sake of the people themselves, for the individual freedom of each person equally. Practically, this means the constitution should provide (a) a list of individual rights that the people retain and that the government is made to preserve, and (b) a list of the rights which the people give to the Union to enjoy exclusively or to share with the National governments,—the division of powers, in short, between the Union and National governments.

The Bill of Rights which the Union would guarantee all inhabitants would contain those rights of the individual which all the founder democracies now separately guarantee. Where these rights are phrased differently in the different democracies, the Union could take the strongest formula, since the Union would be in a much stronger position to guarantee these rights and would be made to further them. It is to be hoped that this world Union would begin, as did the American Union, with a Bill of Rights surpassing that of many of its founder democracies, but if this risked preventing or delaying Union by rousing sterile dispute on fine points it would seem wiser to limit the Bill to the minimum of rights already enjoyed in common.

The Union's Bill of Rights would not end the existing guarantees of these rights in member democracies; it would simply be an added guarantee. The people of member democracies that guarantee rights not included in the Union Bill would continue to enjoy them. Union would prevent no nation in it from giving new rights to its citizens. Instead new rights would be expected to grow and spread among the member nations just as woman suffrage spread from one state to another in the American Union till it became general. The essential is that the Union constitution should leave no doubt that the government it forms is made for the sake of the freedom of all the individuals in the Union equally.

THE GREAT FEDERAL PROBLEM

What shall be the division of rights or powers or fields of government between Union and National governments? We have seen that the main

attack against every proposal for inter-state government always comes from the fear that it creates a super-state, and this fear centers in the question of the division of power between inter-state and state governments. It rises mainly from both the advocates and opponents of the inter-state government approaching this question from the viewpoint of the power the governments concerned gain or lose rather than the object of the division—individual freedom.

If to each field of government we apply the test, *Which will serve our individual freedom best, to give the Union or leave the Nation the right to govern in this field?* we find five main rights that we need to give to the Union. They are:

1. The right to grant citizenship.
2. The right to make peace and war, to negotiate treaties and otherwise deal with the outside world, to raise and maintain a defense force.
3. The right to regulate inter-state and foreign trade.
4. The right to coin and issue money, and fix other measures.
5. The right to govern communications: To operate the postal service, and regulate, control or operate other inter-state communication services.

Manifestly, the Union must provide citizenship in the Union and obviously this brings each of us an enormous gain in individual freedom. Since we remain citizens of our nations in becoming citizens of the Union we lose nothing and only gain. Union citizenship must involve inter-state citizenship in the sense that a citizen in moving from one state to another retains all his Union rights and can change his state citizenship easily. The case for giving the other four rights to the Union is no less clear. We are seeing every day in all these fields that the rights we have granted our National governments to maintain separate armed forces, separate customs areas, separate currencies and separate communication systems have become not simply unnecessary to individual freedom but increasingly dangerous interferences with it.

It is easy to imagine any of the free peoples going to war again to maintain their rights as men. But can one imagine the American, British, French, or any other free people flocking to the colors merely to defend their present practice of taxing without representation each other's citizens who happen to live with them? Can one imagine any of their governments being able to raise an army to fight simply for its right to impose tariffs against the other free peoples?

No free people lacks a proud record of heroes who gave their lives at the stake so that men might have religious freedom. Is there among them

any record of heroes who burned alive so that men might have military discipline and wear military uniforms? Do we call liberators or militarists those who fight for the sake of an army or navy, to whom armed force is a glorious end in itself, not a means to freedom, dreadful even when necessary? The free whatever language they speak hold dear the memory of martyrs who died for freedom of speech and of the press. If there be men among them who would sacrifice their lives merely to establish and maintain different kinds of bits of paper representing money or postage who would hold them dear? Union under the five-pointed star—one citizenry, one defense force, one market, one money and one stamp,—involves no loss of any of those liberties for which our fathers fought and for which we would give our lives today. It means pure gain of liberty without the shedding of blood.

Democracy's experience with inter-state government has shown that these five rights are the main ones we need to give our Union. It suggests that a few minor rights may be given the Union in addition to these, such as the rights to protect authors and inventors by copyright and patent and the right to make bankruptcy law uniform through the Union. Common sense, however, advises strongly against giving the Union even minor rights that the older and most successful existing unions do not have, and in favor of leaning backward to limit the rights of the Union at the outset. The essential thing now is to get the Union established, not to draw a perfect line between the things that belong to the Union and those that belong to the nation. Our immediate aim must be to remove the most immediate dangers to our freedom, and the easiest way to do this is to make no change that is not urgently or clearly needed. Once Union is established time will remain for other changes.

UNITING TO DECENTRALIZE

American genius does not show itself in its Fords and Wall Streets; it appears in its vital force only in its political constitution which balances so well decentralization and unity.—Count Sforza, Revue de l'Université de Bruxelles, No. 2, 1930.

Our object in uniting, we need to remember, is not to see how much we can centralize government but rather how much we can decentralize it or cut it out entirely as unnecessary. Though over-decentralization in five fields drives us now to Union, it by no means follows that centralization is the friend of freedom. The fact is, paradoxically, that what little centralizing we would do in uniting would really be done in order, on balance, to have more decentralization; we transfer five rights to the Union

in order to curb the centralizing tendency in each of our nations which its possession of these rights now causes. We create some new government in order to get rid of much more existing government, to gain on balance more freedom from governmental interference in our lives.

"That government is best which governs least," Thoreau said, for as he explained, "government is at best but an expedient." Before him Paine said in his *Rights of Man*: "The more perfect civilization is the less occasion has it for Government, because the more it does regulate its own affairs, and govern itself, but so contrary is the practice of all Governments to the reason of the case, that the expenses of them increase in the proportion they ought to diminish."

We create Union to free ourselves from some fourteen governmental barriers to our selling dear and buying cheap, to reduce the expense of booming bureaucracy and monstrous armaments, to cut our way out of government gone jungle. *The acme of decentralization is, after all, complete individual freedom.* It is to come nearer to the democratic ideal where each man governs himself so perfectly that no other government is needed that we make our Union.

The five rights we would transfer to the Union are merely means of defending those individual, local and national rights that democrats hold dear,—means, that is, of defending what decentralization we have attained.

Far from weakening these dearer rights we protect and strengthen them by this transfer, whereas failure to make this transfer forces each democracy to centralize, to reduce individual and local rights so as to keep these five national rights, to sacrifice the end to the means. Since this leaves the national rights themselves more exposed to attack than does the Union, failure to centralize the means of protecting and extending decentralization is a losing operation all along the line.

The Union will give *de jure* status to all the existing decentralization that democrats value—to national home-rule for national affairs by whatever system of government, republic, monarchy, or whatnot that each nation desires, to each national language, each national educational system, each distinctive trait that makes each nation, and to the whole distinctive system of local liberties and customs and individual rights within the nation for which each nation stands. All these things now really have only *de facto* status as regards the world outside each nation. How perilous this lack of legal recognition of these rights by the outside world seems to each democracy may be seen by the way each is heavily arming. Only by uniting to recognize and guarantee all these national, local and individual rights can the democracies legalize them even in the democratic world. The practical result of their doing this, moreover, is to make these rights much

more secure as regards the outside nations to whom they would remain only a *de facto* claim until these nations themselves entered the Union.

Particularly in connection with this question of centralization we need to remember that the proposed Union would be unique among unions because of its colossal material strength as compared to outside governments. The strongest existing union, the United States, needs now to have much stronger central governmental powers and to develop much more homogeneity in its population than does this Union. The United States needs to insist on more and more homogeneity among Americans, to invade more and more the fields reserved to their states, to put more and more power in the hands of one man, and to provide a growing array of costly meddling central government organs, if its aim is not merely to defend the individual freedom of Americans against foreign centralizers, but to keep the American Union constantly pitted against other powerful free peoples, such as the British and the French. The United States must centralize more and more if it aims to battle all the time economically and monetarily and financially with all the rest of mankind, and to prepare always to battle separately from them by sea, land and air, cannon, gas and bomb. There is no end to the amount of government required when the aim of government is not only to live in world chaos but to keep the chaos alive too.

Not only would our world Union because of its unrivalled strength need homogeneity in its citizenry and centralization in its government much less than does the United States now, but it would gain added strength to protect the rights of its members by this very lack of homogeneity and centralization. By not merely tolerating but encouraging the existing diversity among and within the democracies the Union, we have seen, would doubly protect the citizen from the internal foes of freedom. He could count on this diversity to shield him from the danger of hysteria sweeping through the Union, and he would be protected as much against narrow-minded parochialism as against stampede.

Decentralization allows the Union to make the most of the fact that the forces and resources of the democracies are so scattered that there is no possibility either of any demagogue within the Union being able to seize all its power, or of any outside aggressor overwhelming the Union even by surprise attack with gas or germs. The Union would have no exposed center or heart as the British Commonwealth of Nations has in England, as France has in Paris, as the United States has in the area between the North Atlantic and the upper Mississippi. Each of these centers would have only fractional importance to this Union. The best the most powerful aggressor could possibly hope to do would be to surprise some outlying fraction of the Union. The rest of the Union would remain mighty

enough to crush him like a cockroach. In these conditions who would dare attack? In union there is strength, but never so much as when union is decentralized as only this Union could be.

HOW SHALL WE UNITE?

When we are laying the foundation of a building, which is to last for ages, and in which millions are interested, it ought to be well laid.—James Wilson in the American Union's Constitutional Convention.

To balance a large State or society . . . on general laws is a work of so great difficulty that no human genius, however comprehensive, is able by the mere dint of reason and reflection to effect it. The judgments of many must unite in the work; experience must guide their labor; time must bring it to perfection, and the feeling of inconveniences must correct the mistakes which they inevitably fall into, in their first trials and experiments.—Hume.

We come to the problem of method: How, concretely, shall we unite our democracies to this desired degree? We can divide this problem in two. There is primarily the underlying political problem of putting these general principles into constitutional form, establishing the Union and its governmental machinery. There is secondarily the practical problem of meeting the various transitional and technical difficulties raised by transfer of each of the five rights to the Union. The better to distinguish between first things and matters of secondary importance we shall consider the former here and the latter in Annex 2.

THE CONSTITUTION OF THE UNION

Those who think through far enough will agree, I believe, that at bottom the only detailed or concrete plan that the Union can need is a draft constitution. For the establishment of the Union eliminates many of the problems for which we now think we need plans and planned management, and it provides itself the mechanism—government—for solving the various problems of transition.

The Convention that framed the Constitution uniting the Thirteen American democracies not only framed no plan except the Constitution, but it had no draft even of a constitution when it began, nothing but the broad outline of the Virginia plan for one—and New Jersey and Hamilton soon produced opposing plans. The situation the Thirteen had to remedy was relatively as complicated as ours, and unlike us they had no existing federal constitution on which to base their planning, for existing or previous confederations, such as the Swiss, were really leagues, not unions.

It is much less difficult to draft an inter-state constitution when man is the unit than when the state is. Organizers of leagues can still find only failures for models; those who would constitute unions can turn now to many time-tested successes. For reasons that will be seen when we study carefully the American Union I believe that we should turn particularly to the American Constitution and experience for guidance.

The drafters of the constitution of our world Union, however, will have the great advantage of including authorities from every successful democratic union, each of which has its own valuable contribution to make. The Swiss themselves are best fitted to tell what they have learned in uniting solid geographical and historical groups of Germans, French and Italians. The Canadians can tell of their union of French and English, the South Africans of their union of Boers and English,—and in the United Provinces and the United Kingdom the Dutch and English have a much older experience to relate. Can it be a harder political problem to draft a constitution uniting Englishmen in England and Dutchmen in Holland now after more than a century of peace between them than it was to draft one uniting Englishmen and Dutchmen in South Africa in the bitterness that war leaves in its wake?

These examples may suffice to indicate the rich store of constitutional experience which, since Hamilton cited the passage from Hume heading this section, has been placed at the disposal of union constitution-makers. They may indicate too the long tradition and discipline and training in self-government on which our democracies can count to aid them in uniting. We have only to organize the Union of unions. Our constitutional problem is not so much the difficult one of creating as the relatively easy one of selecting, adapting, consolidating, perfecting. It is not the venturesome task of sowing but the safer task of reaping the crop already grown by reason and chance, trial and error.

In drafting the constitution of our Union I would suggest that we take pains to avoid the dangerous confusion all unions so far have suffered regarding what they really are. We can do this by having our preamble make clearer than any union constitutions now do what we mean by union —that we men and women are constituting it of ourselves as equal sovereigns for our own equal individual freedom. I would copy the early American state constitutions which with logical clarity began by stating the object for which the government was being organized, namely, the Rights of Man, and then proceeded to organize government as a means to this end.

The Constitution would need to make clear at the outset, too, for reasons already explained, that the Union is organized as the nucleus of an eventual universal world Union of equal men.

WHAT OF INDIA?

At the outset there also rises the problem presented by such possessions of the democracies as India. Whatever we may wish, we must recognize that India's politically inexperienced millions can not at first be included in this Union on the same population basis as the western democracies. To try to do so would prevent our Union. To seek to free Indians this way is to deprive them of all the freedom that the organization of a sound nucleus of world government would bring the whole human species, and to expose them more than ever to the dangers to which all mankind is now exposed. Suppose those founders of the American Union who wanted slavery abolished had sacrificed the idea of union when they found they could not realize it without accepting slavery? Would they have made more freedom thus for any one? They chose instead union despite slavery, and within 70 years tens of thousands of white men were giving their lives to save the Union by freeing the slaves.

It would seem now practically necessary to distinguish in the Union territory between the parts that are already fully self-governing and those that are not, and restrict the right to vote in Union elections and to hold elective Union office to those born or naturalized citizens of the former. This would not mean that those born in the rest of the Union would be deprived of the other rights guaranteed individuals by the constitution, nor of the right to vote and hold office in their country. Instead, the Union's policy should be to train them for admission to the Union as fully self-governing nations. It is true that one can destroy democracy by seeking to spread it too quickly and over-loading the state with too many voters untrained for self-government. It is also true, however, that the only way to acquire such training is to practise self-government, and that an old and well-trained democracy can safely and even profitably absorb a much greater proportion of inexperienced voters than seems theoretically possible. Indeed, the higher the proportion of the untrained that a democracy is able successfully to admit to the vote, the stronger the democracy would seem to be. What better measure of ability to govern oneself can there be than to do it well despite all difficulties?

This whole problem is one of striking a balance, of deciding what proportion of the peoples that for one reason or another are politically weak shall be admitted at the outset to full citizenship. Common sense would seem to suggest both that we start with a low proportion, and that we explicitly state at the start that the Union's aim shall be to increase this proportion thereafter as much as prudent experiment justifies. A policy that deliberately and unequivocally aims at preparing every one in the

Union for full citizenship should transform existing colonial psychology
and make the colonial problem much easier to handle. It would be treating
the politically inexperienced peoples much the same as we treat politically
our own immature sons and daughters. These know that when they come
of age they will enjoy full citizenship rights, and this great section of the
unfranchised has never rebelled against the state nor taken the attitude
the colonially unfranchised often do.

SHALL COLONIES BE CEDED TO THE UNION?

The non-self-governing parts of the democracies present another constitutional problem: Shall these territories remain under their control as now
or shall each democracy on entering the Union transfer to the Union all its
non-self-governing possessions? The latter policy would not be experi-
mental; it was successfully practiced in the American Union. Indeed, the
decision of the various states to transfer their land in the Northwest to
the United States to govern as its Northwest Territory gave the United
States in its league period a common possession and a common interest
that contributed greatly to the establishment and maintenance of the present
American Union.

This policy would require the United Kingdom and France to give more
than any other democracy. It might therefore be called unfair, but the
American precedent was open to the same attack. One needs to take a
broad view in striking the balance between contributions to the Union. For
example, the United States would give to the Union treasury much greater
gold reserves than the British or French.

Moreover, it is much easier to see the advantages the governments of the
various democracies would gain from continuing to hold their colonies than
those their citizens would individually gain thereby. The question for the
individual Englishman, Frenchman, American, Dutchman, etc., is not
whether his national government would lose by his transferring the administration of colonies to the Union but whether he himself would lose on
balance by accepting the Union on this basis.

Transfer of colonies to the Union would not require, of course, upsetting
existing administration. Common sense would advise against any immediate,
abrupt and sweeping changes in this respect, and generally in favor of
leaving colonial administration to the individuals with the most training
for it. Those who believe their national colonial administration is the best
in the world should be among the first to welcome transfer of all colonies
to the Union, since this would give the best colonial administrators a greater
field in which to extend their beneficent influence. If the contrary should
prove true, if their field should diminish once they had to compete with

administrators of other nationalities in the free conditions of the Union, this would seem to mean that their claim to being the best in the world was unfounded. Best must meet perpetual challenge to remain best.

THE UNION LEGISLATURE

The chief technical problem in drafting the Union Constitution is the organization of its governmental machinery, its legislative, executive and judicial departments, and its mechanism for amending the constitution.

Practice is strongly in favor of a two-house Union legislature with one house based completely on the population and the other modifying this principle of equal men in favor of equal states. There can be no argument about the former, for the basic principle of Union requires it, and the practical objections vanish once the right to vote for members of the Union legislature is restricted to citizens of its self-governing member states. If, to prevent having too big a House of Deputies, the constitution allows one deputy for every half million or million citizens, the result in deputies from each of the fifteen democracies would be roughly:

Australia	13	7	Norway	6	3
Belgium	16	8	Sweden	12	6
Canada	21	11	Switzerland	8	2
Denmark	7	4	Union of South Africa *	4	7
Finland	7	4	United Kingdom	93	46
France	84	42	United States	252	124
Ireland	6	3			
Netherlands	16	8			
New Zealand	3	2	Totals	510	277

Those who fear this would give Americans too much weight in the House need to remember two things. One is that this weight would diminish with every new democracy that entered the Union. The other is that there is no more danger of the American deputies or those from any other nation voting as a bloc when elected individually by the people of separate election districts than there is of the New York members of Congress or the Scottish members of Parliament voting as a unit now. Party lines would immediately cut across national ones in this Union as in all others. To have the representation by 1,000,000 (or major fraction thereof) instead of by 500,000 would seem wiser, since the expansion of the Union would soon make the House too big on the latter basis. The million basis would also tend to strengthen moderately the theoretical position of the smaller democracies.

As for the Senate, one of its main purposes in a Union is, of course, to safeguard the less populous against the more populous states, or better, to safeguard all the state governments against the Union government invading their field, or better still, to safeguard the people of the Union

* Based on the white population since negroes there lack the right to vote.

against losing freedom by over-centralization. In the American Union the
method of achieving this purpose consists partly in allowing two senators
to the people—not the government—of each state, no matter what the
number of people in it may be. This might be copied in our Union. The
difference in population between the United States and New Zealand, the
most and the least populous democracies in our Union, is proportionately
about the same as the difference between New York and Nevada.

For my part, however, I would favor a slight modification of this part
of the American system. I would allow two senators to every self-governing
nation of 25,000,000 or less population, two additional senators for every
additional 25,000,000 or major fraction thereof up to a total population of
100,000,000, and thereafter two more senators for each 50,000,000 or major
fraction thereof. This would give two senators to each of the fifteen democracies except France, the United Kingdom and the United States, the first
two of which would have four and the third would have eight. The results
of the two systems may be seen below:

Australia	2	2	Norway	2	2
Belgium	2	2	Sweden	2	2
Canada	2	2	Switzerland	2	2
Denmark	2	2	Union of South Africa	2	2
Finland	2	2	United Kingdom	2	4
France	2	4	United States	2	8
Ireland	2	2			
Netherlands	2	2			
New Zealand	2	2	Totals	30	40

The American method would give the small democracies a preponderance of five-sixths, the other would assure them three-fifths the Senate at
the start, and these proportions would grow with the admission of new
member nations since nearly all potential members have less than 25,000,000
population. It would seem wise to allow the government of so vast a
Union as ours to draw more than the American system permits on the
experience of the democracies most accustomed to government on a big
scale, so long as the Senate's function of safeguarding the small democracies and decentralization is not thereby endangered. Either way the
Senators would be elected at large by each nation, and each senator would
have one vote.

In addition to the safeguard which the second system would provide,
I would have the constitution itself forbid any interference by the Union
with certain national rights, such as language, without the consent of each
nation concerned. This would protect the rights which the system of absolute equality in national representation in the Senate seeks to protect, and
would therefore make its extreme departures from the principle of the
equality of men unnecessary. One of the great advantages of the second
system to my mind is that it would help keep clear that the Union holds

the equality of man superior to the equality of the state. It would thus help save the Union from such dangers as the Civil War which the American Union suffered because its Constitution applied the principle of the equality of the states so far that many concluded that state rights were superior to human rights in it.

PARLIAMENTARY OR PRESIDENTIAL GOVERNMENT?

There are obvious arguments for the parliamentary and for the presidential system of government. The former is more responsive, the latter more stable. One can argue that in this new venture of establishing union on a world scale and among so many historic nations the first aim must be stability. Once the Union is firmly established its government can be made more responsive when the need becomes insistent, whereas if the Union is so responsive at the start as to be unstable it may be too late to remedy this defect and keep the Union together. It is safer to cut cloth too long than too short. Moreover, the establishment of the Union eliminates so much of the work of government today as to make responsiveness less necessary.

On the other hand, one can argue that by eliminating all the burden and waste of unnecessary government and by generally freeing the individual we stimulate enormously the most powerful sources of change. When we study afresh the results of union in America we shall have a better idea of all that this means, how much the Union will change our world and speed change in it, how much we need to make our Union government responsive enough to meet these changes and this quickening tempo of change. The drafters of the American Constitution had no way of knowing how rapidly the United States would grow under the free conditions they provided. We know now from this and other experiences how conducive individual freedom is to rapid growth, invention, discovery, change in everything. We need only look back to see how the tempo of change in the world has been accelerating every generation since government began to be made on the principle of the equality of man and for the Rights of Man. We cannot make the leap forward that this Union makes on the road to freedom without speeding proportionately the tempo of change. Prudence once required for freedom stable rather than responsive government. Now prudence demands greater provision for adaptability.

My own view favors a combination of the responsive and the stable, of the parliamentary and presidential systems,—a combination aimed at keeping the advantages of each, meeting the peculiar needs of our Union, and insuring that its government will not seem too strange to any of the democracies. This brings us to the problem of the executive power. Only here do

I think that we need to invent or innovate in making this constitution, though not very much even here.

THE EXECUTIVE

Because we are unwilling to take change-making as part of our every-day life, changes are forced upon us and we say, "this is a catastrophe." I do not believe that you will ever get civilization or government of any kind on a sound basis until you appoint a cabinet minister on change-making, logical change-making, because you can not keep change from coming.—Charles Kettering, President, General Motors Research Corporation, addressing the American Club of Paris, Oct. 5, 1933.

My suggestion is that instead of establishing a single executive we vest executive authority in a Board of five persons, each selected for five years, one each year, or each elected for ten years, one every other year. This would assure constant change in the Board and constant stability. I would have three elected by direct popular vote. I think it highly essential that there be some officer or officers in the Union elected by and respon-sible to the people of the Union as a whole as is the American President. The other two members of the Board I would have elected in between the popular elections, one by the House of Deputies, the other by the Senate. This should assure a more representative Board. The Board would estab-lish a rotation whereby each member presided it for one or two years. Three should form a quorum of the Board and it should act normally by the majority of those voting.

The Board, I would further suggest, should delegate most of its execu-tive authority to a Premier who would exercise this power with the help of a Cabinet of his own choosing until he lost the confidence of either the House or the Senate, whereupon the Board would name another Premier. I would give the Board power to dissolve either house or both of them in order to call new elections, and I believe it should also have a power of veto somewhat similar to that which the American President has. I would make the Board commander-in-chief of the Union's armed forces, and em-power it with the consent of the Senate to conclude treaties and name all the Union judges.

I would also have it report to the people and the Legislature from time to time on the state of human freedom and of the Union, and on the effects and need of change, and to recommend broadly measures and policies. In short, I would entrust the more general and long term duties of the execu-tive to the Board, and leave the more detailed and short term duties to the Premier and Cabinet.

The aim of this system is threefold: First, to assure the supremacy of

the people and to provide strength, continuity, stability and foresight in the executive while keeping it responsible to and representative of the people. Second, to reassure all those who would be fearful of any one man having too much power in the Union, or of all executive authority being in the hands of, say, an American, or an Englishman, or a Frenchman. Third, to avoid the unhealthy burden now placed on one man by the American system, while enabling the head of the Union to fulfill the liaison functions which the British royal family do to some extent in the smaller British Commonwealth, and which would be much more necessary in the Union. All members of the Board would be expected to travel through the Union, and it would be easy for the Board to arrange rotation whereby one would be visiting the more distant parts of the Union while another was visiting the less distant parts and the other three were at the capital.* Such, broadly are the aims of the system I suggest. I believe few will object to these aims, and certainly I would not object to any other system that promised to secure them better than mine, or nearly as well.

THE JUDICIARY

The essentials to me here are that there be an independent Supreme Court, that no controversies among member states be excluded from its jurisdiction, and that the constitution be made explicitly the supreme law of the Union. To attain these ends I would favor copying broadly the method followed in the American Constitution. No doubt there would be controversy over whether the Supreme Court should have the right to invalidate laws as unconstitutional. I believe it should have this right. The essential purpose of this right is, however, to keep the Constitution supreme—to keep intact the division between the more fundamental law which can be changed relatively slowly, the Constitution, and the less fundamental law which can be changed relatively quickly, the statutes. It would seem wiser to accept any system that gives reasonable promise of attaining this purpose than to delay or sacrifice the Union by controversy over the question of method.

THE AMENDING MACHINERY

Connected with the problem of the judiciary is the problem of how the constitution shall be amended. Many of the objections made to the American Supreme Court would be more justly aimed at the American Consti-

---

* Where should be the Union's capital? There would be advantages in having a permanent one and also in having the Legislature alternate sessions there with sessions in each of the main parts of the Union. This is one of the many questions best left to the Union to decide.

tution's amending mechanism. It makes that Constitution too hard to change, too rigid, and it has for me the further disadvantages of being based too much on the states as corporate bodies. All that has been said of our Union's need to adapt itself more quickly to change than the American Union needed to do when it began applies with special force to the present problem. I would suggest that the constitution be amended by majority vote of the voting citizens on proposals that had gone through some preliminary scrutiny, with several choices open as to the kind of scrutiny. For example, the people might act on amendments proposed by two-thirds the Union legislature with the approval of four-fifths of the Board, or by two-thirds of either House or Senate with the unanimous approval of the Board, or by a special constituent assembly, or by petition of, say, one-fifth or fourth the voters in one-third or half the nations in the Union. It would be expressly stipulated in the constitution, however, that certain constitutional guarantees, such as the right of each nation to conduct its own affairs in its own language and the right of each citizen to freedom of speech and of the press, could not be lessened without the consent of each nation.

Such are the main lines on which the Union could be constituted. Those who desire to see how these proposals look when actually applied will find in the appendix a draft constitution containing them. It may give a better idea of them as a whole, and it provides an easy means of indicating how various minor constitutional problems not treated here might be solved. It should be kept in mind, however, that this draft constitution is not put forward as a hard and fast plan. When there is agreement to organize on the union principle there will be time for discussion of the details of how to do it. This draft is included only as an example of what might be done, an illustration of what Union means, to make the union principle clearer.

TOO "EIGHTEENTH CENTURY"?

I should esteem it the extreme of imprudence to prolong the precarious state of our national affairs, and to expose the Union to the jeopardy of successive experiments, in the chimerical pursuit of a perfect plan.—Hamilton in *The Federalist, LXXXV.*

I would now briefly explain my position better to those who object to my constitutional ideas as being too "eighteenth century" and would prefer to see more recognition given to economic considerations. I would neither stick to nor discard ideas because of their date, I would base my choice on reason and experience and existing practical and political conditions. I would not deny that two plus two make four simply because they made

four in the eighteenth century, and I would not discard the basic principle either of union or of the steam engine because they were discovered in that century. On the other hand, I would not blindly copy past applications even of sound principle. I believe that we can never understand a principle fully or apply it perfectly at first (if ever), that we start with a faulty grasp and application of it, and that as we put this to the test of practice we gain an increasingly better position to understand and apply the basic principle. I find that I am more and more impressed by our need of practical experience in order to learn. Two examples may make clearer what I mean.

When I was a small boy my grandfather, Thomas Kirshman, used to tell me, as he studied the buzzards soaring over the fields and woods of Missouri, that when men learned the principle the buzzards used they would at last begin to fly. He did not live to know that men would begin to fly thanks to what they had learned about some things buzzards do not use—to what they had learned about creating motive power since Watt's time and about applying the principle of the wheel on which Watt built in his time. The fact is that only after they had flown for years with the aid of wheels and engines did men learn of the warm air currents that rise from open fields and of the cold ones that descend toward wooded plots, and begin in gliders to soar like buzzards without wheels or motors.

Similarly, I believe that for our Union to be possible we had to try out the league solution first. Certainly I do not mean to deny by my criticisms of the League of Nations the immense debt that I personally owe to it and to Woodrow Wilson and all the other men who have believed in it and made it possible for me to enjoy the advantage of seeing what could never before be seen—a world organization actually in operation.

I do not doubt that the best way to learn both to understand and to apply better the principle of union is to apply that principle enough to get the Union established. It follows that one should aim primarily at this stage at getting the Union established, and only secondarily at getting it established on what one believes to be the most perfect application of the principle of union. It seems to me that we are more likely to get the Union established by making it an extension of existing applications of the union principle with which people are familiar than by asking men not only to break new ground but to do it a new or unfamiliar way.

That is why I propose establishing the Union on, for example, the familiar "eighteenth century" political basis of a two-house legislature in which the representation of each citizen of the Union is determined by where he lives and not by what he does. I know that the modern tendency is to stress increasingly this latter, "economic," basis and to move toward representing men at least partly by their economic group interests. The

future may well belong to this economic tendency, but obviously at present it is a minority tendency and we have not yet had much opportunity to tell from experience how it will work or whether it will work better than the time-tested and prevailing "political" method.

Whether we organize men on an economic or on a political basis, according to what they do or where they live, by industries or by states, we must still organize them either by the absolutist league principle or by the democratic union principle, we have still only two units to choose between, we must still base our organization on plural man or on individual man as our equal unit, and all that we have said against the former and in favor of the latter method still holds good. Consequently I am quite prepared in principle to organize men partly or entirely by economic groups so long as they are organized on the unionist as opposed to the league principle and unit. And I am ready to go as far in this direction as the majority desires. My objections are confined to the practical side.

Suppose we agree to organize men according to economic groups. There is a basic economic division between consumers and producers but since most men are both how shall be divide them thus? If we organize them only as producers according to what they do, we fall at once into the controversy that has split American labor into the A. F. L. and the C. I. O.,—for shall we organize them horizontally by their craft or vertically by their industry? I do not say that there is no answer to these questions, nor that there may not be two answers that can be compromised. I can conceive of a combination not only of the horizontal and vertical methods, but also of the producer and consumer division, and of the economic and political systems. But all these answers and combinations raise a swarm of questions which invite controversy bound to delay the Union considerably and perhaps fatally.

However fertile this "economic" field may prove to be, we have as yet hardly begun to explore it, and it seems to me that the best way to hasten its exploration—and certainly the best way to get Union now—is to establish the Union on the familiar time-tested political basis with a minimum of innovation, and to leave it to each member state to experiment thereafter as much as it desires with organizing itself on an economic basis. This method allows the various methods of economic organization to be tried out on a small scale. It avoids the dangers of experimenting with one of these methods prematurely on too vast a scale and of delaying or preventing the establishment of the Union by overloading it with innovation. The method proposed is, in short, simply the method of doing first things first.

.   .   .   .

The kerosene lamp became better and better for twenty years after Edison invented the electric light, but that did not save it.

.   .   .   .

When we have a general who insists on devoting an increasing proportion of the national defense appropriation to free public schools we shall be impregnably defended and know military genius. The best defense of any country is a free, well-educated, well-informed, self-reliant citizen. One Lincoln is worth a fleet and army put together and costs far less to produce.

CHAPTER XI

Of Time and Union

It ought to be the constant aim of every wise public council to find out, by cautious experiments and rational, cool endeavors, with how little, not how much, of this restraint [on individual freedom] the community can subsist. For liberty is a good to be improved, and not an evil to be lessened. . . .

But whether liberty be advantageous or not (for I know it is a fashion to decry the very principle) none will dispute that peace is a blessing; and peace must in the course of human affairs be frequently bought by some indulgence and toleration at least to liberty. For as the Sabbath (though of Divine institution) was made for man, not man for the Sabbath, government, which can claim no higher origin or authority, in its exercise at least, ought to conform to the exigencies of the time.—Burke.

THE ETERNAL QUESTION

A policy of national sovereignty and independence has for various reasons proved very helpful in the past to the freedom of every democracy. This has helped lead them all to conclude that continuance of this policy must always prove helpful and never harmful to individual freedom, no matter how conditions change. But the question these democracies face is not whether a policy of nationalism toward all states is always necessary to this end, or never is as regards any of them. The question is whether at the present time and in existing conditions they will secure individual freedom better by practising toward each other a policy of absolute nationalism, or one of cooperation of national units as in a league, or one of union.

Much of the confusion in modern political thought comes from democratic thinkers failing to keep this question always in mind. There can be no more dynamic policy than the policy of freeing man—freeing all the incalculable powers of the individual in his two-billion-fold variety. There can then be no greater mistake than to imagine or assume that this policy can leave anything static, except sound principle. With the spread of democracy and the increasing inventiveness in every field that has accompanied and must accompany this increasing release of human energy, the problem that is always and inevitably coming back to each free people is

the problem of what should be their relations to other peoples, particularly other free peoples.

In 1776 when Britain, to quote Lord Acton's *History of Freedom,* "had been brought back, by indirect ways, nearly to the condition which the Revolution [of 1688] had been designed to remedy forever" and "Europe seemed incapable of becoming the home of free states," the peoples of the Thirteen American colonies manifestly secured their liberty better by separating from a common sovereignty and declaring themselves "free and independent states." Just as manifestly in 1789 in a world of absolutism the peoples of these Thirteen American States secured their liberties better by "sacrificing" the sovereignty of their states to that of the United States.

On the other hand, maintenance of the independence of the United States then was manifestly more in the interest of human liberty than any other policy. A policy of extending that Union to other democracies was then impossible. The only practical way to extend it was the one followed, that of deliberately drawing individuals from all the European states and with them peopling the wilderness,* organizing it piecemeal into states and uniting then with these democracies.

A policy of cooperation with the other nations was equally impossible for the American Union when it began. A policy of entangling alliance with any of the European states was clearly dangerous to the freedom of the Americans. Few will dispute, however, that it was wise for the American people to ally with absolutist France till the Union could do without so dangerous a medicine. After all, that alliance killed only the absolutist partner.

The establishment of the Latin American republics brought the American people a new choice. Union with them was impractical and dangerous when the experiment in free government was so young and communications so slow. Yet it was dangerous too to treat these republics on the same basis as the autocracies of the Old World. Indifference risked bringing absolutism nearer the United States. In these circumstances the American Union took a middle course, still exceedingly bold for a people then only 10,000,000 strong facing the victorious Holy Alliance of Austria, Russia and Prussia. For the Union pledged then in the Monroe Doctrine its full

---

* This free immigration policy was not only a deliberate American policy but one of the things for which we fought to establish our independence from Britain. In our general retreat after the World War from the deepest American principles, we forgot, in adopting then our existing law restricting immigration, that the indictments brought against George III by the Declaration of Independence included this one: "He has endeavored to prevent the population of these states; for that purpose obstructing the laws for naturalization of foreigners, refusing to pass others to encourage their migration hither."

cooperation in guaranteeing the Latin American republics against the restoration of European absolutism.

Later, when a part of one of these republics adjoining the United States declared its independence and was formally recognized in the New and Old World as the Republic of Texas, the American people, changing policy to meet conditions, agreed to unite with the people of this sovereign democracy at their request.

Still later the sons of the men who had seceded from Britain to declare all men created equal decided in four years of Civil War that none of their states had a right to secede and that individual freedom required not only the maintenance of the United States but the admission of the negro slaves to its Union of free and equal men.

The World War faced Americans again with this same problem in circumstances which made two things essential, and looking backward now we may see that they contrived to accomplish both, the one through the President and the other through the Senate.

The first essential was to establish a living institution that could bring out the great truth that the freedom of man had reached the point where it required law and order and government to be organized on a world scale. This institution Wilson did create. The founding of the League of Nations was an achievement for which Woodrow Wilson will always merit well of men. His was a conscious, positive, constructive act done against the indifference or opposition of all his peers in power.

One must measure the grandeur of a man by his contemporaries, for his successors stand upon him. There is no getting away from the fact that Woodrow Wilson got done what man had long dreamed of doing and had often tried to do but never done. Woodrow Wilson worked in a world in which the great conservatives saw no need for organizing world law and order, and the great liberals insisted the most important need was to lay down perfect frontiers and all that, and the great revolutionists at Moscow were interested only in violent overthrow of capitalism everywhere, not in the greater revolution of bloodlessly overthrowing violence itself. History may well rate Woodrow Wilson as a greater conservative than Poincaré and a greater revolutionist than Lenin. He stands out among the great men of his day for among them he alone was wise enough to know that the League with all its faults was at that moment in history worth half a dozen Versailles treaties, and to pay that price so that the great truth in his League might live and grow and make itself known to men as can only things that live.

The other essential was that the great error Wilson's work contained should be brought out before it was too late to avoid the catastrophe to

which great error must inevitably lead. I do not doubt that the United States by joining the League would have enormously strengthened it and changed inestimably for the better the whole course of American and world history since the war. We would all be better off today, but I doubt that our young children would be better off when they take over. I do not know whether or not American entry would have led to detection and correction in time of the error in the league. But I do know this: As long as such error remains, it must grow, and grow to catastrophe. You cannot sow government of the state, by the state and for the state and not reap it. You cannot possibly place the sovereignty of the nation above the sovereignty of man without strengthening the nation at the expense of the citizen.

Had the United States entered the League its entry would not of itself have remedied the fatal flaw in the Covenant, and I fear that it would have glossed it over. By producing temporarily the peace and prosperity men sought, it would have given the Covenant a dangerous prestige and caused men to discriminate less than ever between its truth and its error. I fear the result would have been as it was with the truth and error in the American Constitution: Each would have gone on gathering sinews until our children, when men, would have been flung against each other in catastrophe as terrible as was the American Civil War.

By rejecting the Covenant the United States, without killing the truth within it, hastened the exposure of the error through inducing a relatively harmless breakdown that need not end in smash-up. It so hastened this that the young men who did the fighting and the young women who did the mourning in 1914-1918 could see the error now,—just when they enter the age of governing—and could have it driven home to them in time, precisely as the chaos of the League of Friendship drove home to the generation of the American Revolution that it was not for this they had killed and mourned.

It was essential that the error should be made clear in time for the generation most likely to see and remedy it to act. That this essential was assured was the contribution of Senator Borah and his friends. It may have been mostly blind, it certainly was negative. It was a less meritorious act than that of Wilson for its whole merit depended for existence upon Wilson succeeding in establishing the League. But though the value of a brake depends upon there being a motor, a brake becomes the second essential once the motor runs. It takes no less courage to stand up against a multitude for what one feels is right when one cannot give the best reason why, than when one can. The "irreconcilables," too, served man and truth and freedom.

These examples from one democracy's history indicate that the question,

whether freedom requires a policy of separation, aloof nationalism, cooperation, league or union, can not be settled by a free people once for all toward all the world. By its nature this question must remain open and
require that eternal vigilance which is freedom's price. Free men must be
forever going back to their own basic principles and asking, when a policy is
proposed, "Will it secure better, on balance, the blessings of liberty, not to
our ancestors or the state, but to ourselves and our posterity?"

1789 AND TODAY

Since the first Union began in 1789 the positions of democracy and
absolutism have been reversed. Where there were only one or two sovereign peoples, there is now only one important people, the Japanese, which
is not at least theoretically sovereign,—for even the dictatorships carefully
trace their power to vote of the people. Where government of the people,
by the people, for the people among so many as 3,000,000 men was then
an untried experiment, it has now been tried for more than a century by
several powerful nations. Freedom can count today on a nucleus of 300,-
000,000 men and women whose combined power for defense against absolutism is even more overwhelming than the aggressive power absolutism
enjoyed against the 3,000,000 in 1789. Fifteen democracies are today from
every viewpoint far abler to give the younger democracies everywhere the
protection of a Monroe Doctrine than were the twenty-four United States
in 1823.

In the period when the Monroe Doctrine was proclaimed the United
States appeared no stronger materially than Siam does now. In 1830 its
population was 12,866,000; Siam's in 1930 was 12,000,000. In 1830 American imports totalled $63,000,000; Siam's now are $65,0000,000. American
exports were $72,000,000; Siam's are $69,000,000. But in that century the
population of the United States (only one of our fifteen democracies) increased more than ten times, its trade fifty times, and the individual American now means six times more to the business world than his grandfather
did.

In 1789 the free peoples of today had not ended the long tradition of war
among themselves into which absolutism had kept them plunged. In 1839
most of them were just coming out of that nightmare and into manhood
suffrage. Now these democracies can look back on two things together:
Their first hundred years of manhood suffrage and the first hundred years
of peace among them.

We cannot live in the world of 1789 or 1839, we must live in our time.
Since "from America," as Acton said, the Rights of Man "burst forth like
a conqueror upon the world they were destined to transform," they have

indeed transformed conditions. It is in the light of these changed conditions, and because of them, that the question of the political relations among the democracies needs to be re-examined and answered now afresh by all their citizens:

Does our freedom as individuals still require a policy of national sovereignty toward each other—toward old democracies, not immature ones, or autocracies? Do we still need to suffer all the restraints on our liberty that fifteen sovereignties involve? Absolutism forced its unit on us in the past, but does it now? Since individual freedom so far has gained by every application of the principle of union, can it lose by further application of that principle,—by union of the unions of the free? If our fathers, grandfathers, great-grandfathers could solve the problem of increasing man's freedom tremendously in every way by balancing local and central government as in the United States, the United Kingdom, the United Provinces of the Netherlands, the Swiss Confederation, the Union of South Africa, can we not do as well? Can we follow in their path if we stop now in their tracks?

At a time when our fifteen democracies can by union be almighty on this earth, are we preserving man's freedom by pitting our financial, economic, or other power against each other? If Monroe was faithful to his oath when he warned absolutism to keep hands off untried democracies a month distant from Washington, are Senators and Presidents preserving the Constitution to the best of their ability when they fail to warn absolutism to keep hands off tried democracies not one week distant? Since, for one example, freedom of the press in Holland led to freedom in England and everywhere, is it the Dutchman's right to a free press, or his loss of it, that needs to be feared by free men wherever they may be? Do the Rights of Man ever need protection against the Bill of Rights or *les Droits de l'Homme*?

A policy that asks men to renounce some of their freedom to defend the rest of their freedom from absolutism is understandable. So too is one that would sacrifice the freedom of the state to preserve or extend the freedom of the citizen. But a policy that consists in fifteen democracies each sacrificing the freedom of their citizens in order to preserve the rest of it from each other, to save national democracy from world democracy and freedom from freedom itself—does it make sense? The time for world-wide union of the free for freedom's sake—is not now the time? That could not be the question for 3,000,000 free men in 1789; it can not but be the question for 300,000,000 now.

CHAPTER XII

To Get Union Now

The people gave their voice, and the danger that hung upon our borders went by like a cloud. . . . The Statesman declares his mind before the event, and submits himself to be tested by those who have believed in him. . . . The adventurer is silent when he ought to have spoken.—
Demosthenes.

I have seen war. I have seen war on land and sea. I have seen blood running from the wounded. I have seen men coughing out their gassed lungs. I have seen the dead in the mud. I have seen cities destroyed. I have seen two hundred limping, exhausted men come out of line—the survivors of a regiment of one thousand that went forward forty-eight hours before. I have seen children starving. I have seen the agony of mothers and wives. I hate war.

*I have passed unnumbered hours, I shall pass unnumbered hours thinking and planning how war may be kept from this Nation. I wish I could keep war from all nations.—*President Franklin D. Roosevelt, Aug. 14, 1936.

LET UNIONISTS UNITE

To get Union the first thing those who want it should do is to say so, and unite for it. The way not to get it is to think: "This idea of Union is all right, and I'm for it, and though there are lots of difficulties no doubt they can be overcome some way, but you'll never get most people to believe in it, they're too prejudiced and unreasonable for it to have a chance, and so what's the use of my doing anything about it?" Individuals who take this condescending view of their fellows condemn themselves and form the main obstacle to their own desires. No one can express the individual's will but himself, and so long as individuals do not at least express their will for Union it remains unknown, isolated, lost. So long as most men wait for the majority to make known their will for Union that majority can not possibly be formed.

Union has the great advantage that its supporters do not need to petition governments or wait on diplomats to get it: They need only turn to themselves and their neighbors,—but they must do that. The first necessity then is that Unionists wherever they are should make known their will for

Union and organize their neighborhood, and keep on uniting for Union until they form the majority needed to get Union.

How should Unionists organize themselves? Should they form a new party—the Union or World Union Party—common to all the democracies? Would it be wiser to try to win over and work through existing parties, at least in some countries? The latter course has some obvious advantages, and certain parties may well desire to make the Unionist cause their own. It can conflict, in fact, with the principles of no existing party in any democracy, except those that put the nation above the citizen and are therefore undemocratic. One party in a given country, however, may attack Union because an opposition party has come out for it.

On balance, I am inclined to favor Unionists organizing themselves into a World Unionist Party, or at least forming some common organization to coordinate their campaign in the various democracies. The first step in this direction could be the convoking of a congress of Unionists from the fifteen democracies to form a common center and formulate a concrete program. This congress or the permanent body it organized would be most competent to decide all such problems as whether to form in each democracy a new party, or to work in each through existing parties, or to settle the problem in each country on its merits.

Democracy, however, allows policy to be promoted by men individually as well as collectively. Its true source of power is the free individual, and collective action is only one of the ways open to him. Each individual has an interest in Union, and democracy has freed individuals to advance that common interest by each putting behind it his own peculiar power. Some individuals have a gift for organizing men, others for organizing thoughts; one can express things in writing, another is excellent in impromptu public debate; there are men with special talent in every field,—trade, production, finance, defense, communications, research, popularization. For the establishment of Union there is a need and a place for the special talent and special experience of every individual.

The essential is that each individual, without waiting for any one else, begin devoting some of his individual talent to Union. Let those with a gift for organizing remember that the right of free assembly, which allows them to do the thing they best can do, was established only by union of democrats; let them begin using their gift for the safeguarding and extension of that right by organizing their neighbors for Union.

There was a time when men with the gift of writing or speaking went to the stake so that other men with such gifts might freely use them. To preserve these rights today those with the gift of writing or speaking need only lend to Union some of their gift. Each needs but lend a bit of the thing he is richest in and can best afford to lend. If each who profits from the rights

of Man gives now his mite as he sees best for the cause that made these
Rights possible, he will soon have world Union, and its greater rights for
men.

POSTCARD PLEBISCITE

We can get Union still more quickly by working not only through our
individual selves and through a party, but simultaneously through our
governments. There is much complaint among us that autocracy allows
men to act more swiftly than democracy. Autocracy, however, does not
allow a people to do more swiftly what *they* will; it allows one man to do
his will swiftly with the power of millions whom he keeps from even knowing what their will is. Democracy allows no individual the autocrat's speed
and power of personal action, but it does allow the majority of men to form
their common will and execute it swiftly. Democracy's speed of action is in
direct ratio to the common sense of its citizens.

Though we usually form and express our will by votes on election day,
we can form and express it any day to the representatives we have already
elected. We can be certain that as soon as we make known to them our
majority will for Union we shall have our existing organized power—our
governments—acting forthwith for Union. Democracy is not simply government that bears always on the individual, it consists just as much in
the individual bearing always on the government.

The democracy that permits a book such as this one to be freely written
by any simple citizen and freely read by any individual, makes the speed
with which the common will can be formed depend only on the book's truth
and clarity,—for men will not reject truth that they see clearly. Democracy
makes the speed with which this common will is then expressed and executed depend only on the majority of individuals using a microscopic fraction of their energy and money. It provides the citizen with a cheap and
simple means—even less bothersome than the vote—of bringing his will to
bear at once on his government.

He need only write, telegraph, telephone his Representative, Senator,
Deputy, Member of Parliament, Premier, President. He can reduce his
effort to the point where he need only spend the penny and the minute
needed to send his representative a postal card asking him to favor Union.
The very thing that makes him hesitate to do this—the fact that he can
express only one man's will for Union—is the thing that gives it weight.
A hundred men sending 100 individual postcard messages will outweigh
1,000 men sending the same stereotyped card. The more individually each
man expresses his will the more weight it will have, and the more pennies
or minutes he spends in expressing it, the more weight it will gain, of course.

At most he need spend only a few dollars, only a few hours, to hasten Union. He need only spend a tiny fraction of his money and time to reduce radically his taxes and save his own and his children's lives from war.

Citizens who want Union enough to have that postcard served with the breakfast newspaper only for one week so that the news each day will remind them to send it seven times, can be sure they will thereby cast a weight out of all proportion to their effort—so sharply will this contrast with their usual inertia and lack of persistence. The raindrop on the window seems powerless, but the crudest mill-wheel moves if only enough raindrops take the same canal. It is easier for the democrat to move his government to Union than for the raindrop to spin a turbine. Surely democracy which lets the individual do so much so easily is worth the effort that it requires from any man to save it and extend it.

The more advanced democracy is, the less effort it requires of each citizen, but the greater the responsibility on each to do that little promptly. How great is the responsibility for man's vast future it places now on each of us we may see by looking backward.

IN MAN OUR TRUST

"Ours is not the first modern world—there was Rome." Of all I heard Dean Carlyle say at Oxford this I remember. There was Rome (it came to me long after) and had the men of Rome held the ground that Man had won then for Man, where might not we be now? Had Rome not fallen, would Man have needed 2,000 years to step from Aristotle on to Descartes, and seven generations more to step from Descartes on to Darwin?

Had the men of Rome only held this ground—but Rome fell, and when Rome fell then fell not only civilized man, but all the barbarians whom they were civilizing, and American Redskins of whose existence they were not aware. When Rome fell, truly you and I and all of us fell down, for then fell down our species. It has not reached today the point it could long since have passed had Rome not fallen.

Fifty generations have lived and toiled and died since Rome fell, and slowly coral-like man has raised another and a far better Rome. It is the freest and the most extensive and the most marvelous and the most delicate civilization our species yet has known. Beside it Rome seems as barbarous as the world Rome ended seemed to Rome, and as unfree as our civilization should seem to our children.

With the fruit of past labor, with the slavery fruits of war, Rome bridged streams with massive stone. With the fruits of future labor, with the fruits of plants unplanted, we have flung strong spans of steel across great harbors. In the first Rome men knew how to make one hundred do the work of

one hundred. Our Rome has been made possible because with our greater freedom we have found how to make one hundred do the work of one thousand by credit—which is to say by faith in our future, by faith in Man.

Thus Man has freed the power in his arm until a child's finger on a button in London can start gigantic machines in Australia. Man has given his legs the seven-league boots he dreamed of in his fairy-tale age. He has come to throw his voice across oceans of which the first Rome never dreamed, to attune his ear to voices coming at once from the same room and from the antipodes, to sharpen his eye until he has discovered and had to name worlds of tiny animals and enormous stars that Adam never saw. Man has freed himself not only to enter the heavens alive, but to fly upside down as the birds themselves cannot fly.

Thus have men built up a civilization that seems too solid now to fall. And it is at once the strongest and the most fragile civilization that Man has ever made, the one in which the individual is most independent and dependent. We have not placed our world on the shoulders of an Atlas; we have pyramided our world on credit—on faith, on dependence of our neighbors (and we have for neighbors men not only next door but next continent), on dependence on ourselves, on dependence on Man and freedom for Man. Democracy is based on faith in free and equal Man, faith in Man's vast future.

For ten years now this confidence, this credit, this faith upon which our Rome is built has been crumbling away. Who can guarantee us that this crumbling can go on and our world remain? And if it fall? If it falls, then we can prophesy with certainty. If our democratic civilization falls, then will fall not only Germany, or France, or Russia, but Europe, not only Europe but America, Asia, Africa. The fat and the famished, the advanced and the retarded, the capitalists and the communists, the haves and the have-nots, the unionists and the nationalists,—they will go down together into the new dark ages, they and their children's children, for how many generations?

MAN'S WORST WEAKNESS

Our Rome need not fall. To live and grow to greater marvels it needs but the faith that made it, the faith in Man. Man's worst weakness is that he is always under-estimating Man. He has never seen too large, he has always seen too small, too small. He has never had too much faith in what Man could do; he has always had too little.

Since time began, the western world lay there across the sea, but even when Columbus came he saw himself as the discoverer not of a new world but of a new route. The kettle steamed through thousands of years of hu-

man slavery; then came Watt—and which would amaze him most today: The automobile or the negro owning one? Once a man believed that Man could make a ship go without sails against a river. Other men called his ship *Fulton's Folly*. But he kept faith in Man, in one man,—himself,—and *Fulton's Folly* went paddling up the Hudson. Fulton saw far for his time, but doubtless he himself would have called it folly to believe the oil he used to cure a cold in the head could ever drive gigantic ships across the Atlantic in a hundred hours.

The fathers of the American Republic, the leaders of the French Revolution, the authors of the Bill of Rights, the political liberators of men everywhere had faith in Man—but they had no idea of all the forces they were freeing. They had no idea of all the rapid growth in civilization, all the transformation of the world, all the victories of men over autocracy and Nature that would come from freeing those then called *la canaille*. Washington, Jefferson, Hamilton, all voiced despair of the American Union even after its establishment, but they are not remembered for their doubts. They are known for what faith they showed in Man.

Man has still to find the limit of what he can do if only he has faith in himself. And yet each generation has seen wonders done by men who believed in Man. Man's greatest achievements have been the work of some obscure man or handful of men with faith in themselves, helping mankind against mankind's stubborn opposition. These inventors, discoverers, artists, statesmen, poets,—each of our benefactors has always had to over-come not only Nature but his own species. And always these lone men with faith have worked this wonder. As Andrew Jackson said, one man with courage makes a majority.

We have seen a village unknown through all the ancient Roman era become in a century Mecca to a world greater than Rome ever ruled, because there lived there then one man with faith in himself. We know what marvels one single simple individual with faith in Man can work—one Mohammed, one Joan of Arc, one Gutenberg, one Paine, Pasteur, Edison. What we do not know is what marvels could be done if the fifteen elected leaders of the 300,000,000 free men and women once worked together with the faith of one Columbus. We know that, working together,—which means depending on each other,—the Wright brothers did one of the many things that Man had always dreamed and failed of doing. But the Wright brothers were two simple citizens; they were not fifteen leaders in whom millions of men already trusted.

"As I stand aloof and watch [Walt Whitman wrote] there is something profoundly moving in great masses of men following the leadership of men who do not believe in man."

Yet the leaders who have believed in Man and have appealed not to his

lowest but to his highest instincts have always in the end been not only followed but alone remembered by all mankind. There is nowhere a monument to those who burned Bruno at the stake; there is in Rome a monument raised, in 1889, which says: "To Bruno, the century he foresaw, here where he burned."

As the dust are all those of our species who said that Man could never bring the lightning down against his other natural foes. Green still is the name of Franklin. Who were those twenty-seven men who, preferring the freedom of New York to the freedom of New Yorkers, came so near to preventing the American Union? It is their opponent, Alexander Hamilton, whose name still evokes eloquence in Europe as in America.

The difficulties that now seem so certain to keep us apart,—will men remember them a generation hence more than they now remember those that seemed to make the Union of Americans impossible in 1787? Will our own children be the first to honor those who kept Man divided against himself, at war with himself and a prey to ignorance, poverty, disease, premature death?

DECLARATION OF INDEPENDENCE

If we are to save our own world, we need Union, and we need it now. If we are to save ourselves none of us can dodge or divide his individual responsibility, or delay. But the individual on whom the most responsibility must lie in each democracy is the one who has asked and received from his fellow citizens the post of guardian of their liberties. Among these few, the most responsibility must lie upon the one freely chosen and freely trusted by the most men and women.

For our unending nightmare to end before another night only that one man is needed. He needs but invite the chief guardians of fourteen other democracies to confer with him on how best to unite the free and safeguard and extend their common heritage. Who could refuse without betraying his trust? Who would not accept at once such an invitation if it came from the President of the American Union?

For the condition of the whole human species to change overnight immensely for the better, the American President need only invite the fourteen other leaders of democracy to join him in declaring the undeniable: That their common supreme unit of government is the individual free man, that their common supreme end of government is the freedom of individual man, and that their common means to their common end is the union of free men as equals; that the existence of a democracy is proof in itself that the people of it want Union, that Democracy and Union are one and the same; that the responsibility facing 300,000,000 free men today is the one

that faced 30,000,000 in 1861 and 3,000,000 in 1787—the responsibility of choosing for themselves and their children whether to slip backward with the misery-making absolutist principle of the sovereignty of nations, or to continue forward with the richest political principle men have ever found, the principle of free union through the equal sovereignty of man. The American President need only ask the others to join him in making this Declaration of the Dependence of free men on themselves and on each other, and in convoking then our Union's constituent assembly.

If he fears that even after the events of September, 1938, men will call his move premature and will not see in time what nationalism means he can recall Isaiah: "A people . . . which remain among the graves and . . . which say, Stand by thyself, come not near to me; for I am holier than thou. . . . These are a smoke in my nose. . . . Ye shall all bow down to the slaughter . . . ye shall be hungry . . . ye shall be ashamed . . . and leave your name for a curse. . . .He who blesseth himself in the earth shall bless himself in the God of truth . . . For behold, I create new heavens and a new earth."

If he fears that men will call him mad, he can reply with Lafayette: "If it be a wild scheme, I had rather be mad that way than to be thought wise on the other track."

He can ask as Lincoln asked on the eve of war: "Can aliens make treaties easier than friends can make laws? Can treaties be more faithfully enforced between aliens than laws can among friends? Suppose you go to war, you cannot fight always; and, when after much loss on both sides and no gain on either, you cease fighting, the identical old questions as to terms of intercourse are again upon you."

He can answer with that Great Emancipator: "I have only to say, let us discard all this quibbling about this man and the other man, this race and that race and the other race being inferior, and therefore they must be placed in an inferior position. Let us discard all these things, and unite as one people throughout this land, until we shall once more stand up declaring that all men are created equal."

He can turn then to Washington's Farewell Address and repeat: "These considerations speak a persuasive language to every reflecting and virtuous mind, and exhibit the continuance of the Union as a primary object of patriotic desire. Is there a doubt whether a common government can embrace so large a sphere? Let experience solve it. To listen to mere speculation in such a case were criminal. We are authorized to hope that a proper organization of the respective subdivisions, will afford a happy issue to the experiment. It is well worth a fair and full experiment."

The President has his responsibility, but we each have ours, too. He must depend on us, as we on him.

There is no need, and there can be no excuse, for democracy and its great civilization to crash from failure to act in time. There is no need whatever for millions of men to bow down again to slaughter, hunger and shame. We can escape these. We can leave our name for a blessing. We can hasten man's vast future. There is need only for you, too, to stand up for Union now.

. . . .

> *Our cause is ripe:*
> *The enemy increaseth every day;*
> *We, at the height, are ready to decline.*
> *There is a tide in the affairs of men,*
> *Which, taken at the flood, leads on to fortune;*
> *Omitted, all the voyage of their life*
> *Is bound in shallows and in miseries.*
> *On such a full sea are we now afloat;*
> *And we must take the current when it serves,*
> *Or lose our ventures.*
> *Then, with your will, go on.*
> Shakespeare, *Julius Caesar*, IV-iii.

PHILOSOPHY

CHAPTER XIII

Of Freedom and Union

One's-self I sing, a simple separate person,
Yet utter the word Democratic, the word En-Masse.

Of physiognomy from top to toe I sing,
Not Physiognomy alone nor brain alone is worthy for the Muse,
I say the Form complete is worthier far,
The Female equally with the Male I sing.

Of Life immense in passion, pulse, and power,
Cheerful, for freest action form'd under the laws divine,
The Modern Man I sing.

Whitman, opening Leaves of Grass, 1867

Out of the trouble and tragedy of this present time may emerge a moral and intellectual revival; a religious revival, of a simplicity and scope to draw together men of alien races . . . into one common and sustained way of living for the world's service. We cannot foretell the scope and power of such a revival; we cannot even produce evidence of its onset. The beginnings of such things are never conspicuous. Great movements of the racial soul come at first "like a thief in the night," and then suddenly are discovered to be powerful and world-wide. Religious emotion . . . may presently blow through life again like a great wind, bursting the doors and flinging open the shutters of the individual life, and making many things possible and easy that in these present days of exhaustion seem almost too difficult to desire.—H. G. Wells, *Outline of History.*

The real question is whether the free and civilised peoples of the earth can become a true community by giving up their unfettered individual sovereignties and by forming a union to stand against war. . . . The effort to get it might be risky to the point of mortal peril. I think it would be a risk worth running. And I do not believe that the world will ever find peace in freedom along any other road.—Wickham Steed, in *Headway,* January, 1939.

CHAPTER XIII

Of Freedom and Union

If you would be freer than all that has been before, come listen to me . . .

I swear I begin to see the meaning of these things . . .

I swear nothing is good to me now that ignores individuals,
The American compact is altogether with individuals,
The only government is that which makes minute of individuals,
The whole theory of the universe is directed unerringly to one single in-
dividual—namely to You . . .

I am for those that have never been master'd,
For men and women whose tempers have never been master'd,
For those whom laws, theories, conventions, can never master.

I am for those who walk abreast with the whole earth,
Who inaugurate one to inaugurate all.

I will not be outfaced by irrational things,
I will penetrate what it is in them that is sarcastic upon me,
I will make cities and civilizations defer to me,
This is what I have learnt from America—it is the amount, and if I
teach again.
                    —Whitman, *By Blue Ontario's Shore.*

And now, having devoted twice six chapters to the work of the day, we may, perhaps, go on with it better if first we have a Sunday here to consider more broadly what we have been doing, to treat more deeply of the relation between the individual and society, and to get a better understanding of our philosophy of freedom and union.

OF FREEDOM

One can not repeat it too often: There is nothing so fertile in marvels as the art of being free.—De Tocqueville.

We have too petty a notion of freedom. We are bound to, since freedom is so great and growing. And yet our understanding of it need not be so petty. We tend to see it too narrowly on its political side. If we

213

call that view old-fashioned our revolutionary up-to-dateness often consists in emphasizing instead its economic side. We divide and argue as if political and economic freedom were not complementary but mutually exclusive, and on this confusing basis we debate again the eternal question of the relation of the individual and the collectivity.

Even when we see that political freedom no more requires sacrificing the collectivity to the freedom of the strongest individuals than economic freedom requires sacrificing the individual to the collectivity, that political and economic freedom are parts of a whole and that the relationship of the individual and society which serves freedom most on the one side serves it most on the other too,—even when we see this we have too petty a notion of our freedom.

We talk, for example, as if freedom of trade were simply a problem for the legislator and economist, a matter of freeing trade from this or that tariff or other legal or theoretical barrier. We talk as if the steamship that freed man from the accident of wind and the accident of calm had done nothing to free trade, nor the express train that freed the producers of perishable foods from the tyranny of time and northern tables from the monotony of winter. We forget the air-driven drill and the dynamite that enable us, when a mountain bars our road, to take a short cut through it. We forget a host of things that free us from the limitations of tongue and ear and eye, and let seller and buyer find each other swiftly anywhere on earth. Yet trade can lose its statutory freedom and be encumbered by politicians and economic experts with all sorts of man-made barriers, and still grow greater because other men have been freeing it from more stifling natural barriers.

As it is with trade, so it is with everything. The story of the freedom of man, of the freeing of man by man, is the whole story of man. It is the story of the invention of language, of the freeing of man's tongue to tell his thoughts to his neighbor and of the freeing of his ear to understand his neighbor's thoughts, of the freeing of his thoughts from space and time and the tricks of memory and death by the invention of writing. It is the story of the freeing of his tongue, ear, eye, mind by the invention of grammar, and still more by the invention of paper, and still more by the invention of printing, and still more by the discovery of America and of electricity and rubber, and by such political inventions as the freedom of the press and democracy and Union and such mechanical inventions as the steam engine and the locomotive and the high speed newspaper press and the telegraph and photograph and phonograph and telephone and airplane and moving picture and wireless and talking picture and television.

This is not even a meagre outline of the freeing of man (insofar as

he is free) in respect of his mind and thoughts and tongue and ear and eye. And were it complete it would outline only the freeing of these with respect to communication—for there is not a word in this about the freeing of the eye to peer into the worlds of microbes and of stars, nor the freeing of the ear to the harmonies of music, nor the freeing of the mind from error thanks to logic and from terror thanks to the accumulated experience of generations, nor the freeing of the mind to think honestly about anything regardless of the taboos of society or the self-interest of the body. And when we have outlined this vast field we have only begun: We have still to tell of the freeing of the power in the arm of man from the time he extended it with a club or rock on through to where he extends it with a bullet or electric button, of the freeing of man from his pulmonary handicaps until he can cross the ocean in a submarine, and of the freeing of his skin from the cold and the heat, of his stomach from famine, of his body and mind from disease,—and when we have told all this our tale of the freeing of man by man remains a fragment. It is a tale that can never be told, and not only because of its vast range and the intricate inter-relation of every detail to the others and to the whole. It can never be told because in the telling it is growing; somewhere, wittingly, unwittingly, some of the two billion of men and women are at work freeing man, adding to a glorious tale new glories that men will not be free enough to recognize or use perhaps for a hundred years to come.

It is a myriad-sided never-ending task and tale and joy, the freeing of man by man; and it is the myriad-sided never-ending variety among individual men and women, the rich resources given mankind by the fact that no two individuals are precisely the same, that each one forms a distinct combination of character, talent, knowledge, skill, tastes, curiosity, heredity, environment and physical, moral and mental strength,—it is this that allows the task to be advanced and the tale to be faintly imagined and the joy enjoyed. It is because the democratic principle of the equality and rights of man allows mankind to free all this power it has in men, and to let men enjoy themselves freeing mankind still more, that it is the most fertile and powerful political, economic, social, and philosophical principle that men have ever discovered.

To think, as so many seem to think, that this principle depends for its success mainly on all men exercising all the rights it gives to vote or govern in things political, or to innovate as one pleases in things political, economic or social, is to miss the point. The power in this principle lies instead in its guarantee by society to the individual of his right to do freely that which most interests him whenever it most interests him, and its guarantee to all other men of their right to judge freely then his work.

Government of gasoline and electricity by the people does not consist in every man being able to build an automobile or dynamo, any more than the government of microbes by men consists in every one of us having a thorough medical and scientific knowledge. Hardly more does government of the people by the people consist in every man interesting himself deeply in political problems and trying to work them out himself.

We govern the power in gasoline, first, by insuring any man who is interested in the problem of governing that power the freedom to tackle it as hard as he pleases, and, secondly, by retaining the power to pass judgment broadly on the solutions brought us by these men who are engineer-minded. One such man has it clear in his mind that gasoline can be so governed as to run a wagon, but he can not make it clear to the rest of us, for we are not engineer-minded to that degree. And so to make it clear he makes us the first automobile, and when we see it running then we see the man is right and we admit it can be done. But it still is not at all clear to most of us that his automobile is safer than a horse, or cheaper, or faster, simpler, better. The more engineer-minded men, however, see that all this is true, too; in a widening circle this type of man becomes interested in the problem of man governing gasoline. These men fight out among themselves the technical questions, and when and as long as they all agree,—as, for example, on pneumatic tires— we readily follow them—no buyer now demands solid tires on a pleasure car.

But when these men of technical sense disagree they come to us, the men of common sense, and ask us, not to solve their problems, but to pass judgment on their different solutions. And through purchase we accord our highest prize in the long run to the engineer who has solved the problem most clearly—for that means he has solved it in a way that those of us who are least mechanically endowed can understand is the safest, cheapest, fastest, simplest, best solution.

The government of gasoline by man began with a contraption so simple in its structure that one could see or hear its every organ, but so complicated in its operation that even the genius who contrived it could never be sure of getting home without a horse. But by the democratic process of freedom mankind develops a machine so amazing that it makes the gasoline not only drive it far faster than a mile a minute but light its way at night, herald its arrival, and stop it shortly,—a machine so complicated structurally that no one genius could ever have developed it and so simple to run that a child can run it. Gasoline is being governed by the people when any man without engineering knowledge can make it take him where he wants to go with a touch of the finger, a touch of the foot, and

a few simple rules such as: Obey the indicator when it warns that the governor needs more gasoline to govern.

In all this the thing to note is that the human freedom that government of gasoline by the people brings is achieved, first, by freeing all engineer-minded men to tackle this problem, and second, by keeping the rest of mankind free to pass judgment on their work. It is achieved by this system which discourages the non-engineer from trying to solve engineering problems while discouraging the engineer from turning to the best engineer as his supreme judge; this system which forces the best engineer to make himself so clear that a moron can see his solution is the best and which assures him that the greater his technical achievement the more he will gain the votes of the simplest laymen.

This is noteworthy because this system is the one through which government by the people for the people has been established, insofar as it is established, over everything they govern, whether it be gasoline or electricity or microbes or animals or music or fire or water or wind or earth or light. It is, too, the system whereby government of the people by the people for the people has been or is being established. This last is only the most difficult and the most productive of man's problems in government, because it means the government of the most powerful of the elements by the most marvelous and unaccountable among them, the government of the governors by the governors, the government of man himself by man himself for man himself. It is a never-ending problem if only because the more constructive man becomes the more destructive he is able, too, to be.

The way to solve the problem of self-government is to follow the same principles that have led to government by the people of everything from animals to gasoline, while carefully avoiding an error, tricked out as truth, which appears at this point and on which despotism, benevolent or malevolent, is based.

So well hidden is this trap that Plato himself fell victim to it. In his argument for government of all men by the wisest men Plato seems to base his reasoning on the analogy of the government of sheep by men: The statesman, he says, is after all only the shepherd of the human flock, and the conclusion seems to follow that since it is absurd for the sheep to elect and direct the shepherd the democratic theory is absurd. And so Plato divides his ideal state into three great specialized classes, rulers, fighters and farmers. He thinks out elaborate machinery, first, to make sure that the human shepherds shall never be responsible to the human sheep but only to other shepherds, and that the philosophers need answer only to the philosophers, and then to safeguard everyone from the dangers he sees in this. And so men less wise and generous defend the principle

of government through dictatorship by a single autocrat, or by an hereditary despot, or by some single class of men, whether the propertied or the proletariat, the oldest families or the *giovinezza*, the chosen Aryans or the chosen Jews.

The error in all this is the same. There is a difference between the shepherd and the statesman, and it is a fundamental difference. The shepherd is a man governing, for men, a different animal, the sheep. The statesman is a man governing, for men, these same men.

The fact that in all cases, except that of man himself, the government by man of whatever he seeks to govern, whether sheep or gasoline, is invariably marked by his refusal to consult the wishes of the governed, does not make this refusal the *sine qua non* or cause of success; it makes it simply a worse trap for human reason. The essential thing is not this negative detail that the shepherd and engineer are not answerable to the sheep and gasoline, but the positive principle that the men who are shepherds and the men who are engineers are answerable to other men,— in last analysis to all other men, and not simply to the shepherds and sheep-owners or to the engineers and owners of oil wells. The essential to be remembered is that success comes from the fact that the supreme judges of the specialists are not the best of specialized minds but the commonest of lay minds, and that the specialists must bring the government of sheep and gasoline by men to that point of perfection where a child can govern them.

The way, then, to solve the great central problem of freedom, the problem of government in all respects of the people by the people for the people, is neither to depend on the bulk of men, who have no particular aptitude for or interest in the problems of politics, to work out the solution, nor to make those who have this aptitude and interest, those who are the best political engineers or philosophers or statesmen or rulers, answerable only to themselves. The solution is to assure man, alone and in society, equally the rights of man. It means freely allowing any one who is politically-minded to devote himself to political problems as much as he pleases, while reserving the right of passing judgment freely and frequently on his work to the rest of men,—to the engineer-minded, farmer-minded, artistic-, financial-, economic-, business-, doctor-, research-, artisan-, manual-, and other-minded men who compose the common political men.

These men do not want to think out their political problems for themselves any more than the man with a bent for governing men wants to work out for himself the problem of the automobile. The man who delights in making the soil grow two ears of corn where one grew before does not want to stop and fumble with the problem of how to distribute

the extra ears, or of how to make his own body cease growing a cancer. The cry for leadership in politics is simply the demand by us all that our political inventors and explorers invent and discover for us as all our other inventors and explorers are doing—as each of us who is following his natural bent is doing. We are tired of seeing them come whining to us with their difficulties and with their problems to solve, instead of bringing us their solutions to judge. We want them to stop blaming our stupidity when we reject their truths, we want them to get down to their business of making their political truths so clear that a child can understand them.

They need not worry then about our verdict. They need only fear that we will vote so overwhelmingly for their truth as either to handicap by our gratitude their further search for truth, or to cause us to over-reach their truth and fall again into error. When our vote is expessed by purchase we vote as readily for the man who makes his truth most clear in automobiles or oil or steel or other things that we load him now with a tremendous fortune liable to give him a diseased idea of his own importance, or dull his children's enterprise. Or we force him to leave the thing he can best do and try to solve a problem for which he may have no aptitude,—the problem of the distribution of wealth, of making the most of it to bring more freedom to himself and children and everyone by en-couraging art, scholarship, medicine, industry, men. When the vote is by applause instead of purchase we fill the lives of our Lindberghs with so much applause that we deprive them of that freedom to live and act as simple folk which allowed them to do their greatest work.

When a Washington's firm grasp of truth liberates us our gratitude is such that, to show our pious respect for him, we make it heresy to follow his example and meet the problems of our time so boldly as to rebel against the "thus far and no farther" of the past. When a Lincoln makes the equality and rights of man clearer we are so grateful that we make a myth of a man who was proud of being a common human man, we forget that in so doing we fall into the very fault from which he sought to save us—that of disprizing or dishonoring members of our own species. What Jesus rebuked the Jews for doing to Abraham, the Chris-tians soon were doing to Jesus, and for the same reason, to show their gratitude.

We are so ready to admit any man's truth if it is only made clear enough, so grateful to those who make it clear and so cursed with an in-feriority complex about our species, that great teachers and liberators who seek to bring men to a truer concept of the equal dignity and rights of man need to guard against our deifying them more or less, or other-wise emotionally clouding over their central truth,—that Man, as Paine said, is Man's "high and only title, and a higher cannot be given him."

There is no more effective way than this democratic way for each of us to free ourselves from the tyranny of poverty, and disease, and ignorance, and matter, and time. There is no simpler, no safer and no cheaper way. No elaborate machinery of selection and reward is required: This is simply a question of freeing men so that their nature can most naturally take its own course. Everyone wants to do what gives him joy, and everyone is doing best his share in society when he is doing that which gives him the most joy.

The profit motive? True, it exists, and it is a mistake to rail at it or try to remove it. Whether he measures it in money, power, or whatnot, man will seek profit, and he should, for it is the fuel that moves perhaps the greatest force on earth, individual enterprise. Profit is but the surplus difference between what one puts into a thing and what he gets out of it, and nothing living grows except by getting back all it expends and something more. It is not profit we need weed out but the three evils, too much profit, too little profit, and dead loss,—for each of these dulls or kills individual enterprise. Provide a condition of freedom and security for the individual to develop his natural talent and let him profit enough materially from his work to live fairly well and he needs little or no further encouragement to bring us the best he has. He is not working for money beyond what he needs to live comfortably and do his work.

The proof is that when he finds some way of further freeing us we cannot keep him silent with bribes or even with comforts. He will do without comfort, spend all his money, borrow all he can, slave through day and night, wear himself out, risk his life, he will do anything he needs to do simply to solve a problem he has freely set for himself and force us by our common sense to agree that he is right,—that we *can* free ourselves from malaria by killing a certain mosquito, that we *can* free ourselves from earth and fly. Men who are doing what they can do best we do not need to encourage with millions in money; we can not contrive to discourage the men who are doing what they were made to do.

Every revolution, every great human crisis invariably shows that there is far more talent scattered through our species, and in the most unexpected places, than we imagine. There seems to be no limit to the power of individual enterprise, and there is no resource in which we are richer than individual men and women, and none we use less or waste so appallingly. We deal with refugees as if men were liabilities instead of assets.

All manner of means for freeing men are to be found widespread among men. We had no way of divining that the man who would give us paper would be born in China, and that an Arab would bring it to us, an Englishwoman would give us a Turk's idea of vaccinating against

smallpox, an Italian would give us wireless, a German Jew would find the cure of syphilis with the help of a Japanese, and that negroes instead of white men would be the first slaves to establish an enduring republic of self-freed slaves. No one could have predicted that a Pole would be the writer who would bring the salt of the sea best in English to the English, or that a Dutch dry-goods merchant would be the man to make the lens that freed our eyes to discover the miscroscopic world. We can no more tell today what bargeman on what river will rise to steer our freedom through a dangerous civil conflict than our great-grandfathers could tell that a lanky Mississippi raftsman would be the man to save from suicide the first great union of the free.

We have no way of telling from what family, nation, race or class our future liberators will come, or from what farm, village, city, country, empire. We have no way of knowing that our cook will never change one day into a poet, our miller into chemist, our farmer into flier.

Yet there are some things we know, for they have been proved a million times. We know that men will not stay put, that great changes are continually happening in them, that the liberating genius of man is concentrated in no family or place but is scattered generously through the whole species. We know a ray of it was here yesterday, there today. We can divine only that it may be somewhere else tomorrow. We know that not even one beam of it is the monopoly of any man.

We know that our greatest liberators are those who make their liberating truth most clear to all of us. Their greatness is in proportion to the speed with which they can get us voluntarily to absorb and assimilate their truth as fully as they have themselves. The sooner they can free us from the need of their expert services, the more they allow us to build further on the top brick they have laid until that top brick becomes indistinguishable from all the bricks above and below and around it.

We are beholden the least to those who seek to maintain themselves longest in a position of superiority to us and convert a truth they have found into a permanent source of tribute to themselves. Our true benefactors never seek to impose themselves or their children on us, never seek in any field, political or other, to be answerable to us only once for all time, or to alienate in the slightest those inalienable rights of man that allowed them to do themselves whatever they have done. The mark of the spurious liberator, of the autocrat in every field, is the desire to make oneself more and more indispensable to mankind. We know that our true liberator frees us more and more from dependence on him and seeks only to enable others to outstrip him,—he is a man of the great, proud line of Whitman:

I am the teacher of athletes;
He that by me spreads a wider breast than my own proves the width
of my own;
He most honors my style who learns under it to destroy the teacher.

We know all this and in our hearts we know too that for each of us
to gain the most freedom we must all keep all the doors to life forever
freely open to every man and woman.

At the heart of our freedom, then, lies the democratic principle of the
equality and rights of man, the freedom of the individual to follow his
natural bent and to bring his findings to mankind for judgment and to
pass judgment on the findings of his fellows. And at the heart of the
rights of man lies the freedom of speech and of the press. Do you still
think that freedom of speech and of the press is concerned simply with
politics and words? Read then this letter written by the School Board
of Lancaster, Ohio, in 1826 and unearthed in 1920 by the *Cleveland Press*:

You are welcome to use the schoolhouse to debate all proper questions
in, but such things as railroads are impossibilities and rank infidelity.
There is nothing in the Word of God about them. If God designed that
His intelligent creatures should travel at the frightful speed of 15 miles
an hour by steam, He would have clearly foretold it through His holy
prophets. It is a device to lead immortal souls down to hell.

The glory of Elizabethan England to me is Peter Wentworth. He was
the one who reminded the House of the rumors of what the Queen would
do to those who opposed certain bills, and of her messages commanding
Parliament not to consider certain measures, and who then spoke out:
"I would to God, Mr. Speaker, that these two were buried in hell, I mean
rumors and messages." For this the House itself sent him to the Tower.
When he came back a year later he spoke again for the right to speak
freely in at least the House of Speech, and again he was sent to the Tower.

The glory of Elizabethan England is likewise John Stubbs and his
printer, and those who stood with them. John Stubbs wrote a pamphlet
protesting against Elizabeth's proposed marriage with Alençon, and for
this he and his printer were condemned to have their right hands cut off.
The lawyers and judges who protested were put in the Tower, and the
right hands of John Stubbs and his printer were cut off at the wrist by
a knife driven through with a mallet. With his left hand John Stubbs then
waved his hat and cried, "God save the Queen!" And though her Star
Chamber might a little while continue to assert the need of limiting "the
excessive multitude of printers," her cruelty shocked and his fortitude

encouraged people, and their children rose up in one hundred years and made the first king subject to the first Bill of the Rights of Man.

And now their children's children and all of us may go freely to the National Portrait Gallery in London and find one small room on the top floor big enough not only for Elizabeth and the great men of her time (not Wentworth, not Stubbs), but also for Henry VIII and the greater of those whose heads he had cut off. But as we go on down chronologically through the rooms and centuries, and the crude absolutist method of men governing men by cutting off their heads and hands gradually gives way to men governing men by the free speech principles of the Wentworths and by the free press principles of the Stubbses and by the other rights of man they led to, the scene changes. Where there were only a few portraits for each reign, and these only of monarchs, princes, ministers, generals, priests, with now and then a writer, poet, artist, or scholar, the number of portraits grows, and the variety with it more and more, until on the ground floor we find the nineteenth century needing room after room to house the great of England. There the monarchs, generals and priests become a minority amid the Shelleys and Jane Austens and Butlers, the Disraelis and Gladstones, the Benthams and Mills, the Stephensons and Faradays and Listers and Huxleys and Darwins.

Such is the great flowering of the genius of man that every people has enjoyed and is enjoying as they have enjoyed and are enjoying equally the rights of man.

In another gallery I looked at Leonardo's works after coming up through the centuries at the Italian Art Exposition in Paris in 1935, and it dawned on me that before his century the best eyes in Italy had been blind to the beauty in the play of light, blind to shadow. I walked back then through the centuries seeking shadow: Cimabue, Giotto, blind to shadow; Uccello discovering perspective but ignoring shadow; then here and there a painting with here and there a shadow,—the shell in Botticelli's *Birth of Venus* casting a shadow, but not Venus nor any of the figures nor the trees, no real perception of shadow there. Shadow always everywhere and everyone blind to it until somehow one man saw shadow clearly, and then everyone thereafter seeing shadow.

Why did we need so long to make the simple, invaluable wheel? Could man ever help but see the circular? Nature is all curves. It would seem that man must have made the wheel long before achieving that miracle of abstract reason, the brick. For men could not see so easily the square, cube, or straight line in Nature. These man created. Yet America knew the square before Columbus came, but not the wheel. Ages before mentioning the wheel, the Bible celebrates in the tale of Babel not only the confusion of tongues but the discovery of how to "make brick" and all

it meant to men—how since "this they begin to do . . . now nothing will be restrained from them" while "the people is one" and "have all one language,"—not even the achievement of the great ideal that mankind then at once magnificently set out for: The building of "a city and a tower whose top may reach unto heaven."

The fact is that the wheel, despite all Nature's hints, also required a miracle of pure reason. To turn the first natural disk into the first wheel one had to see something that was there no more and no less than the straight line. Something invisible, abstract, yet so tangibly there that one needed only to put finger and thumb on it to make all men see— the axis, and wheels everywhere.

The marvelous thing about us is not simply that it took so many men for one to see the axis. It is perhaps even more marvelous that it took only one to see it and demonstrate it clearly for each of us to see it at once, and for all of us to keep it forever after. It is this marvelous power in our species that democracy harnesses through its equal interest in and equal freedom for every individual.

Underlying alike the brick and the wheel is a greater miracle—Man's creation of the straight line. How could it have taken us eras to see a truth so simple and precious as the straight line? How many simple things of truth, of beauty, of priceless value, lie today around us all, unseen, awaiting the marvel of sight by some one becoming sight by all?

Surely in such a world we can not fail to keep building on the simple truth of which we have had such proof: That Man's vast future lies in the democratic philosophy that would give every one an equal chance, an equal freedom to tell us all whatever truth he alone has seen or believes that he has seen, an equal obligation to express his truth with that clarity and simplicity that makes us all see it and thereby proves it true, and an equal right to refuse to accept whatever one alone still doubts is true, an equal veto against whatever one alone believes is false.

OF CAIN AND ABEL, SOCRATES, JESUS AND MOHAMMED

To understand is what is hard. Once one understands, action is easy.— Sun Yat Sen.

*We learn to understand the new by studying the old.—*Confucius.

We shall now combine our individual power into one great power which is this confederacy and we shall therefore symbolize the union of these powers by each nation contributing one arrow, which we shall tie up together in a bundle which, when it is made and completely bound together, no one can bend or break . . .

This bundle of arrows signifies that all the lords and all the warriors and

all the women of the Confederacy have become united as one person.—
Laws of the Confederacy of the Five Nations, or Iroquois Indians.

Man's freedom began with men uniting. Both love of kin and love of country have served our species as a means of freeing man by uniting men. Blood patriotism built the family into the nomad tribe and allowed man, through the taming of the horse, sheep and cow, to free himself from some of his natural limitations. As he freed himself from subjection to the accidents of the hunt, he settled down and land patriotism rose to free him and his beasts from Winter's hunger and cold and from the accidents to which the hunter and nomad herdsman are prey. It grew through blood barriers, brought tribes together, tied the nomads not only to the land but packed them together and built the City. It grew through centuries of warfare between nomad and husbandman, which (as I learned from George Cram Cook one day in the ruined temple of the Delphic oracle) are compressed in the tale of Cain and Abel.

Cain was the first man known to love his country. Before his time there was no fatherland. There was only father. The nomad patriot abhorred the thought of being bound to the land where he happened to be born. He roamed the earth. Love of a common father and common aversion to the land held together the nomad tribe. Then came Cain.

Cain settled down. "Cain was a tiller of the ground." He brought to the Lord Judge the fruits of the soil as his offering. But Abel remained "a keeper of sheep," and "brought of the firstlings of his flock and of the fat thereof. And the Lord had respect unto Abel and to his offering: But unto Cain and to his offering he had not respect. And Cain was very wroth." Neither the Judge who in favoring the conservative had promised the innovator, "If thou doest well, shalt thou not be accepted? and . . . thou shalt rule over him," nor the tribal bond of blood could prevent the conflict. "Cain rose up against his brother, and slew him . . . and builded a city."

The city united more men in a closer compass than the flock or farm, and with it rose great empires, Nineveh, Babylon, spreading through mankind the fruits of the city's work in freeing man from his limitations. So it was that human wisdom grew strong and brave enough in Athens to take "Know thyself" for motto and to begin to think and talk in terms of individual freedom and universal union. It looked upon the slaves tilling the earth and revolted against the dogma that man's freedom must remain bound to the soil. It questioned the love of country on which the city's civilization was based, and asked as did the philosophers whose horrified countrymen called them Cynics, dogs, "Why should I be proud of belonging to the soil of Attica with the worms and slugs?" And it realized

primitively, as Plutarch said of Alexander, "the Cynic ideal on its political side by the foundation of universal empire."

"The Cynics," says Professor Barker, "were descended from Socrates; and the Cynics were cosmopolitans, who found their own reason and knowledge sufficient for their needs, and, craving no guidance or instruction from any city, took the world to be their home." With them, as he points out, "two new ideas are entering the world, both destined to a long history—the idea that all men are naturally equal, and the idea that they are all by nature brothers in a single human society . . . While the city-state lay dying, and while Aristotle busied himself with medicines and dietaries, Diogenes [greatest of the Cynics] lifted up his voice, and cried—The King is dying, is dead: long live the new King of the world."

Then came Jesus teaching men to render unto Caesar the things that are Caesar's and unto God the things that are God's,—to decide each in his own conscience which things are Caesar's and which things are God's, to decide each for himself what he owes to the gods of other men and what he owes to the god within himself.

Jesus went unto the mount of Olives . . . saying, I am the light of the world: he that followeth me shall not walk in darkness, but shall have the light of life.

The Pharisees therefore said unto him, Thou bearest record of thyself; thy record is not true.

Jesus answered . . . Though I bear record of myself, yet my record is true . . . And ye shall know the truth, and the truth shall make you free.

They answered him, We be Abraham's seed, and were never in bondage to any man: how sayest thou, Ye shall be made free?

Jesus answered them, . . . I speak that which I have seen with my Father: and ye do that which ye have seen with your father.

They answered . . . Abraham is our father.

Jesus saith unto them, If ye were Abraham's children, ye would do the works of Abraham. But now ye seek to kill me, a man that hath told you the truth, which I have heard of God: this did not Abraham . . . Your father Abraham rejoiced to see my day.

Then said the Jews . . . Thou art not yet fifty years old, and hast thou seen Abraham?

Jesus said unto them, Verily, verily, I say unto you, Before Abraham was, I am.

Then came Mohammed to be hailed too as a liberator, and first by the slaves, and first of all by woman. He came into a society where a man inherited his mother as part of his father's property, wore sackcloth and ashes when a girl-child was born, and buried alive in the sand the sex

that brought poverty-ridden men more mouths to feed. From the beginning of his first Sura Mohammed stood out against that society "in the name of the Compassionate, the Merciful, the most Beneficent, who hath taught the use of the pen." Among his earliest prophecies was the prophecy that a day would come "when the female child that had been buried alive shall be asked for what crime she was put to death" and each individual "soul shall know what it hath produced." He freed the girl-child from burial alive, and her mother from slavery, and through him tens of millions of women received economic rights that Christendom did not allow until modern times. He freed not only man from the myth that he was made of earth but woman from the myth that she was made of man. Mohammed rationally taught (Sura 46:46), "He hath created the sexes, male and female, from the diffused germs of life." He freed woman from the burden of original sin, placing it equally on Adam and Eve in Sura 87. Where Paul taught the Christians:

Let your women keep silence in the churches: for it is not permitted unto them to speak; but they are commanded to be under obedience, as also saith the law. (I Cor. 14:34)

Mohammed preached a single standard of morality for man and woman, repeatedly bracketing together the two sexes as in Sura 103:

Truly the men who resign themselves to God, and the women who resign themselves, and the believing men and the believing women, and the devout men and the devout women, and the men of truth and the women of truth, and the patient men and the patient women, and the humble men and the humble women, and the men who give alms and the women who give alms, and the men who fast and the women who fast, and the chaste men and the chaste women, and the men and the women who oft remember God: for them hath God prepared forgiveness and a rich recompense.

It would seem that Mohammed had eliminated every possibility of ambiguity, yet—such are the wonders of propaganda—Christians generally condemn this early feminist as a man who degraded woman and left her out of paradise.

The truth that Jesus brought to make men free was so misunderstood that his followers soon came to glory in filth of body and ignorance of mind* as signs of grace. They converted one of the most liberating of doc-

* J. A. Symonds (*Renaissance in Italy*, 160-61) gives some amusing examples of how the monks paraded their lack of grammar: "I warn the curious reader," writes a certain Wolfherd in the Life of St. Walpurgis, "not to mind the mass of barbarisms in this litle work; I bid him ponder what he finds upon these pages, and seek the pearl within the dung-heap." Gregory the Great goes further and defies the pedantry

trines into an authoritarian institution and a dogma that has kept many men and women from striving after and enjoying truer and freer lives by promising them paradise when they die if only they suffer till then the evils of this world. The freedom Mohammed brought was corrupted until Mohammedan came to connote the seclusion of woman, and Islam, which means "to make peace," came to connote Holy War. "For eleven hundred years," sadly notes that devout Catholic, Lord Acton, "from the first to the last Constantine, the Christian Empire was as despotic as the pagan." The Moslem empires fared no better.

Yet the teaching of Jesus with its appeal to the individual and to all mankind, instead of to the rulers of men, or to this or that tribe or nation of men, survived to do great service to human freedom. So, too, with the teachings of Mohammed: They led to the wisdom of many of the Cynic and other Greek philosophers being saved from the Christians, and to the printed Bible being made possible by the bringing of paper from China to the West, and to Voltaire pointing to the Turks,* when he wrote his *Essay on Tolerance*, as an example for the world to follow.

Like the means of uniting men that preceded it the modern dogma of nationalism is but an idea of men, no more, no less. It is a combination of the patriotism of blood and the patriotism of land, of the ideas of *jus sanguinis* and *jus soli* as the lawyers who try to separate them say,—a confused and confusing mixture of our throwback to the nomad bound to his beasts and to the peasant bound to the soil.

It is historically a *parvenu*. It was not known in the time of Jesus nor during the long centuries when what a European believed about God mattered more than his blood or land. As for the Moslem world, until the Turkish Republic was established Islam asked the traveller for his religious belief rather than his nationality; it organized men politically in its empires by religions and not by nations. There was so little nationalist patriotism in the great century of discovery that scarce an important explorer sailed under the flag of his birth, and a Portuguese captain, Magellan, angry

---

of pedagogues. "The place of prepositions and the case of the nouns I utterly despise, since I deem it unfit to confine the word of the celestial oracle within the rules of Donatus." . . . Writes a fanatic of Cordova . . . "let the foaming and bespittled grammarians belch, while we remain evangelical servants of Christ, true followers of rustic teachers."

* When I was in Ankara in 1921 I found above the Speaker's chair in the Grand National Assembly of Turkey this verse of Mohammed: "Solve your problems by meeting together and discussing them." I found a woman, Halidé Edib Hanum, occupying a far more important role in that revolution than any woman held in the American Revolution, and when I remarked that the Turkish girls' schools I visited were better than the boys', Lieutenant Tewfik Bey answered: "You see, we think that if the mothers are well educated, the sons will surely be."

when refused an increase in pay in Portugal, went over to Charles V of Spain and, to prove to him that the Spice Islands were not in the zone the Pope had given Portugal, set out on the voyage that proved the world is round.

Nationalism really began to flourish only in the nineteenth century when it did for freedom the great service of uniting the numerous petty states of Italy and Germany into two great peoples. It rose as a means of securing those wider and stronger political organizations which the steam engine and other inventions were making more and more necessary. It rose too as a democratic offshoot, as a lever for supplanting absolute royal sovereignty with popular sovereignty, and alien rule with home rule.

Nationalism reached its crest early in our century when the major nations were united to the point where further application of this principle was bound, because of the multiplicity of small nations in such states as Austria, Russia and Turkey, to begin dividing the world more into small compartments than integrating it on the greater scale that the gasoline engine and electrical and other inventions were making increasingly necessary. Since nationalism united men by making all important not Man's need of union but things separating one group from others, it could not possibly unite into one state the groups it had united as nations, except by the imperialist methods to which the greater nations turned. Its stress on points of difference between nations, once this stress had brought most of their nationals together, could only keep mankind divided and make for greater misunderstandings, quarrels and wars.

Nationalism's main positive, constructive, integrating work being done, all the human force and sentiment and gratitude which its liberating work had gathered behind it could only pour into and operate the negative, destructive, disintegrating principles inherent in it from the start. And so we had the World War of Nations, for the place in the sun of big nations, for the rights of small nations to independence and self-determination, and, as the need of organizing the world to prevent a return of this nationalist inferno grew more imperious, for a league of nations.

This period of transition was marked, as all such periods must be, by both the forces involved, by the one ending and by the one beginning. The constructive, liberating side of nationalism in its death agony served human freedom by creating in the League and International Labor Organization and Court and Bank the first such world institutions to live, and by thus preparing the way for the Union of free men.

It served human freedom in other ways too. It replaced the remaining hereditary autocracies in the West—Russian, German, Austrian and Turkish—with more democratic governments. It restored to the human equality and dignity that all men crave such peoples as the Poles and Czechs,

whose position became intolerably inferior once the theory of nationalism succeeded religion and dynasty as the basis of politics and the popular criterion of liberty. It gave new life to other peoples such as the Chinese and Turks and made them a better medium for their own westernization than imperialism could possibly have been.

But when all is said, it remains true that in our generation nationalism reached its logical limits, its constructive elements began to wane and its destructive ones to wax, until its spiral definitely turned downward. It is operating less and less to bring men together and more and more to keep men apart. It has turned against both society and the individual, it has changed masters and quit serving the freedom of man to serve the freedom of the state—as was shown so strikingly when 3,000,000 Sudetens were deprived of their individual freedom and delivered to autocracy in the name of democratic self-determination. Like everything that has outlived its usefulness nationalism has changed from a beneficent into a maleficent force; it can only lead backward and downward now those whom it helped prepare for that greater union of men which their civilization and machines demand so impatiently.

The political theories which the tribesman and the countryman and the nationalist represent have in common not merely their high motive but their basic method. They all seek, however unconsciously, to free man from the tyranny of accident by getting and keeping men working together and they all try to unite men by subjecting them to the same thing, to one accident, the accident of how or where they happened to be born. They all try to subject men to this accident and make it the all-determining thing for each individual by circling it with magic or mysticism.

Nationalism was saved for a while from its basic irrationalism by its early connections with democratic rationalism. Its rapid degeneration now may be seen from the way it is galloping back behind Guide Hitler to the nomad's belief in the superiority of the tribal blood and tribal gods. Such priestcraft may still be necessary among the more backward peoples—and it is for each people to say for itself through its institutions and its leaders how politically backward it is.

But while nationalism was growing there was also growing up another means of uniting men, democratic Union. It stemmed from Socrates and Jesus rather than from Cain and Abel. It grew out of the Renaissance that ceased appealing to Aristotelian authority and returned to the democratic appeal to reason that produced Greek philosophy and made Athens great in the days when Pericles said, "These things are made for men, not men for them." It rose too from the Reformation that sent the individual back from the authority of the Pope to the Word itself, and to its doctrine that "the sabbath was made for man, and not man for the sabbath," and its

insistence on the equality of the soul of man and the importance of the humblest person.

It came up with the English and the American and the French revolutions to unite men for their *Bill of Rights*, for the principle that *all men are created equal*, for the ideals of *Liberté Egalité Fraternité*. The men it has freed no longer need mysticism to keep them together, they need only Union now to bring them all together to free mankind still more. They have now enough experience behind them and intelligence in them to understand that freedom lies in free men freely uniting, trusting in each other and depending on each other. They are mature enough to understand that the way to man's freedom can not possibly lie in worshiping the accident of birth. They know that freedom for each can lie only in men freeing all the billion possibilities that the billions of men can alone supply for the billion-sided task of freeing man from accident's arbitrary rule. They know that to free man from the accident of death they must begin by freeing his mind from the accident of birth.

OF UNION

Liberty and Union, now and forever, one and inseparable.—Webster.

There never was an independent man, or nation, or empire, and there never will be. To think these possible is foolish. It is worse to believe that one has achieved them, to glory proudly in one's independence or his nation's. It is shameful.

There is no shame in admitting one's dependence on his fellows, and the dependence of one's nation on one's species—dependence not only on the living but on the billions and billions of men who have brought us painfully up. We need not blush to remember that in the sweat of arms like ours was paved the path on which we stroll, that through a human patience perhaps surpassing ours our enemy the wolf was made our friend the dog, that we owe much to the boldness of Xerxes in defying the gods by throwing the first bridge across the Hellespont, and to the courage of the Spartans at Thermopylae and to the wisdom that Socrates by his way of dying carried far beyond the grave.

We need not hang our heads in recognizing that minds and hands like ours are somewhere in nearly everything we see and are protectingly around us wherever we may be, that they discovered the microbes that cling to fingers and made the waxed paper and invented the machines to put it round the food we announce "no human hand has touched." There is no shame in being mindful of our dependence on the men who today are tapping the rubber tree in the tropics, trapping the fox in the Arctic, brav-

ing the explosive gas of the coal mine, feeding the hungry silkworm, watching the whirring spindles, cleaning the streets and the surgeons' lances, tracking the storm to its lair in Greenland and fever to its marsh in Africa, guarding the thoroughfare we crowd and the lonely reef that lies in ambush for us.

The shame lies instead in forgetting all or anything we owe our species, in exaggerating what little mankind owes to us, in combining ingratitude, conceit and usurpation to make a patriotic virtue, and in professing that we are self-made and independent. The shameful thing is for a man to think that mankind is in his debt when the balance is struck between what mankind has done and is doing every day for him, and what he has done to make his species freer and happier. It is still more shameful to act as if mankind were so much in his debt as to justify his receiving, and his children and his children's children receiving, millions more than other men, or political, social or other title and position whose possession needs no further justification—no matter how many other benefactions other men confer thereafter on society. The shame is not lessened when such delusions of grandeur are enjoyed by masses of men instead of by individuals, when a whole nation assumes that it has given more than it has received, that there is something naturally superior and peculiarly sacred in it, that it is the Elect of God or the Chosen People, that it was meant to be the lord of others. These are the things that are shameful in men, and they are shameful because they are so tawdry and false and unworthy of a species whose name gives us the adjective, *manly*.

The freedom of man goes hand in hand with the inter-dependence of men, whether organized as a democracy or union or on some other basis or tacit. This is true in every field, it has always been true, and the more our freedom and self-reliance has grown, the more inter-dependent we have become and the more we have needed union with more men.

It is a common thing to find a man who treats all the rest of us as stupid, as obstacles in his path from which he longs to be free. Each of us has sometimes felt that way about some or all of the rest of us. It is natural that we should, that each man should always be ready to indict the mass of mankind as stupid. We are so made that all of us are ignorant and awkward and stupid in far more ways than we are skilled and wise. That in itself tends to make us esteem more our own wisdom where we have it. The fewer the things in which we are wise the more value we set, of course, on our wisdom and the more irritating becomes the stupidity of our fellows in the field where we are wiser.

But the interesting side of this is the other side of the medal, for it is the positive side. Though a man may be stupid in no matter how many things, he is almost certainly more skilled or wiser than most of us in some

few things, or at least in some one thing. "In every god there is something divine," Anatole France remarked, and we can add that in every man there is some of Man. I once had a cook who I thought was a hopeless moron until one day she made an apple pie. It was the one thing she knew how to do, it was her specialty, but she could do it so succulently well that one forgave her a heap of other things.

The man who was no good at pie-making would be a fool not to depend on her for apple pies, and the one who could make pies but not so well would be a fool not to depend on her for instruction. This example being typical, we can smile while minorities of different experts nearly 2,000,-000,000 strong accuse our (and their) species of a hundred million stupidities. We can be sure our species will survive and each of us will grow richer and wiser and freer so long as we enjoy this wealth in minorities of experts—and are not so stupid as to try to be independent of any of them.

Put in other terms, the wildest reactionary is never 100 per cent conservative, and the wildest revolutionary is never 100 per cent rebel. Our Neville Chamberlains are the first to rebel at the cut-and-dried methods of diplomacy, our Lenins are conservative not only in their habit of dress but in a host of other things. Conservatism and radicalism partly result from men differing in the velocity of their adaptability to change, and from this standpoint the most hide-bound among us would appear a flighty revolutionist to his own great-grandfather. Some of course in every generation adapt themselves to or welcome change in general relatively more than others, but usually we are each conservative about many things and actively rebellious against only a few. And generally our radicalism comes out in the things we know the best, and we resent change most in the things we know the least or have just gained knowledge of.

But the result of our division into conservatives and rebels is that though we can not depend on ourselves not to atrophy or grow stagnant or lax or careless in some directions we can depend absolutely on our species never lacking plenty of men either to rebel against every conceivable obstacle to the freedom of man, or to conserve every bit of the freedom won by yesterday's rebels until those of today prove the new bit of freedom that they bring is really worthy of acceptance. This may not conduce to our independence, but can we have a better way than this to free ourselves?

It is not our greatest men who think it beneath them to acknowledge their dependence on others. They teach us not to depend on ourselves alone if we would free what is individual in us, but to study diligently other men who are masters, for, as Sir Joshua Reynolds said, "The more extensive your acquaintance with the works of those who have excelled, the more extensive will be your powers of invention . . . and what may

appear still more like a paradox, the more original will be your conceptions."

As it is with those lonely venturers, our great men in every field, so it is with those who are pioneers in the narrower sense of the word. If any man can be called independent it is the pioneer who goes out into the wilderness and carves out his home, the man of the type of Mr. Bulow, the Connecticut farmer who took Brillat-Savarin on a turkey hunt in 1794 in the forest near Hartford, and who, the great epicure narrates, thus described himself:

"You see in me, Sir, a happy man, if there is one under Heaven: Everything around you and every thing you have seen in my home come from my own property. These stockings, my daughters knitted them; my shoes and my clothes came from my flocks, which contribute, too, with my garden and poultry-yard, to supply me with plain and substantial food."

Yet in the next breath Mr. Bulow (with Shays's rebellion and the hard times of the Confederation only seven years gone and the American Union only five years old) attributes his happy lot to union with and trust in his fellows, saying:

"The great thing about our government is that you can count in Connecticut thousands of farmers as contented as I am, and whose doors, like mine, are never locked. Our taxes are next to nothing, and as long as they are paid we can sleep soundly. Congress favors in every way our budding industry . . . All we have comes from the freedom we have won and founded on good laws."

It was these pioneers of Connecticut who were among the first to sacrifice the sovereignty of the state and ratify the Constitution of the United States. Their forebears, the first men to pioneer in Connecticut, Lord Acton notes, "possessed so finished a system of self-government in the towns, that it served as a model for the federal Constitution." As early as 1638 a pioneer was preaching in the primeval Connecticut forest the dependence of men on each other, and of their rulers on them, saying: "The choice of public magistrates belongs unto the people, by God's own allowance. They who have the power to appoint officers and magistrates, it is in their power, also, to set the bounds and limitations of the power and place unto which they call them."

It was precisely in these conditions, when civilized man was thrown in the American wilderness most upon his own resources that the elemental fact of his dependence on his fellows was most driven home to him, and men came to realize that their freedom lay in trusting in each other, in pulling together, in uniting freely on the basis of the equal rights and dignity of each of them. It was in these pioneering conditions that these

American colonies, before they constituted their Union, united under state constitutions that form the first written constitutions in history superior to and limiting the government and alterable only by the people themselves. When enlightened men were most alone against the world in America they put first things first and began most of these state constitutions by asserting first the Rights of Man, and then providing in the second part a broad plan of self-government designed to secure through the Union of men their inalienable rights to individual freedom.

As the pioneers moved westward through the American wilderness enlightened men for 200 years had to depend on women to do not only a woman's work but a man's work too,—to seize the reins and drive the covered wagon while the man stood off the Indians, to take his rifle and defend the children when he fell or was away. Pioneering conditions made so clear the dependence of men and women on each other that there finally began in the Rocky Mountains, with man's free acknowledgment of the equal right of woman to the vote and to everything else, the liberation of half the human race. There never were men more independent than the cowmen and prospectors and homesteaders of Wyoming in 1868, and they were the first thus to recognize and extend their dependence on women.

Our freedom has always been inseparably bound to our faith in our fellows, and the more of them we have trusted, and the more implicitly, blindly, we have depended on each of our fellow-men—no matter what race, nation, class or sex—the more we have been rewarded with freedom. Truly of the stuff of dreams is our species made.

Men talk excitedly of crime waves. We are so good at heart that for every house built as a prison there are a hundred thousand homes where live law-abiding men. No country needs more than a tiny fraction of its population for police, and the freer the people the fewer the police. There were 160 crimes for which men were put to death in England when Blackstone wrote and George III reigned. In that century when England grew such men as Paine and Burke a man guilty of high treason was cut down when half hung, disembowelled and his bowels burned before him, and his body then was quartered. The law for pressing with weights a prisoner who refused to plead was not repealed until 1771, and down to 1790 Englishwomen who murdered their husbands were publicly burned to death. There is no such ferocity now in England, and though the population is far greater there is much less crime and only one prisoner to 4,000 people. There is also now far more freedom and trust by Englishmen in each other.

Two hundred, one hundred, fifty years ago one finds everywhere in every field far less dependence of men upon each other, and far less free-

dom. Then perhaps ten or a dozen men entrusted themselves for fifty miles to a stage-coach driver with four or six horses, after making inquiry, and scrutinizing their man. Now a thousand men rush into a train and are whisked off sixty miles in an hour. They may do it twice a day through every year or they may cross a continent without ever going up to the locomotive to see what manner of man is there with his hand on the reins of hundreds of horses, with his eye now on his watch and soon searching vigilantly through the mist for the signal lamps.

They may do this all year without it once occurring to them that they are all trusting their lives to a man at the throttle, and to the unknown men who made his watch, and to the man at the throttle of the train hurtling toward them, and to the maker of his watch, and to distant train dispatchers and their watches and clocks, and to the signal men, and to the brakemen, and to the long line of men who made and inspected the making and also the operation of the brakes and the wheels and the cars and the locomotives, and to the men who made and inspected and laid the rails, and to the section hands and the track-walkers, and the bridge-builders and the tunnel-makers. We can not enjoy the freedom from the horse's limitations that a train gives without trusting our lives blindly to the good faith of thousands of unknown men.

While the passenger must have faith in these thousands, they have to trust in millions of passengers having faith enough in the railway to use it. The *Great Eastern*, that 1857 fore-runner of our Atlantic liners, failed not because she lacked room for passengers,—she was longer than nearly all the ocean greyhounds afloat sixty years later,—but because she lacked passengers. She failed because ocean travellers then did not have enough faith in steamships, in their makers and their crews and in men generally.

The train and the ocean liner are two of many wonders that are possible only through the willingness of men to depend utterly on their fellow-men. Wherever we go, whatever we do, we do, we need but keep our eyes open to see the same phenomenon of freedom for each man through faith in every man.

It is in every item in our newspaper as it is in every bed in our hospital. Our newspapers, now that they reach to the ends of the earth for men who are interested in and need to know everything on earth, require for their functioning far more confidence all round than ever before, far more faith in unknown men. The statesman, the banker, the businessman who closes his door on the press, who impatiently tries to dodge when the newsmen surround him may not realize, when he suppresses or distorts or falsifies to them the news of what he has been doing, that he is hurting most himself. Yet however important he may be he has only a few items of news to give compared to all those he needs to get, and the more he

handicaps the newsmen in their work of accurately and quickly reporting the essentials in every field to everyone, the more he contributes to a condition that poisons the air which he himself must breathe.

The newsman who jazzes a story to sell himself to the editor and public, or who is not alert for the true interest and essential in everything, or who fails to do his best to put himself in the shoes of those whose actions or words he is reporting so as to understand the gist of what they are trying to tell the world,—the newsman may not realize it either but the worse he does his job the more he hurts himself, if only because he too must depend on the newspapers for his facts. No men, indeed, depend upon newsmen more than do the newsmen.

Our great-grandfathers rarely trusted their lives to men they did not know, our grandfathers did so only sparingly, but we are doing it all the time, many of us nonchalantly many times a day. Yet it is now, and especially among the more trusting peoples, which is to say the freer peoples, that the death rate is far lower and the span of life is growing. We eat and drink almost anywhere on earth without the fear that man once had that strangers might poison him. We pile into elevators and go dizzily down, we dodge through streets crowded with cars more powerful than the monsters of antiquity, we jump into taxicabs without worrying whether the driver may possibly be drunk—and we never suffer half the qualms that grandfather did.

In his time there were never on the roads nearly so many horse-drawn vehicles as there are now horseless ones. When he was out driving with his girl in the buggy he did not need to trust that the men driving the few buggies he met would keep to their side of the road and not run into him and kill him. He could depend on the other man's horse and his own horse not colliding even if both drivers went to sleep, and he could be reasonably sure that an accident would not be fatal.

Paradoxically the more that men depend upon machines, the more they must depend on men, and on more men. The number of slaves who labored up the Great Pyramid is small compared to the world-scattered, ungeneralled army of free men who now help bring each tourist to see that work of autocrats and slaves.

The doing of a book may seem an independent enterprise, one requiring few hands compared to those needed to bridge the Golden Gate. Yet I would sooner try to count the hair of my head than the men and women who have lent a hand merely on the mechanical side of the writing of this book: The men who felled the trees, who brought them to the paper mill, and mined and smelted its minerals and provided it with chemicals and fuel and grease, who loaned the money to build the mill and provide the machinery for it, who ran the mill and distributed the sheet of paper on

which these words are now being written by a typewriter,—and all the world-scattered men who put that typewriter on this desk (among them far away natives who helped bring it bits of rubber and provided its inked ribbon (we must count in too the cotton-pickers).

And then there is the host of men behind this desk, this chair, this house, this fountain pen, this ink, and behind the universal postal system that carries this "manuscript," and the machines that set in type every letter in it, and the presses that print that type,—and the tale is neither finished nor even complete as far as it goes.

And when we have finished with the mechanical side there would remain the substance of the book. That seems to be something independent, personal, but the book is studded with allusions to only some of those who have lent me a hand. If I sought merely to list all the men and women, great and obscure, known and unknown to me, whom I thank for encouraging me and helping give this book what substance it has, there would be no space left in it. Even to express my thanks I must depend on Lincoln who solved the problem so well when he wrote in his letter to Conkling and the "unconditional Union men" of 1863:

Thanks to all—for the great Republic, for the principle it lives by and keeps alive, for man's vast future,—thanks to all.

I can not even number the individuals, living and dead, upon whom I have had to depend, and upon whom I am glad to depend to bring before your eyes these words:

Let us then all keep clearly in our minds and tightly in our hearts that in Union there is freedom, and that each shall be the freer and happier the more we all recognize our dependence on the individual and the more we each recognize our dependence on each other and on all our species. We are all the losers when one of us is not doing the work that is joy for him, and we are all the gainers when he is doing what he loves to do, for he is then doing his share best. The more deliberately and fully and trustingly we unite with each other and depend upon each other for our freedom, the more we shall solve the problem of so arranging our society that each lives in it more happily and freely. For freedom is like love, the more of it we give, the more of it we can enjoy, and love is like union, too. True love can not do without union, nor can there be full union without love, nor freedom without either, nor either without freedom.

We have too long forgot that freedom and love were born together, and we have yet to learn that they can not live and grow without each other. As a child sometimes sees deeper than a man, so Man, when he was making words for those ethereal solid things that he has never touched and always reached for, saw into them more deeply than we do, and he

made his word for *love* his word for *free*. We have too long forgot that we began *to free* with the Gothic *frijon* and the Sanskrit *pri*, which means, *to love;* we have yet to learn that not simply through the Gothic *frijonds* up from the Sanskrit *priyon* for *beloved* but from the very nature of things stem together *friend* and *freedom*.

Man has on earth no one but Man to help him, and what a mighty, what a generous, what a kindly and abiding and dependable friend and liberator is Man to Man. Man has already wrought miracles of Man by Man for Man. These are great and they are but a hint of those that will be done when our Union opens Man's vast future as each Man pledges each:

Thy freedom is my freedom as is my freedom thine.

Man

Here in a thimble
seed of Man
enough to fill every womb in the land
womb within womb
seed within seed
all in a thimble
Say
what shall we say
of Man?

Myriad myriad
seed of Man
born and dead and back in the land
myriad myriad
still to be sown
and then one day Man shall be grown
Man who shall be
finally free
Then he shall say
　　　　who he is
　　　　why he is
　　　　all he is
　　　　Man.

ANNEXES

These annexes deal with matters that are of secondary importance at this stage of the Union, or illustrate concretely certain points in the book with a view to making these points clearer.

ANNEX 1

Illustrative Constitution

The draft constitution that follows is meant to make the proposed Union clearer by illustrating how the democracies might unite. I would stress what I have already pointed out in Chapter X. This draft is not intended to be a hard and fast plan. Practically all of its provisions, however, are time-tested.

The draft is drawn entirely from the Constitution of the American Union, except for (1) a few provisions that, although not drawn from it, are based on American practice (notably Art. II, sections 1, 2, 4, 5), and (2) a few innovations: These latter are given in italics so that they may be seen at once. Most of the draft taken from the American Constitution has been taken textually, though its provisions have sometimes been re-arranged with a view to greater clarity and condensation, and once or twice they have been made more explicit and somewhat expanded. The Preamble is the only serious example of this last. In the American Constitution the Preamble reads:

We the People of the United States, in order to form a more perfect Union, establish Justice, insure domestic Tranquility, provide for the common defence, promote the general Welfare, and secure the Blessings of Liberty to ourselves and our Posterity, do ordain and establish this Constitution for the United States of America.

No important element in the American Constitution has been omitted. The draft follows:

ILLUSTRATIVE CONSTITUTION

We the people of the Union of the Free, in order to secure freedom equally to every man and woman now and to come, to lessen ignorance, poverty, and disease, to insure our defense, to promote justice and the general welfare, to provide government of ourselves, by ourselves, and for ourselves on the principle of the equality of men, and to bring peace on earth and union to mankind, do establish this as our Constitution.

PART I

THE RIGHTS OF MAN

ARTICLE I.—In the individual freedom this Constitution is made to secure we include:

1. Freedom of speech and of the press and of conscience.

2. Freedom to organize ourselves for any purpose except to change by violence this Constitution and the laws made under it; freedom to assemble peaceably and to ask redress of grievances and make proposals.

3. Freedom of our persons, dwellings, communications, papers and effects from unreasonable searches and seizures, and from warrants unless issued upon probable cause, supported by oath or affirmation, and particularly describing the place to be searched and the persons or things to be seized.

4. Freedom from ex post facto law and from bills of attainder.

5. Freedom from suspension of the writ of habeas corpus except when public safety may temporarily require it in case of rebellion or invasion.

6. Freedom from being held to answer for a capital or infamous crime except on indictment of a grand jury—save in the armed forces in time of war or public danger—and from being twice put in jeopardy of life or limb or liberty for the same offence, and from being deprived of life, liberty, or property without due process of law, and from having property taken for public use without just compensation.

7. The right when accused of any crime to have a speedy public trial by an impartial jury of the country and district wherein the crime shall have been committed, as previously ascertained by law, and to be informed in good time of the nature and cause of the accusation, to be confronted with the witnesses against one, to have compulsory process for obtaining witnesses in one's favor, to be under no compulsion to be a witness against oneself, and to have the assistance of counsel for one's defense.

8. Freedom from excessive bail or excessive fines or cruel and unusual punishments.

9. Freedom from slavery, and from involuntary servitude and forced labor except in legal punishment for crime.

10. The right to equality before the law and to the equal protection of the laws.

11. The preceding enumeration is not exhaustive nor shall it be construed to deny or disparage other rights which we retain.

PART II

THE GOVERNMENT OF THE UNION

ARTICLE II.—THE PEOPLE OF THE UNION.

1. All persons born or naturalized in the self-governing states of the Union are citizens of the Union and of the state wherein they reside. All citizens above the age of 21, except those in institutions for the feeble-minded or mentally deranged or in prison, are entitled to vote in all Union elections, and to hold any Union office for which their age qualifies them.

2. All other persons in the territory of the Union shall enjoy all rights of citizens except the right to vote in Union elections. The Union shall seek to extend this right to them at the earliest time practicable by helping prepare their country to enter the Union as a self-governing state.

3. *The self-governing states of the Union at its foundation are Australia, Belgium, Canada, Denmark, Finland, France, Ireland, the Netherlands, New Zealand, Norway, Sweden, Switzerland, the Union of South Africa, the United Kingdom, and the United States of America.*

4. The non-self-governing territory of these states and of all states admitted later to the Union is transferred to the Union to govern while preparing it for self-government and admission to the Union.

5. *Before casting his or her first vote each citizen of the Union shall take this oath in conditions to be prescribed by law:* "I do solemnly swear (or affirm) that I will preserve, protect and defend the Constitution of the Union of the Free against all enemies, foreign and domestic."*

6. Treason can be committed only by citizens against the Union and can consist only in levying war against it or in adhering to its enemies, aiding and comforting them. No one shall be convicted of treason unless on the testimony of two witnesses to the same overt act or on confession in open court.

ARTICLE III.—RIGHTS OF THE UNION AND OF THE STATES.

1. The Union shall have the right to make and execute all laws necessary and proper for the securing of the rights of man and of the Union and of the states as set forth in this Constitution, and to lay and collect income and other taxes, duties, imposts, and excises, provided these be uniform throughout the Union, and to incur and pay debt, provided that no money

---

* The American Union requires this oath only of naturalized citizens or of citizens entering the Union service or applying for a passport.

shall be drawn from the treasury except by lawful appropriation and that an account of all receipts and expenditures be published regularly.

2. The Union shall have the sole right to

a. grant citizenship in the Union and admit new states into the Union;

b. treat with foreign governments, provide for the Union's defense, raise, maintain and control standing land, sea and air forces, make war and peace, regulate captures, define and punish piracies and felonies committed on the high seas, call forth the militia to execute the laws of the Union, suppress insurrections and repel invasions, organize, arm, discipline, and govern such part of the militia as the Union may employ, and punish treason;

c. regulate commerce among the member states and in the Union territory and with foreign states;

d. coin and issue money, regulate the value thereof and of foreign money, provide for the punishment of counterfeiting, fix the standard of weights and measures;

e. own and operate the postal service and own, operate or control all other inter-state communication services;

f. grant authors and inventors exclusive right to their work for limited periods;

g. provide uniform bankruptcy laws throughout the Union;

h. govern any district the Union may acquire for its seat of government or for forts, magazines, arsenals, dockyards, and other needful Union plant.

3. The Union shall have no right to establish a Union religion, grant hereditary or noble titles, levy any tax or duty on inter-state commerce, subject vessels bound to or from one state to enter, clear, or pay duties in another, grant preference by any regulation of commerce or revenue to one state over another.

4. The rights not expressly given to the Union by the Constitution nor forbidden by it to the states or the people are reserved by it to the states respectively, or to the people.

5. The Union shall guarantee to every state in it a democratic form of government and shall protect each of them and all the territory of the Union against invasion; and on application of the state legislature or executive the Union shall protect each state against domestic violence.

6. Each state has the right to maintain a militia and a police force, but may engage in war only if actually invaded or in such imminent danger as will admit of no delay.

7. Each state has the right to guarantee to the people in it greater rights than those enumerated in this Constitution.

8. No state has the right to

a. abridge the rights, privileges and immunities of citizens of the Union;

b. exercise, except temporarily by consent of the Union, any of the rights given by this Constitution to the Union alone;

c. raise any barriers to inter-state commerce or communications without the consent of the Union;

d. adopt any law impairing the obligation of contracts;

e. enter without the consent of the Union into any pact or agreement with another state or foreign power.

9. Full faith and credit shall be given in each state to the public acts, records and judicial proceedings of every other state in the Union.

10. The citizens of each state shall be entitled to all privileges and immunities of citizens in the several states.

11. A person charged in any state with crime who shall flee and be found in another state shall on demand of the executive authority of the state from which he fled be delivered up to it.

ARTICLE IV.—THE LEGISLATIVE POWER.

1. The legislative power of the Union is vested in the Congress, which shall consist of a House of Deputies and a Senate. Each shall choose its own officers, judge the elections, returns, and qualifications of its own members, determine its rules of procedure, have the power to punish its members for disorderly behavior, to compel their attendance, and to expel them by two-thirds majority; keep and publish a record of its proceedings, meet and vote in public except when two-thirds shall ask for a private meeting on a particular question, vote by roll call when one-fifth of the members ask this, form with a majority a quorum to do business though fewer may adjourn from day to day, act by majority except where otherwise stipulated in this Constitution.

2. The Congress shall meet at least once a year at a regular date it shall fix. During a session neither branch shall adjourn more than three days or to any other place without the other's consent.

3. Members of Congress shall not be questioned outside their branch of it for anything they said in it, nor shall they be arrested on any charge except treason, felony, or breach of the peace, during attendance at a session of Congress or while going to and from it.

4. No member of Congress shall hold other public office in the Union or in a state during his term, *except in the Cabinet.*

5. The Deputies shall be at least 25 years old, and shall be elected directly by the citizens every *third* year.

The number of Deputies from each state shall be determined according to population, a census being taken at least every ten years, and shall not exceed one for every *1,000,000* inhabitants or major fraction thereof, though each state shall have at least one.

6. Senators shall be at least 30 years old, shall have resided since at least 10 years in the State by which elected, and shall be elected at large from each state directly by the citizens every *eight* years, except that in the first election half the Senators of each state shall be elected for only four years. There shall be two Senators from each state *of less than 25,000,000 population, and two more for each additional 25,000,000 population or major fraction thereof.*

7. To begin with the apportionment of Deputies and Senators shall be:

Australia	7	2	Norway		3	2
Belgium	8	2	Sweden		6	2
Canada	11	2	Switzerland		4	2
Denmark	4	2	Union of South Africa		2	2
Finland	4	2	United Kingdom		47	4
France	42	4	United States		126	10
Ireland	3	2				
Netherlands	8	2				
New Zealand	2	2	Totals		287	42

8. To become law a bill must pass the House and the Senate and be approved and signed by *a majority of the Board.** If *a majority of the Board* shall return the bill with its reasons for not signing it, the bill shall become law only if passed again by House and Senate by two-thirds roll-call majority and if a *member of the Board* shall ask to be heard by House or Senate during its debate thereon he shall be heard. A bill not returned by the Board within fifteen days (holidays and Sundays excepted) after presentation to it shall be law, as if signed, unless adjournment of Congress shall have prevented its return. This shall also apply to every order, resolution, or vote to which the concurrence of the House or Senate may be necessary, except on a question of adjournment, and to every expression of the Union's will, unless otherwise provided herein.

9. The Congress shall have the power to declare war, make peace, and exercise all the other rights of the Union unless otherwise provided herein.

10. The Congress shall have the right to admit new states into this Union; but no new state shall be formed or erected within the jurisdiction of any other state nor any state be formed by the junction of two or more states or parts of states without the consent of the state or states concerned.

ARTICLE V.—THE EXECUTIVE POWER.

1. The executive power of the Union is vested in the *Board. It shall be composed of five citizens at least 35 years old. Three shall be elected directly by the citizens of the Union and one by the House and one by the Senate. One shall be elected each year for a five-year term, except that in the first election the citizens shall elect three, and the House shall then*

* The executive, see Art. V. The United States Constitution gives to the President the powers this paragraph gives to the Board.

elect one for two years and the Senate shall then elect one for four years, and the Board shall then by lot assign terms of one, three, and five years respectively to the three Members elected by the citizens.

2. *A majority of the Board shall form a quorum, and it shall act by majority thereof unless otherwise provided herein.*

3. *The Board shall establish a system of rotation so that each Member may be President of it one year.*

4. The *Board** shall be commander-in-chief of all the armed forces of the Union, shall commission all officers of the Union and appoint ambassadors, ministers and consuls, may grant reprieves and pardons for offences against the Union, shall have the power to make treaties by and with the advice and consent of the *Premier and Congress,†* and to appoint with the advice and consent of the Senate the justices of the Supreme Court and of all lower Union Courts, and to make any other appointments required of it by law.

The *Board** shall from time to time report to the people and Congress on the state of the Union, *its progress toward its objectives, and the effects and need of change,* and shall recommend to their consideration such policies and measures as it shall judge necessary and expedient; it may require the opinion of any one in the service of the Union on any subject relating to the duties of his office.

The *Board** may convene extraordinarily Congress, adjourn it when its two houses cannot agree on adjournment, *or dissolve it or either branch of it for the purpose of having it elected anew as shall be prescribed by law.*

The Board* shall receive ambassadors and other public ministers.

5. *The Board shall delegate all executive power not expressly retained by it herein to a Premier, who shall exercise it with the help of a Cabinet of his choice until he loses the confidence of House or Senate, whereupon the Board shall delegate this power to another Premier.*

ARTICLE VI.—THE JUDICIAL POWER.

1. The judicial power of the Union is vested in a High Court, and in such lower courts as the Union may from time to time establish by law. All Union judges shall be appointed for life. The number of High Court judges shall be fixed by law, but shall not be less than *11*.

2. The judicial power extends to all cases in law and equity arising under this Constitution, the laws of the Union, and treaties made by it; to all cases affecting ambassadors, other public ministers, and consuls; to all cases of admiralty and maritime jurisdiction; to controversies between two or more states; between a state and citizens of another state; between

* President, in the United States Constitution.
† Senate, in the United States Constitution.

citizens of different states, and between a state, or citizens thereof, and foreign states, or persons.

3. The High Court shall have original jurisdiction in all cases affecting ambassadors, other public ministers, and consuls, and those in which a state or a foreign state shall be party; in all the other cases before-mentioned it shall have appellate jurisdiction, both as to law and fact, under such regulations as shall be made by law.

ARTICLE VII.—THE AMENDING POWER.

1. The power to amend this Constitution is vested in *the citizens of the Union acting by a majority of those voting on proposals made by two-thirds majority of the House and of the Senate with the approval of three-fifths of the Board, or by two-thirds majority of either House or Senate with the unanimous approval of the Board,* or by a special constituent assembly established by law, *or by petition signed by at least one-fourth the voters in one-half the states. No state, however, shall be deprived without its consent of its right to have its own language and its own form of democratic government.*

ARTICLE VIII.—GENERAL

1. This Constitution, and the laws of the Union which shall be made in pursuance thereof; and all treaties which shall be made under the authority of the Union, shall be the supreme law of the land; and the judges in every state shall be bound thereby, anything in the Constitution or laws of any state to the contrary notwithstanding.

2. All persons in the service of the Union, and the legislative members and executive and judicial officers of each state, shall at the beginning of each term renew their oath to support this Constitution.

3. All Union elective offices, unless otherwise stipulated herein, shall be filled on the same day throughout the Union, to be fixed by law; the exact date when their terms shall begin and end shall also be fixed by law, as well as the manner for filling vacancies.

4. All persons in the service of the Union shall be paid from the Union treasury as shall be fixed by law, but the compensation of no judge shall be decreased during his term nor shall that of any elected officer of the Union be increased during the term for which he was elected.

5. Any one in the service of the Union, on impeachment for and conviction of treason, bribery, or other high crimes, shall be removed from office and may be disqualified from holding office again, and if convicted remains liable to indictment, trial, judgment, and punishment according to law.

The House shall have the sole power of impeachment and the Senate

the sole power to try an impeachment, and it shall convict only by two-thirds majority of the Senators present sitting under oath or affirmation. The Chief justice shall preside when a President *or Member of the Board* is tried.

6. No religious test shall be required as a qualification to any office or public trust under the Union, nor shall there be any official Union religion.

ARTICLE IX.—RATIFICATION

1. The ratification of this Constitution by *ten* states, *or by France, the United Kingdom, and the United States,* shall suffice to establish it among them.

. . . .

An endeavor to conciliate mankind, to render their condition happy, to unite nations that have hitherto been enemies, and to extirpate the horrid practice of war, and break the chains of slavery and oppression.—Paine's description of his *Rights of Man*.

. . . .

They are two to one against us. . . . Tell them that the Convention shall never rise until the Constitution is adopted.—Hamilton when asked by a friend what to tell New York City about the prospects of the New York State Convention ratifying the American Constitution. In six weeks he changed a hostile majority of two-thirds into a favorable majority of three.

ANNEX 2

Transitional and Technical Problems of Union

The difficulties involved in creation of the Union's common citizenship, army, market, money and stamp may frighten or discourage many. Three things may help reassure them.

First, our choice is not between difficulty and danger with the Union and ease and safety with any other course, but between greater and lesser difficulty and risk. What we face in securing our freedom by the Union is trifling compared to what we face in trying any other course.

Second, the difficulties in uniting are mainly if not entirely transitional ones that will soon end. The difficulties in any policy that fails to establish one citizenship, army, market, money and stamp are inherent and unending.

Third, many of the difficulties and risks liable to be held against the Union will be imaginary, or rather, will arise only from the faulty imaginations of those that see them. Many will spring from the assumption that we need ideal union from the start and must solve every problem not only perfectly but at once. Or they will come from forgetting that our aim is not to make everything uniform, orderly, neat, but to make the world safe for more variety, more individualism, more democracy. Only part of the present disorders needs ending as hindering rather than helping this end, and much of this part can safely be left to the Union to deal with later. The only problems needing consideration now are those that absolutely need consideration if the Union is to be established.

We shall now briefly consider the main transitional and technical difficulties involved in establishing the Union citizenship, defense force, money, and communications system, and then discuss less briefly our hardest problem, the establishment of a customs union.

CITIZENSHIP

Some nations may fear that one citizenship, because it brings free movement of men within the Union, will cause them to be flooded with emigrants from other parts of the Union. Experience does not justify this fear. If possession of freedom of movement involved necessarily the use of it the German Swiss would have flooded long ago the French and Italian cantons, or the French would have emigrated from Quebec to other parts of

Canada. Why should nations fear great migratory movements within this Union more than the American states fear such movements from the other states of that Union?

Union by bringing opportunity for freedom and prosperity equally to men wherever they are tends to keep them settled; acute migration problems derive from conditions that force men to leave in order to be, or hope to be, free and prosperous. The relatively small part of the total population that would be shifting from nation to nation in our Union would, moreover, be better balanced than it is now, for there would be more migration among the scientists, engineers, doctors, artists, etc. Men from the nations in the Union that excel in certain things would be in demand in other nations in it that are retarded in these things. To make teachers freer to teach and students freer to learn is to cause some migration, but not an immigration problem, certainly not one dangerous to freedom. It is true that the United States raised some problems when it granted the emancipated negro slave the right to move about as freely as the whites, but this policy has never raised anything like the problems which were raised by its extreme opposite—by the fugitive slave law which sought to fix the negro in the South.

There is, too, the question of what to do about all the immigration officials, passport officials, customs officials, and all the other government officials, civil and military, high and low, whom the Union will make unnecessary. The practice in relieving the unemployed which nationalism has given every democracy should make it easy for each of them to handle its share of a problem so relatively small. The great stimulation to business which the Union would give could be counted on to provide productive work soon absorbing these superfluous officials.

DEFENSE

How should the great reduction in defense forces which the Union permits be carried out? Should at least some of it be erected by each nation in forming the Union or should it all be left to the Union government to do? The latter would seem the more reasonable. How much reduction should there be? How far should the process of eliminating duplication be carried? Such questions could be left to the Union.

How shall the Union take over the existing defense establishments? The Act enabling the Republic of Texas to enter the American Union shows how easy it is to do this. It provided that Texas should cede "to the United States all public edifices, fortifications, barracks, ports and harbors, navy and navy yards, docks, magazines, arms, armaments, and all other property and means pertaining to the public defense belonging to the said

Republic of Texas." Our Union might of course permit minor exceptions enabling nations to retain things of historic and sentimental rather than military value. The less of this the better, however, especially as concerns things reminiscent of the wars between our nations. Pride is at the root of the desire to retain these things, and the individual will be safer if he puts his pride less in what the nation has done to keep men apart and more in the Union and all that men in every nation have done to make the Union possible.

What of the fact that some democracies have volunteer armies and others universal service? Which system should the Union adopt? It would seem possible for each democracy to continue provisionally its present system until the Union adopted a common one, if not till the admission of new states solved the question by making nothing necessary except a small volunteer force. The Union's least secure period would be at the outset and its most exposed territory then would be on the European continent. But this very territory would enter the Union best prepared to defend itself, thanks to universal service there. Even if the Union adopted a volunteer policy at the start it would take some time to organize it and in that time the Union would be strengthening itself with new members. The advantages of universal training can not be lost quickly even by abolishing conscription. The European situation is such that as the Union spreads it could always count on having a citizenry trained for the army at those frontiers where and when the Union needed this most.

What of the command of the Union army, navy, air force at the start? This does not need to be accorded to one man; it could be given provisionally at least to a supreme defense council composed of the officers commanding the armed forces of the democracies now. Common sense would give a preponderating position in this council to the democracies contributing at the start the greatest armies, navies, air forces. One would expect the Union to begin by turning most to the French—as the British have already done—for army leadership and to the British—as the French have already done—and to the Americans for navy leadership. It would thus enjoy the services of the most experienced military experts precisely where it would need them most. Since the military would be subordinate to the civil power, and since the greatest democracy could not dominate this power and the smaller democracies would be safeguarded by their strong position in the Senate, there could be no valid objection to the Union organizing its defense on the basis of merit rather than national pride. The better the Union officers, the more its armed forces could be reduced with safety.

The Council would have to work out a new defense policy, of course. That should be child's play for its members. They now have the problem

of defending the same individual freedom with a fraction of the Union's resources, and with no guarantee all the other democracies will even remain benevolently neutral should their nation become engaged in war.

But organizing an army of Americans, British, French, Dutch, Belgians, Scandinavians, Swiss, etc.,—is it not too difficult to get men of so many nationalities and languages to form a coherent fighting force? It is difficult but by no means impossible to do this even by the league or alliance system, as the World War showed. It is much easier when one changes the political governing unit from state to man. The French with their Foreign Legion and the United States with all its forces have shown how easy it is to weld the greatest mixture of men into an effective force, provided only that one can organize them on a man to man instead of state to state basis. Our Union's task at the outset would be little more difficult in this respect than that of Switzerland with its three nations. There would be no need of or advantage in mixing all the troops at the start; one could begin with a judicious mixture among the officers and gradually extend this.

Finally, there is the fear that it will be too hard to get the different democratic peoples to defend each other, especially the more distant or least exposed ones. This fear is another hangover from the habit of thinking of world organization in terms of states instead of men. Just as an international and a union army are poles apart, so too there is basic difference between a league which expects Americans, for example, to cross the sea to defend France while the French remain free to carry on whatever foreign policy they desire, and our Union where every American, Frenchman, Englishman, Dutchman,—where every citizen would have an equal voice in determining the Union's foreign policy, where there would be no French or American or British or Dutch territory or policy to defend but only the Union's. When all the land of the free would be one common land of theirs, one could rely on plenty of the brave rising from every nation in it to defend the whole or any part of it.

Many may fear that the American people will be less disposed to defend the European part of the Union than the contrary, but I do not believe it. The American people are much more accustomed than any other to think in terms of union. None could be depended on to understand more easily than Americans why the men of Maine should agree to aid Texas if attacked as a member of the Union and why they should refuse to make this pledge to the people of Texas as an independent republic. It is true that geographical position does enter into such considerations, that the Americans of the West were more reluctant than those of the Atlantic seaboard to come to the aid of the British, French and Belgian democracies in 1917. It is also true that once a government elected by the whole American people decided to enter that war to make the world safe for democ-

racy, no state held back and the people in each sought to outdo the others in assuring victory for the Union cause.

In considering all defense problems, moreover, it should always be remembered that the mere formation of the Union will greatly diminish the danger of war, and that as time consolidates the Union and spreads it through mankind this danger will steadily disappear. Though prudence requires preparation now for the worst, there is reasonable hope that once the Union is formed the dangers for which it must prepare will not actually arise.

MONEY AND DEBTS

The monetary problem, now so perplexing even from a short-range view, would be among the easier problems for the Union. It would be mainly a question of establishing a common Union currency and pooling behind it the existing reserves of the member democracies and of all new members as they entered the Union. It would seem wiser not to take the pound, dollar, or franc as the Union money but to avoid all national feeling by giving the Union currency a new nomenclature and valuation. The suggestion was made several years ago in the Bank for International Settlements that the unit for a world money could be one gram of gold, to be called the *gramor* after the shorter French name for gold, *or*. The Union might adopt this idea.

The change to the Union money would be inevitably gradual. People in each nation would continue for some time to quote prices and do local business in terms of the old national money, but everyone would soon learn the exact relation of the new to the old currency. When Austria established its postwar currency with the new name of *schilling* and with this unit worth 10,000 of the old *kronen*, it showed how easily such changes can be made. From the first the money that changed hands was expressed in schillings though people continued for some time to buy and sell in terms of kronen. The old habit slipped off and the new one on sooner than many expected. Now Austria's money has been changed again, this time to the Reichsmark.

The pooling of the gold reserves in the Union need not involve necessarily shipment or concentration of gold. It would require essentially only the political act or transfer of ownership to the Union, and creation of a Union central bank or reserve system which would have for branches the existing national central banks. That done, it would seem safer to leave the gold scattered than to concentrate it.

Should the Union take over the debts with which the democracies enter it, or should each of them keep its own? It would not seem wise for the

Union to take either all or none of this burden. Nations have incurred debt to obtain the armaments or colonial territory which they would have to hand over to the Union; it is only fair that the Union should assume such debt.

As for the "War Debts," they could be settled by the Union taking over and consolidating the entire debt of each democracy incurred as a direct result of the World War, for without their common victory then the Union would not be possible now. This would of course involve each nation handing over to the Union all its foreign war credits or reparation claims. If this operation when worked out increased or decreased too unreasonably the actual per capita war debt burden that each democracy is now bearing it should not be hard to adjust the extremes. No people in the Union would draw real advantage from a solution saddling any people in it too heavily or too lightly per capita with debt at the start. Too great disparity in this tax burden would tend to stimulate unhealthily such compensating movements as migration from the poorer to the richer nations.

The debt operation I suggest would really give advantage not to any nation or its government but to all the individuals in the Union who own the bonds that the "War Debts" represent. These bonds are widely held everywhere by individuals with such small capital that they must put their savings into the safest investments. My suggestion would make these bonds even safer, and would therefore benefit most the small investor.

COMMUNICATIONS

Uniting the postal services seems to present no serious problem. Some new postage rates would need to be made. The American Union finds it possible to have a flat three-cent letter rate throughout its vast territory, and the world finds possible a flat five-cent letter rate around the planet. The Union could have a flat rate of three or four cents, or it could modify the latter with a three-cent continental rate. It would seem best, however, to fix a cheap flat rate throughout the Union to encourage communication among the democracies and knit together the Union. The money saved on armaments would cover probably a thousand times any loss this involved.

Electric means of communication present a somewhat more complex problem because some nations now own and operate these while others leave them to private companies. This complication is not very serious. The two systems now cooperate very well together and there is no reason why they should not work together even better under the Union. The only essential is that power to control rates and regulate all electric means of communication should be vested in the Union. In this field, too, it would

seem wise to encourage communication by cheap rates, especially cheap press rates.

As for the communication of goods and men, the establishment of the Union would appear to be relatively simple. At sea it would mean opening coastal shipping in each democracy to the others, but this does not seem liable to work any violent change in the existing services. Shipping firms that now need the protection of coastal regulations to live would probably find the loss of their privileged position more than offset by the increase in trade Union would bring. All transoceanic shipping that was confined exclusively to intra-Union trade would become part of the coastal shipping of the Union, subject to the Union's regulations as regards manning, hours, working conditions, etc. These regulations should eliminate much of the argument now in favor of protecting the national shipping of the various democracies against that of the others. The rest of this argument should be eliminated with the Union's elimination of each democracy's need to protect its shipping as a measure of national self-defense.

Similar unification of river, rail and road communications would be still simpler. It would be mainly continental and would seem to require little immediate change in existing regulations for international traffic, except the abolition of all such customs formalities as automobile trip-tyques.

There remain air communications. Far from bringing civil aviation any hard problem the Union would go far to free it from the bewildering vexatious labyrinth of national regulations with which the needs of national defense now afflict it.

FREEING $50,000,000,000 OF TRADE

Many will consider that the change from protection to free trade is the greatest difficulty confronting the Union. Much of this difficulty, too, is imaginary. Here again the problem is mainly transitional, at worst only a small minority would be injured, this minority would soon be absorbed in the productive mass, and help given it meanwhile would bring the majority no new burden but would instead reduce and liquidate an existing burden.

The more agricultural among the democracies may fear that the Union would freeze them in their present state and prevent their developing a more diversified economy. United States history may soothe such fears. Union there has not kept the textile industry from spreading to the South from New England; Ohio and Illinois have not needed tariffs against Pennsylvania to develop their steel industry. The automobile industry has flourished most not in the older manufacturing states but in Michigan, and when the motion picture industry came it, too, picked a non-industrial state, California, for its home. Certainly the less industrial countries would

seem to have a much better chance to develop rapidly as sharers in the business expansion that the Union and its great free market would bring than as independent nations walled in—and out—by tariffs.

Industrial democracies may fear that the Union would lower their standard of living. To oppose the Union on this ground is to argue that the people of any state in the American Union would be far more prosperous today had the Constitution preserved each state's right to raise tariff walls instead of sacrificing it to extend the citizen's right to trade.

The term, *national standard of living*,—like so many other terms now glibly used in discussions of world problems,—covers usually a wide range in standards within the nation and gains its significance from national sovereignty rather than from itself. There always has been a wide disparity in standards of living in, for example, the United States, if only as a heritage of slavery, and this disparity remains not only between sections but within states. Is this range of standards of living in this one democracy really less than the range in the so-called national standards of living of the fifteen democracies forming our Union? Is the difference between the American and the Belgian, French, Irish, British, or any other standard of living in our Union greater than the difference between that of, say, Iowa, and Mississippi? Is it so much more that those enjoying the highest standard in the United States need a tariff to protect them against the lowest standard in our Union, when the Iowans never needed a tariff's protection against Mississippi to attain and keep their higher standard?

The Union, instead of being faced with fifteen different national standards of living, is really faced with fifteen ranges in standards whose highs and lows are probably not nearly so far apart as is generally imagined. For a simple explanation, assume that these ranges run from 1 to 10, the standards of living in some democracies running the whole range, those in others running from 1 to 7 and those in still others ranging from 4 to 10. Does this not make clear that what the Union does is merely to swell the number of people having each existing standard, not to create a new problem?

Abolition of trade barriers within the American Union did not result in lowering the higher standards of living in it: Instead it has raised gradually both the higher and the lower standards. The surest way to protect the workers with the higher standard would seem to be to raise it in this manner, or to bring up to it as many workers elsewhere as possible. Tariff protection not only keeps the cost of living higher for the protected worker, but, by preventing sales by the foreigner, helps keep the foreigner's standard low. It thereby reduces his power to buy what the protected worker makes and tends to cut the latter's wages and standard of living. The Union policy doubly protects the worker, for the Union not only provides

a market for all but facilitates raising the standards of workers throughout its territory by law, and in this and other ways builds up buying power everywhere.

It has been hard to end child labor among the forty-eight American States, but it has been impossible to end it among the sixty states of the International Labor Organization. For seventeen years this League organ has tried to get the world to put in force the 48-hour week convention. The American States, thanks to their Union, improved their worker's standards much more radically in a year—only to face the problem of how to keep those standards alone in a nationalistic world. That seems an insoluble problem—without the Union to help eliminate the cut-throat competition among the democracies that nationalism encourages.

We come to the general, usual fears of change. There are always those who want to be reassured against loss from change even when they run no real risk, or much less than their present risk against which they can gain no reassurance. There are those, who claim the right to be guaranteed against loss from change made by majority vote though they ask no such guarantees against loss from change made without majority vote, from change resulting from failure to act in time. There are also the marginal enterprises in each democracy that need protection to exist, the people whom the Union would really force to change more or less their occupations.

Although it may be practically and politically wise to make imposing safeguards to reassure or compensate this opposition to the Union, it would no doubt be found in practice that only a very small minority in every country was adversely affected even for a few years by the change to the Union,—and none to the degree to which most will be affected by continuance of the present policy of disunion. It would also be found no doubt that the cost of tiding this minority through transition took but a fraction of the gain in prosperity which would be obtained from the Union.

The maximum foreign trade our fifteen democracies have achieved under national sovereignty was that of 1929 when it amounted to $44,000,000,000 gold or $75,000,000,000 devaluated. One can estimate that $50,000,-000,000, devaluated, of that trade was inter-democracy trade which the Union would make domestic trade. These fifteen could do this $50,000,000,-000 trade among themselves in 1929 despite tariffs, they quickly cut this down to $15,000,000,000 while increasing the monetary and other barriers to trade, and they have subsequently raised this to $22,000,000,000 in 1937, regaining some of their trade by lowering these barriers. Is it then unreasonable to expect them to regain the rest soon by freeing this great market of all barriers and endowing it with one stable money and cheap, simple communications? Yet, in merely regaining the 1929 level they

would be more than doubling their present prosperity, as measured in value of inter-democratic trade.

Even if they thus gained only some twenty billion dollars in trade could they not easily afford to set aside a billion or two to tide them through transitional difficulties? And are transitions caused by a healthily rising prosperity ever really hard or costly? Does not nearly everyone take care of himself in such conditions?

There is, moreover, good reason to trust that our $50,000,000,000 area would soon pass its 1929 peak, double it, triple it, and continue upward. When we study afresh the results of union and disunion in the United States we shall see this reason better. True, we have no good figures that are exactly comparable. We do not know what the trade among the Thirteen American democracies aggregated before their Union. Its rise, however, is reflected by the fact that the foreign trade of this same territory quadrupled in the first ten years of the Union. If the trade of thirteen weak, isolated democracies quadrupled in ten years of Union despite all the artificial and natural barriers to trade at the end of the 18th century, is it unreasonable to expect as much for our Union which would practically own the earth, be secure from foreign danger, have no rival,—and whose people would have ten times more cause for confidence in their future than they had in 1929 or the American people had in 1789? Would any producer who could not find buyers in this huge market nor make a living in such transition conditions deserve much attention? Would he deserve our sacrificing the Union for the sake of his pocketbook?

Many will find in these considerations sufficient answer to such questions as: What will happen to those farmers in Switzerland who are used to growing wheat and can no longer do so if tariffs go? What of the watch-makers in the United States who presumably can not survive Swiss competition in a free market? To reassure those others, however, who will multiply such questions in each democracy we need to consider in more detail the problems such interests present.

These interests, we have said, will form at worst a small minority. This is not merely because the trade expansion which the Union brings is bound to benefit most of its citizens. There is another reason. Each of our democracies even now sells most of its exports to the other fourteen despite trade barriers. That shows both that the major part of their export trade would be freed by the Union, and that this major part needs no protection. For if a democracy can sell a commodity now in this democratic market *despite* barriers, it could surely continue to sell it there *after* the Union removed the barriers.

It would seem to follow that in each democracy all those producers of commodities that now can be exported profitably to the democracies, or

elsewhere, would not only survive the Union but flourish on it. Study of the situation from this angle suggests that allowance must be made for some subventioned exports that could not survive, but that even so a large part of the people in every democracy is represented by the producers of these commodities whose surplus—which may be only a small fraction of the national production of them—is now profitably marketed abroad.

One example may suffice. The chief exports of the United States according to the League of Nations yearbook, *International Trade Statistics,* which names no export of less than $5,000,000, or animals, meats, lard, fish, wheat, flour, rye, other cereals, fruits, nuts, refined sugar, other foodstuffs, furs, fodder, tobacco, wood and manufactures thereof, copper including ingots, wire, plate, etc., iron and steel including manufactures, other metals, petroleum, coal, cotton, chemicals, leather and manufactures thereof, cotton and other textiles, rubber manufactures, paper and printed matter, electrical machinery, farm implements, office machines, motor cars, other vehicles,—and a number of other commodities that together make 10 per cent of American exports. Consider how many Americans are directly or indirectly engaged in producing all these commodities whose export all the existing trade barriers have failed to stop, and which should boom with the removal of those barriers. One may then get an idea of how few Americans could possibly be hurt by the Union. The list varies with the democracies but the conclusion remains the same—none could possibly be adversely affected by the Union except the small minority which can not even sell their produce at home to the nearest, most friendly consumers, their fellow citizens and neighbors, without tariff protection against other democratic producers.

Moreover, this minority, it is important to remember, would not be in difficulty long. Take the extreme case of the Swiss wheat-grower whose business the Union would presumably ruin. It does not follow that he himself would be ruined or torn from the soil. The Union would at the same time stimulate the Swiss specialities, such as watch-making, cheese-making, lace-making. This would give work to the farmer's sons and daughters whom tariffs have deprived of their jobs; he would have fewer mouths to feed at home and more to feed in town with vegetables and other fresh foods. The probability of his finding an easier livelihood in truck-farming would be increased by the fact that the rise in prosperity through the Union would bring Switzerland more tourists. This would expand its hotel business (now at 20 per cent capacity), increasing the demand for fresh foods while tending to reduce the supply by drawing people from the farm to work in the hotels. This process would be speeded by the fact that the tourist influx would cause much constructive work

of all kinds for the development of the scenic and playground resources of the Alps.

Production, it is often forgotten, is not an end in itself but a means to consumption. Economic thinking that thinks always in terms of work and never in terms of play is hopelessly wrong. A rise in independent leisure spells prosperity as a rise in dependent idleness spells depression. The more leisure the world gains, the more access to its natural playgrounds can be cheapened by various capital improvements, and the more these playgrounds can be put within reach of more and more people.

Consider what only one detail in this widening world of play that the Union opens—skiing—means economically, keeping to the same example, Switzerland. The rise of this sport has added snow and mountains to the list of valuable raw materials, and no country is so rich in these as Switzerland. Others may have more mountains, but they are not so high or not so open or not so sunny or not so easy to get at or not so close to great populous regions as those of Switzerland. The business that this sport of skiing brings with it ramifies amazingly. We may profitably glance at the work which this play brings for it is typical of many economic developments in every democracy which the Union will encourage.

Skiing brings the woodworker skis to make and the metal worker, fixtures; the textile worker has to supply ski clothes and the shoemaker ski shoes. Back of each of these are foresters, miners, farmers in many lands. There is transportation to be supplied: Rail, air and motor to the mountains and then snow-trains, motor buses, funiculars and "air ferries" or *"téléfériques"* to the mountain tops. There are roads to be kept open from the snow, new highways to be blasted through the mountains, service stations and garages to be multiplied in mountain villages, hotels and restaurants and refuges to be erected in hitherto forgotten valleys and peaks. There are food and drink and fuel to be supplied, and guides and ski instructors. Almost everyone seems to benefit from the spread of this one sport. Even the doctors have broken bones to set, the insurance agent new policies to sell.

The sport of skiing rose even through the depression and with it rose all this business. In the years while people were talking of the imminence of political revolution and economic collapse in France skiing was developing there so fast that one Alpine village, Mégève, had to erect scores of buildings and two "air ferries" in a vain attempt to keep up with the rising demand. With prosperity this sport is bound to leap forward with all it means to business.

Give the people who can grow wheat more cheaply than the Europeans their natural market so that they can prosper and travel, and there is no need to worry about the European wheat-grower's future. He can

make a living much more easily then merely exploiting in one way or another the play resources in which his country is really wealthy. He too can then begin to travel and enjoy overseas the beauty of unbroken, unending fields of golden wheat, a sight as rare to him as the Matterhorn to the plainsman.

What is true in this example seems true for all the minority interests adversely affected by the Union. One can reasonably expect them to be reabsorbed soon into healthy activity by the development of the natural advantages that each country enjoys and by all the new activities which the Union would open, particularly through the greater leisure it would permit.

Financial aid to tide these interests through transition would mean no additional burden to the majority in each country—the great crowd of producers who can produce so well that even now they can sell their surplus against world competition. *These producers already support the minority; they pay for its inefficiency by the various tariff and monetary schemes for keeping excessive the prices of what efficient producers need to buy while keeping low the prices of what they have to sell.* This process eats into the good producer's profit from two sides, raising cost of production and lowering demand, all for the sake of a minority that can not stand alone.

The amount which the inefficient are thereby already costing the efficient is incalculable, and there is no possible shifting of this burden under the present system. Far from shifting it to the foreigner, a tariff ties it on the home producers by forcing them to consume goods they would otherwise buy more cheaply from the foreigner. When a thing can not stand alone, the only thing that can possibly hold it up is a thing that *can* stand alone with strength to spare. There is, moreover, nothing transitional or temporary about this burden now. It is a permanent part of the nationalistic system and it has been growing instead of declining in the past decade.

The question facing members of the efficient majority in each democracy is simply this: Shall we continue to pay more and more to protect this parasitical, loud-mouthed minority, or shall we definitely free ourselves from this burden by establishing the Union, and speed its establishment by arranging to use some of the profits the Union will bring us to help the parasites through the few years necessary for them to be absorbed in sound production? The choice is between bearing the existing burden forever or only a little while longer.

It should not be hard to work out in detail provision for this transitional relief; here again it may be noted that nationalism has given every people plenty of experience in handling relief problems.

Should the transition of the fifteen from trade barriers to free trade with each other and one tariff policy toward the outside world be accomplished abruptly, at one step, or gradually, by stages? "There is no greater mistake than to try to leap an abyss in two jumps," Mr. Lloyd George has said. It may be, however, as great a mistake to try to leap it from a standstill when it is too wide to jump without a running start. There are arguments for both ways of effecting this change to the Union.

A system could be worked out whereby each of the democracies would reduce by stages its barriers to trade with the other fourteen, say 10 per cent the first six months or year, 20 per cent the next, then 30, and the remaining 40 in the fourth period. But this seems to me unnecessarily complicated, particularly since much confusion would rise from the necessity of working out simultaneously the Union's tariff relations with the rest of the world.

My tentative suggestion would be that, in agreeing to the principle of the Union, all should agree that its abolition of customs frontiers should take effect on a definite day. This day might be six months or a year after the Union government had decided on what its commercial policy toward the outside world should be, which policy should also take effect the same day. This would seem to be the method of abrupt change, but the abruptness is really confined to the legal side of the operation. The method suggested allows plenty of time for adaptation between the taking and the application of the legal decision. It would require time to debate and decide what the Union's foreign commercial policy should be, even if the final decision were to adopt (as would seem wise) the simple policy of free trade with all the world, or the maintenance of merely a revenue tariff. Even before this could be decided time would have been needed to work out the Union's constitution, get it ratified and the Union government elected. During all this unavoidable delay a good deal of voluntary adaptation to the coming change would be going on. It would be induced particularly by two things:

First, the rise in prosperity would not be delayed until all these changes were effected in practice or worked out on paper. The decision in principle to unite would stimulate confidence and hope sufficiently to start an upward movement, and this in itself would ease transition and simplify the working out of the practical details of the Union. The process of economic forces transforming—to return to our example—the Swiss wheat-grower into a truck farmer would therefore immediately begin its work. Second, the certainty that on a definite date cheap wheat would enter Switzerland would strongly encourage the Swiss wheat-grower to begin planting something else.

Even on the day that the change to free trade went into effect the

degree of abrupt change practically felt would probably surprise more by its smallness than its greatness. Once the mind is made up, one can change a law abruptly but one can not thereby effect abruptly great practical change. Such change involves change in men's habits, and that always takes time and comes about gradually in practice even when no provision for this is made.

This is especially true of all constructive change, all improvement, all growth. Destructive change may be effected with relative abruptness. A sapling can be felled at one stroke, but an inch can not possibly be added at one stroke to the girth of its trunk. All one can do is to stimulate the tree's own natural process of growth. This applies even more to the affairs of men. An earthquake may wreck a city in a moment and effect great practical changes in the lives of a million men, but these men cannot rebuild the city except gradually no matter how determined to do it they are, or how united. It is only when one is pursuing a policy of contraction, of negation, of destruction,—such as the policy of nationalism today,—that one needs to worry about safeguarding against abrupt change. Nature can be trusted to make transition gradual when the policy is positive, constructive, natural.

To illustrate: Suppose (what is really very doubtful) that Americans could, practically, supply from their factories in the United States all the automobiles the fifteen democracies can now absorb. Yet the demand for automobiles at the time the change to free trade began would be much more than now, because of the period of rising prosperity preceding it. Suppose the Americans were able to meet this demand, too. If they sought to meet it without establishing European factories, they would be getting into economic difficulties, for it is cheaper to ship the materials than the finished product. If they could make a profit shipping motor cars from Detroit to France, they could make a greater profit by getting the steel in Lorraine, having the materials they could not get more cheaply in France shipped there and making cars in France too to meet the rising demand. They would thus be giving more employment there and increasing on both the economic and the psychological sides the demand in France for their product.

This would not mean that the French maker would be driven necessarily out of business, let alone abruptly, or what is more important, that his plant would be closed and his workers thrown out of employment. His costs meanwhile would be falling through the effects of the Union. This might offset the American automobile maker's advantage, for his costs would be increasing if he sought to supply the whole world. To mention one item, shipping is limited and the more of it he sought to take

from other commodities (also desirous of reaching their market) the more ocean freights would rise.

Suppose Detroit could still deliver all the cars demanded in France—and everywhere else in Europe—more cheaply than the maker on the spot could. There would remain the problem of distribution and service and this would require building up a greater organization than the French makers now have, and this takes time and money. When all this was done, there would still be business left the French maker. For one thing, there would remain all the tens of thousands of his sold cars to help protect him for several years. At worst, from his viewpoint, these might all be traded in for American cars, but even then they would have to be re-sold and kept running, and the demand for their parts would continue.

There are, moreover, all sorts of uneconomical factors that enter into the buyer's psychology. There is habit to make many people reluctant to change their make of automobile. There is national or local pride. The irrational belief that has been propagandized into the people of every nation for generations that everything done by a fellow-national is better than the same thing done by the foreigner is not going to vanish the day that the Union is established. It is going to remain and do yeoman service to the European automobile maker and the American dressmaker and other producers (for the example applies to many producers of many things in many countries) in tiding them through the Union's transition period.

These are only some of a host of factors that combine to make this transition gradual in practice no matter how abrupt it may be on paper. There would seem to be no need to arrange for a gradualness that is bound to occur.

However carefully one does make such arrangements, however great the assurances and reassurances and safeguards and super-safeguards the unionist provides, one can be sure there will still be plenty of pother and crying-before-hurt. The delusion will still be popular that there is security only in continuing our present ills. We shall long have with us the slave who has no time to fear his burden will break his back, because he is too occupied by fear of catching cold if the burden is removed.

One can be sure that the fearful minority will fill the air with cries—and there is one thing more incredible than the amount of noise a small minority composed of silly and selfish interests can make. It is the readiness of the majority on whom they are imposing not only to believe them without checking their figures, investigating their motives or remembering their past record, but to suffer for them as if silliness and selfishness were the great patriotic virtues and vital interest they pretend to be.

Unionists need not be worried by the genuine technical difficulties to be solved in uniting the democracies into one market. Customs unions have already been made successful, time and again, and the task at hand is much less complicated than it seems, far less complicated than the task of trying to make the existing system work. Unionists need be concerned still less by all the imaginary complications that will be conjured up. They have hysteria and parasitic interests and pedantic experts and inertia and lack of constructive imagination and the present against them. But on their side they have the facts, and both the past and future.

.   .   .   .

We must see things in time perspective.

ANNEX 3

How National Sovereignty Wrecked the Gold Standard

Slowly, painfully, by differing and even by contradictory methods in the various national economies, the world is coming nearer to some degree of economic equilibrium, but it has not yet arrived . . . No decisive lead has been given to coordinate the various efforts. Whereas one national economy has gained or seemed to gain, another has lost or seemed to lose, frequently as a consequence of the repercussion upon it of a nationalistic policy followed by a neighbor. The world is still waiting for a courageous move which, whatever risks it may appear to involve, holds out the hope of founding reconstruction on a firmer ground of monetary stability than the shifting currency values which have hampered economic revival to date.—Leon Fraser, in his 1935 Report as President of the Bank for International Settlements.

The basic reasons for the fatal role that national sovereignty plays in the monetary question were explained in Chapter IV. To make clearer why the confidence which monetary stability requires can not possibly be long maintained while the great democracies remain sovereign over their money, we shall now briefly examine in more detail how confidence in the gold standard as an international money was in fact destroyed. We shall see better then that we have had before the Munich accord the kind of reasons and reasoning that encourage some now to believe that we can have peace and prosperity in our time without union.

The run on the gold standard began in Austria in May, 1931. That year had begun well. "In the spring of 1931, as in the spring of 1930," says the League of Nations, *World Economic Survey, 1931-32,* "there seemed to be a definite easing of economic and financial conditions. The early months of the year were calm, there was some return flow of capital to Germany and of gold to Great Britain, security prices rose somewhat in most countries in the spring, and money-market rates were extremely easy in the chief financial centres." The Board of the Bank for International Settlements, which includes all the big central bank governors of Europe, found conditions so improved that it unanimously voted March 9, 1931, to encourage resumption of long term investment by investing publicly

some of the bank's money in fifteen year German mortgage bonds.* Hitler was then a minor figure, Japan had not seized Manchuria, the London Naval Treaty had been concluded, the World Conference for the Reduction and Limitation of Armaments had been convoked for 1932, and the latest cause for optimism was that the British had persuaded the French and Italian governments to initial in February the Bases of Naval Agreement.

The fact, however, was that under the rules of national sovereignty things were going well only from the viewpoint of the sovereignty and power of the United States, Britain and France. They were going badly from the viewpoint of the sovereignty and power of Germany, which, because of its weakness, was also feeling most the pinch of depression.

Armament lies at the heart of world politics under the existing principles of sovereignty, for armed force is the final instrument for maintaining that sovereignty and all its policies. It is not merely security and advantage in war time that armed superiority gives, but constant security and advantage in the day in and day out diplomatic bargaining. When one really has this armed superiority one does not have to flourish it, to sabre rattle in order to profit by it. In a game based on armed power relative strength is everything, and in 1931 the question of the relative armed power of each nation was the issue that was scheduled to come up in a year in the Arms Ratio Conference, *alias* the Disarmament Conference.

The year 1931 that had opened so auspiciously was, in short, the last year in which each power could manœuvre—as was its duty under the national sovereignty rules—for position at the coming conference. Each had to prepare then or never so that any reduction in armaments should result in improving its own degree of armed strength and lessening that of its possible enemies. Britain and France had won the first move, for one effect of the naval agreement with Italy was to isolate Germany in the coming Conference. Germany counter-moved only one month later by suddenly announcing, March 21, the signing of a protocol for customs union with Austria.

While Germany was pursuing primarily political aims in this ostensibly economic move, Austria was seeking means to improve its bargaining position in the trade negotiations it was then vainly carrying on with its neighbors. Its government knew better than any other how dangerously exposed it was financially and economically. The best card Austria had to play—and frequently played—in diplomatic negotiations then was to raise the threat of *anschluss*, and this customs union protocol threatened it more effectively than had any previous move. It is hard to believe

* See *The New York Times*, Mar. 10, 1931.

that its Berlin or Vienna authors then thought for a moment that their neighbors would allow this union. Nor is it likely that they failed to realize that a bilateral union made in the spirit behind this one ran dangerously contrary to the spirit of the movement for European federation Briand had then got started at Geneva.

The results followed swiftly—and have been continuing ever since, for the present troubles in Europe can be traced back directly to the chain of events started by this Austro-German protocol or, if one prefers, by the Franco-Italian naval agreement preceding it. The protocol at once set Europe by the ears. It enabled the French nationalists finally to discredit Briand and prevent the consummation of his naval agreement with Italy, which fell to the ground at once. It dealt the Committee of Inquiry on European Union a blow from which it, like its founder, never recovered. Six months before this move Stresemann had died; ten months after it Briand, already forced from office, followed him. By September the customs union protocol had been declared illegal by the Permanent Court for International Justice. But the mere announcement of the protocol had succeeded in its political purpose for it had effectively torpedoed the Franco-Italian naval agreement and rescued Germany from its isolation. When the Disarmament Conference opened Germany enjoyed some support from Britain and much from Italy, both of whom hoped thereby to induce France to come to terms with them.

This may seem to have nothing to do with the gold standard. It had enough to do with it for England itself to go off gold six months after the signing of this customs protocol.

A few weeks after the protocol was announced a high official of the Bank for International Settlements told me that this protocol had "hit on the nose the hope of restoring long term investment just as it was getting its head out of water." Since then no German bonds, and almost no fifteen year bonds of any country have been issued in the foreign market.

France and the new states of Central Europe, having no security that Britain or the United States would help defend them against a German attack, sought to protect themselves against the danger of Germany strengthening herself by *anschluss* with Austria. Their first necessity was to get Germany and Austria to agree to submit to the Court the question whether this protocol was in violation of Austria's treaty obligations. France and its friends brought financial and economic pressure to bear. As one of the statesmen directly involved later admitted to me, "we combined, as always in politics, against the weaker of the two, Austria."*

In these circumstances it became publicly known in early May—about

* This statesman has lived to grow into a greater statesman and yet see the stronger combine much more ruthlessly against his own country.

six weeks after the protocol was announced—that the balance sheet of
the great Creditanstalt Bank of Vienna, drawn at the end of 1930, showed
it to be in very bad condition.* "The importance of this news from
Vienna which travelled round the world's financial centres like a seismic
shock, lay less in the event than in its general significance," notes the
League's *World Economic Survey, 1931-32.* "It was instantly realized
that not only other banks in Austria and foreign countries, but virtually
the whole industrial structure of Austria, and other Eastern European
countries, would be involved. It was equally evident that neighboring
debtor states, and particularly Germany, would be at once exposed to the
danger of panic withdrawals of capital."

One will understand still better the general significance and effect of
this disclosure if one keeps in mind two things in addition to the technical, financial and economic situation that one can find in the *Survey.*
One is the political situation just described, to which the *Survey* devotes
only these few cushioned phrases: "The Austro-German protocol announcing the plan of a customs union appeared on March 21, 1931. The
European political situation was strained and international economic cooperation became more difficult. Soon after the Creditanstalt difficulties
were announced, a renewed run began on the Reichsbank."

The other thing, which the *Survey* does not mention at all, is that all
financial centres knew that one of the legendary names in the financial
world was involved in the crisis, for the Creditanstalt was the Vienna
bank of the Rothschilds. When the Austrian government had to advance
$14,000,000 to the Rothschild bank, it is hardly surprising that creditors
everywhere in the world began to wonder what must be the condition
of the other banks in this region.

No doubt others placed in the same conditions as the German and Austrian governments, or those of France and her allies, would have done
about the same as each side did to protect the interests of their sovereign
states. No doubt the German government was not aiming then at immediate *anschluss*, to say nothing of war, but merely at dissolving the
opposing diplomatic combination. No doubt the French government had
no intention of really ruining the schilling, to say nothing of the gold
standard. No doubt it too sought only to break up without war the opposing combination by making the Austrians and Germans merely fear their
currency would again be undermined. No doubt both sides planned to
keep things in bounds and were merely manoeuvring, playing with fire
within the accepted national sovereignty rules or the Great Power game.
The result, however, was that Americans and Englishmen and Dutchmen
and Swiss and others suddenly realized that the financial position of

* See Geneva despatch, *The New York Times,* May 13, 1931.

Austria and Germany was rotten. They had no means of knowing how far the political playing with fire might go (there were rumors of war then as now), and they had no means of controlling the situation or protecting their investments in these countries—except by selling out and withdrawing the money. They began to sell and withdraw. And the foreign run on Austria and Germany began.

THE SHORT TERM FLAW

At this point there was a discovery that accelerated and spread financial panic everywhere until the situation got out of hand. A tremendous flaw was found in the gold standard: Its main safeguard, the 40 per cent ratio of gold reserve to currency, was not the safeguard it appeared to be for it left completely out of account the fact that any country's foreign short term indebtedness could be quickly converted by foreigners into the country's currency and the currency converted into gold and withdrawn. The fact that gold coin nearly everywhere had been withdrawn from circulation after the war had led the League's Gold Delegation to hold in 1930 that "an internal drain can not take place" and that modern gold reserves were mainly required "to meet possible deficits in the international balance of payments."* This report, however, gave no hint of what was to happen four months later. The experts who wrote it mentioned short term debt incidentally and only once or twice. It had apparently occurred to no one that the world had become so inter-dependent that panic among distant† Americans over Austrian stability could lead, through this process of turning short term credits into currency, to Austria losing her gold reserve without the Austrian government inflating or Austrian citizens starting a bank run.

In 1931 almost no account was taken in any country of its own short term indebtedness, or of that of any other country. The first attempt anywhere even to collect information on how much the country owed and was owed at short term was made, I believe, by the Federal Reserve Bank of New York in 1930, and that was still a crude isolated pioneer effort when the bubble burst in Austria. Not only in Austria, but even in England neither the central bank nor the government then knew how much short term paper the country owed abroad. The Bank of England did not begin regularly securing reports on this subject until January, 1932—after the gold standard had broken down. Most central banks now have some information on their country's short term position, but even this helps little for they keep it mostly secret. The Federal Reserve now

---

* Gold Delegation, Second Interim Report, C. 75. M. 31, 1931-II, p. 16.
† Geographically, not electrically distant.

has an idea of how much short-term money Amercians have loaned in, say, Belgium, and the Bank of England knows how much has been loaned there from England, and the Bank of France how much from France, but none knows how much all others have loaned; only the Bank of Belgium has an idea of how much Belgium owes all the world at any given time. The example is generally true of all countries.

The creditor world still has little means of knowing how much short term debt each country has at any given time. Yet experts agree that this knowledge is at least as essential to confidence in a currency as the fact which the world does know—how much sight indebtedness (paper money) each country has at any time. One of the chief aims of the Bank for International Settlements has been to make itself the clearing house for this short term debt information, but it still falls far short of the information any government needs to safeguard its currency. Banking and business and political conditions make it extremely difficult to assure the world adequate timely short term debt information—and the principle of national sovereignty makes it even harder to obtain reliable information in time of emergency. Yet that is precisely the time when it is most needed.

This problem of short term debt remains one of the great obstacles to the permanence of any restoration of the gold standard under the existing conditions of national sovereignty. But in 1931 most bankers no more suspected that this problem existed than a baby suspects typhoid germs in water. The huge debt load on Austria had been built up because the individual American and British and other lenders had no idea how much short term money had already been lent Austria even by their own countrymen, let alone the world, and because the Austrian government did not know how much the Austrians had borrowed. The danger in this ignorance was discovered only when foreigners, fearful of the schilling breaking, began to sell their Austrian short term paper at a discount for the sight paper (schilling currency) that could be converted into gold, or dollars or pounds or francs at gold parity, and taken out of Austria.

It then began to be realized that if it was true, as the gold standard premise held, that a minimum of 40 per cent of gold against obligations convertible at sight in gold was necessary for confidence in a currency, then the gold standard conclusion—that one could have confidence in a currency that totalled, say, 100,000,000 schillings so long as its gold reserves totalled 40,000,000—was wrong. For if the country had a foreign short term debt of, say, only 300,000,000 schillings, one must add this to the 100,000,000 and admit that really 400,000,000 of paper had been issued against the 40,000,000 of gold, and the true ratio was only 10 per cent.

Moreover, the long term foreign indebtedness could also be similarly converted, by the creditors selling the bonds at a discount and exchanging their schillings for gold. The long term factor could be measured and was not so dangerous at first—but it played an increasingly important role in the run on the pound in February, 1935 and on the Swiss franc in April, 1935. But there was no means of knowing in 1931 whether the short-term paper totalled, say, 100,000,000, or 300,000,000, or 700,000,000 or more—whether there was enough gold to satisfy 40 per cent, or 20 per cent, or 10 per cent, or 5 per cent of Austria's foreign creditors, or still less.

A more disconcerting financial discovery could hardly be imagined. And so the run on Austria swiftly gathered force despite the millions that the big central banks and the Bank for International Settlements poured into Austria to stop it. It is not surprising that once this appalling miscalculation in the gold standard rules had been discovered, foreign short-term creditors of Germany began to "play safe," and that a worse run swiftly developed there.

All this in turn reacted on the political factor, which blossomed quickly (June 1931) into the reparations-war-debts-private debts-political security tangle among the three great democracies. Britain was seeking to relieve the pressure this Austrian run brought on the pound by getting rid of the war debt claims of the United States and the reparations claims of France. The United States as the biggest private creditor of Germany, holding the second mortgage on her, was seeking with the Hoover moratorium to save this interest by lifting even the "unconditional" part of the French reparation first mortgage on Germany—but without renouncing the American war debt claims. France, as Germany's biggest public creditor, was seeking to protect the unconditional reparations against the private holders of the German second mortgage and to get Britain to secure France politically against Germany and to get the United States to cancel war debts—both in exchange for French concessions on the reparations side. Each of the three governments, in short, was defending what any one playing under the national sovereignty rules would have deemed to be the immediate interests of the State. Each was simply doing its duty.

While all this was inevitably stirring up bad feeling and suspicion in each people with regard to the others, and while each government was bringing all the pressure it could on the others, the French and Americans, who had a great deal of money in London, began to discover (thanks to what the Austrian and German breakdown revealed) that London had been lending long and borrowing short—and no one knew how much— and also that the British budget was getting more and more out of balance. French, American and other private citizens began hastily to take

their money away from London. The *Banque de France* and the Federal
Reserve Bank of New York rushed in with loans to Britain totalling
$130,000,000. The British public did not become panic-stricken over sterling,
but—as in Austria and Germany—foreigners who had no voice in sterling
or British policy preferred to play safe.* In less than four days, more
than $200,000,000 of short-term funds were withdrawn from Britain.

Two days later, Sept. 21, 1931, Britain suddenly abandoned gold.
That dealt a staggering blow to confidence in the international gold
standard. Though the United States later dealt it a blow that was worse
in some ways, it did not rock and move the world as much as did England's
abandonment of gold. The consternation it caused everywhere showed how
little it was expected, *despite* the run on London. It forced thirteen countries off gold within six weeks and others, including Japan, followed in a
few months.

"This very considerable breakdown of the world's monetary mechanism was important in itself," notes the *World Economic Survey 1931-32*.
"Even more important in the immediate situation, however, was the reac-
tion upon the remaining gold standard countries and upon the financial
structure of the world as a whole. When Britain went off gold, all the
European stock exchanges except those of Paris, Milan and Prague, closed
for various periods; bank rates rose, foreign exchange restrictions (ranging from limitation of imports to moratoria) were imposed in thirty
different countries, tariffs were increased, contingent, priority and quota
systems introduced. Partly as a result of these trade restrictions, the
financial storm burst with redoubled force on Germany . . . New York
was for a few weeks subject to much the same kind of run as London
and Berlin had experienced. In October a "gold rush" set in which had
the net effect of reducing the United States stocks by $715 million."

WHAT BRITAIN DID TO CONFIDENCE

Why did the British decision so shatter confidence? Britain for generations had been the world's greatest trading and financial power. It had
practically given the world the international gold standard. It had built
up carefully the greatest reputation for financial trustworthiness in the
world. It had shown before that it held that reputation very dear and
would make sacrifices to keep it. Britain had brought the pound back
to its old value in 1925 at tremendous cost to its business interests.

* Snowden as Chancellor told the House of Commons Sept. 21, 1931: "We consulted the banks as to the origin of the heavy sales of sterling and the banks assured
us that as far as they can judge the selling was predominantly on foreign account
and there was no evidence of any substantial export of capital by British nationals."

The gold standard's 40 per cent minimum ratio* meant, if it meant anything, that at worst one was sure of having two chances in five of saving his money, of being among the 40 per cent of the holders of paper who got paid in gold. It was based, as we have seen, on a miscalculation which made the real ratio much lower, but this does not change the implication in it that, in an emergency, the promise to pay in gold would be kept to the bitter end, nobly, self-sacrificingly.

Certainly the implication was not that as soon as a country's reserves fell to about 40 per cent it was entitled to suspend gold payments. The requiring of a minimum reserve was never intended as a guarantee to the central bank that, if the worst came to the worst, it at least could always keep 40 per cent of the security it had promised for its notes. No one could trust the currency of a country that proclaimed: "We have gold now for 55 per cent of our currency but if our ratio ever falls to 40 per cent we shall cease paying gold." That would be a ratio of 15, not 40 per cent.

Britain had the highest reputation for financial integrity. It had a special responsibility to the world. Not only were many business transactions between non-British countries done in sterling,† but Britain had encouraged other countries to tie their currencies to sterling through that post-war invention, the gold exchange standard. By this device weak countries could form their metallic reserve of pound, dollar and other notes rated "as good as gold." The result was that Britain had not only the safety of sterling but of other currencies directly in its keeping.

The world knew in September, 1931, that Britain was having economic and financial difficulties, but it knew also that the British had enormous assets and resources and plenty of credit in New York and Paris.

The world expected Britain to make a titanic struggle to overcome any panicky fear of sterling. It expected every English sovereign to do its duty at every monetary Trafalgar. If they all perished, it expected Britain to use its credit or sell its assets—as individual Englishmen in similar straits had often done—until it had made good every promise. The world expected England to stand behind English money as unflinch-

---

* The usual ratio figure, 40 per cent, is used for simplification, although all countries did not have this figure and British law did not provide for a minimum reserve on a percentage basis. The Currency Act of July 2, 1928, allowed the Bank of England to issue a maximum of £260,000,000 of fiduciary notes (backed by securities other than gold beyond the total value of its gold reserve). In practice this works out near enough to the fixed percentage for the present purposes.

† For example, even in 1923 when the pound was off gold and the dollar seemed supreme, I found American tobacco buyers in Greece paying for their purchases not in dollars or drachmas but sterling.

ingly, as self-sacrificingly as it was to seeing the English "bobby" stand
behind English law. These may seem romantic ideas now, but on such
ideas confidence is built. Would men trust the captain who always kept
one life boat reserved for himself as they trust a captain who was rescued
drowning when his ship went down? The world's utter consternation when
England quit gold showed how heroically high it had held the name of
England and how much it expected from England.

What the world saw was that Britain quit gold with a reserve of £133,-
628,000 and its credit still good. It is true the £130,000,000 London had
borrowed from New York and Paris almost equally the remaining British
gold reserve, but it can not be seriously maintained that this wiped out
that gold reserve or that it was Britain's last liquid asset. The fact is that
the Bank of England statement two days after gold payments stopped
listed the gold reserve at £133,628,000—not at £3,628,000 as should have
been done if the rest belonged instead to New York and Paris. If the
gold reserve was wiped out by these loans, then it was wiped out before
these loans were made—indeed, it never really existed—since the possible
claims against it were always far greater than it was.

New York and Paris, moreover, were not pressing London to pay back
the £130,000,000 then, and did not do so later. How little the National
Government (which used the emergency very effectively to hold elections
and win overwhelming power) used Britain's inherent strength to keep its
gold obligations may be seen from the fact that in six months the £130,-
000,000 was repaid,* an unknown amount of gold was diverted from the
reserve into the equalization fund—and still the reserve was almost
as great as when it had fallen so low that, presumably, gold payments had
to be stopped.

The British in quitting gold sought to improve their competitive commercial position in a declining world market.† The world awoke Sept. 21
not only to find that the historic champion of sound money had quit gold
but also to learn the almost equally disconcerting news that the historic
champion of free trade had become protectionist, doubly protectionist, in
the most lightning-like and thorough way possible. For currency depreciation acts both as a subsidy for every export and a tariff against every
import. The pound immediately fell 25 per cent, making British goods
25 per cent cheaper for all gold countries—and their goods 33 per cent
dearer to the British. By quitting gold the British government thus en-

* All was repaid except a fraction of the French loan which, it is worth noting,
was not repaid simply because it was in a form that could not be redeemed so soon.

† Those who believe the British left gold from purely monetary reasons and with
no deliberate intention to profit thereby will do well to turn back and read again
such contemporary things as the inspired and other comment in the London press
when it announced the abandonment of gold.

couraged all the world abroad and at home to follow the nationalist slogan and "Buy British."

All the major currencies were then still on gold, for previous experience of inflation had led Austria and Germany to shun the temptation to seek a temporary trade advantage in depreciation and to keep their currencies at gold parity by extraordinary measures of control and "standstill" arrangements. It was Britain of all nations that introduced into the depression that poisonous weapon of national commerce, monetary depreciation. Being the first to use it Britain profited by it more than did those who followed.

In self-defense rivals then invented contingents, quotas, etc., to keep out such cheapened goods, but they could not remove the barrier that depreciation raised against the sale of their goods in Britain nor the premium it put on British goods there. Britain, having hitherto had the least trade barriers, benefited most of all from the protective side of depreciation, from its stimulation to domestic trade and private building.

Despite the great improvement in Britain's position and the talk of "recovery" that monetary policy helped bring, Britain has stubbornly refused (except for a brief interlude immediately after the dollar quit gold) to listen to the urgent pleas of the United States or France for stabilization. But Britain has not refused to use its managed currency as a means of pressure on other countries for political and other ends.

There is no doubt whatever that the monetary policy Britain followed can be defended on the ground that the superior interests of the nation required it. Certainly I would be the last to argue that this policy violated the basic national sovereignty rules of the game. Nor would I dispute that the British National Government, however much one may criticize it for not having tried harder to change those shortsighted rules of the jungle, is entitled to have its monetary policy judged on the basis of these existing rules. One can strongly argue that, considering the practical dangers and possibilities in 1931, Britain in leaving gold chose the lesser evil not only for Britain but for all the world. Any other government of equal intelligence would probably have done the same in those conditions.

We are not concerned here, however, with the morality or immorality, the merits or demerits of Britain's action in leaving gold. No such red herring should be allowed to divert us from the point—the effect of Britain's action on confidence in the stability of the gold standard or of any other international money based on national sovereignty. If Britain could thus in its national interest and to its national profit break its promise to pay in gold, what country could people trust to keep on gold? In what country could one have faith that the guarantees of the international gold

standard—these promises to mere foreigners—would always resist the
imperious demands of national policy? In the United States?

WHAT THE UNITED STATES DID TO CONFIDENCE

The United States proceeded to deal at least as shattering a blow to
confidence as Britain had. Britain was in a much more exposed position
than the United States, had stood a relatively greater run, had twice
borrowed before quitting gold, owed war debts to the United States, and
by the most generous calculation had only 41 per cent cover when she
left gold. The United States left gold when it was the world's chief creditor
and had the greatest gold reserve in the world, and a gold reserve ratio
of 55 per cent.* The effect was aggravated by the fact that it suddenly
suspended gold payment while Messrs. MacDonald and Herriot were
at sea on their way to Washington at Washington's invitation to discuss
stabilization. Later it was further aggravated by the United States dis-
regarding the most solemn "gold clause" contracts and deliberately depreciating the dollar, deliberately using the currency as an instrument
both of domestic and foreign policy.

It is true the United States was undergoing an exceptionally severe
internal crisis when it definitely went off gold—although it had already
been able to resume gold payments after the temporary suspension while
the banks were closed. It is true the American internal debt situation
remained bad, and that there were strong demands in Congress for inflation or devaluation. Though financial conditions might have permitted
keeping the gold clause in contracts with foreigners, regardless of the
measures taken to meet the domestic situation, it would have been extremely hard, to say the least, to persuade Congress to pay foreigners
in gold and Americans in paper. It is true, too, that Britain would not
even consider stabilization until the United States quit gold.

There is no more point in denouncing the Washington than the London
government for what it did, and I would repeat that we are not here concerned with weighing the virtues or vices of the policy of any government.
We are concerned solely with systems of government, and particularly now
with the idea that the gold standard can be made a stable international
money again with nothing more behind its guarantees—in the last analysis—than the quixotic idea that in a grave emergency independent
sovereign states can be depended on (as can some independent sovereign
men, at least), to sacrifice themselves if necessary merely to keep their
word even to strangers.

* Federal Reserve report Apr. 16, 1933. The ratio on March 1 before the first
temporary suspension of gold was 50 per cent.

The United States perhaps dealt confidence in this system the worst blow of all, for, until it left gold, all financial centres felt there was no need to worry about a currency until the gold ratio began to fall within a few points of the minimum. Even then, it was felt one could count on each country making at least as much struggle as Britain had made to pay its obligations to foreigners. But after the richest power on earth left gold without warning and while it still had 55 per cent of its money backed with gold and unlimited credit in the world, there was nothing left to trust in this system. All the rules had been made ridiculous. Thereafter no matter how big a gold reserve one amassed, one could not be certain this would protect one from a run by one's neighbors—for the neighbors could not be certain this big reserve would protect them from a sudden willful depreciation.

If a domestic situation could arise in the wealthiest country such as to lead it to repudiate its gold obligations to foreigners, it was bound to arise thereafter with the same results in other countries, and it did. Why should it not do so again in the first crisis after any restoration of the gold standard—if that standard continues to be based on national sovereignty?

.   .   .   .

Nationalism would now fetter man's genius in the name of man's freedom.

.   .   .   .

The work of deepening and extending the range and the meaning of Democracy and Citizenship, Liberty and Law, . . . would seem to be the chief political task before mankind in the new epoch of history on which we have suddenly entered.—Sir Alfred Zimmern, prefacing the second edition of *The Greek Commonwealth*, Dec. 2, 1914.

ANNEX 4

How National Sovereignty Wrecked the Locarno Treaty

The Locarno experiment is worth examining in more detail than was practicable in Chapter IV, because this treaty, for ten years the key piece in the post-war European balance, was the only experiment ever made in regional collective security. Though the present study of the Locarno treaty was written in 1936 it may be the more timely now when there is talk of peace in our time through a Four Power Pact. The reader can judge for himself how far this analysis has been borne out by subsequent events.

. . . .

The Locarno treaty provides an object lesson in (a) the inefficacy of collective security even on the smallest basis and under most favorable auspices so long as it is not backed by definite collective war plans, and (b) the practical impossibility not only of getting such war plans made but even of obtaining unambiguous commitments to enforce the treaty effectively. It shows throughout how the principle of national sovereignty itself upsets attempts to harness it to peace.

The Locarno experiment was made under most favorable auspices because each party to this treaty had from beginning to end as strong a national interest in its success as can reasonably be expected.

To Germany, which took the initiative that led to Locarno, this treaty was a powerful guarantee at the outset against another Ruhr occupation and against separatism in the Rhineland, and, later, against France and Russia resuming their automatic pre-war alliance. For under it France could not aggressively invade the Rhineland without running the risk that Britain and Italy would carry out their pledge to defend Germany.

To France, Locarno gave in addition to the Covenant's general pledges— whose weakness we have already seen—a more definite and extensive legal commitment from Britain than France had obtained before the war, and also a guarantee from Italy. As diplomatic weapons go, the Locarno treaty with all its faults was by far the best France had, for it tied Britain most.

To Italy Locarno gave, in addition to the prestige of acting as guarantor

of France and Germany, valuable practical support on the Brenner. For Locarno by keeping the Rhineland unfortified kept Germany open to legal invasion by France when called by the League Council to defend the independence of Austria against German attack. Conversely, German fortification of the Rhineland by protecting Germany against such French invasion facilitates German action in Central Europe. German possession of Austria would tend for nationalist reasons (Italian annexation of the Germans of South Tyrol) and for trade reasons (the need of an Adriatic port) to aim German policy thereafter toward controlling the Trentino and Trieste.

To Britain Locarno gave the deciding voice in Europe by making both France and Germany look to London. First, the treaty was a guarantee against Germany either attacking the Channel region or becoming too powerful in Central Europe, because by keeping the Rhineland unfortified it effectually laid Germany open to French attack whenever Germany lost London's favor. This became all the more important when France, after vain efforts to gain an automatic commitment from Britain, fortified the frontier. The effect of these forts is double. On one hand, they give France a better springboard for plunging into Germany. On the other hand, just as one forces water to go either over the dam or around it when one dams a stream, the "Maginot Line" forces Germany in any attack on France to strike directly by air and indirectly by land through Belgium, Holland or Switzerland.

The Maginot Line thus practically makes German war on France all the more dangerous to Britain, since it develops the air weapon to which Britain is most vulnerable and tends to make the fighting occur in Britain's continental front yard. German fortification of the Rhineland only accentuates this for it frees more German forces for invasion by air and by Belgium, and it forces the French, too, to develop their air arm and look to Belgium. For France to sink into a position where it can give no effective aid to Poland, Czechoslovakia, etc., is to let these countries fall, for all practical diplomatic considerations, under German control. The more Germany thus builds up its position in Central Europe the more dangerous the position of France and therefore of Britain becomes.

During this stage Britain and France can buy peace for themselves by merely granting Germany a free hand in Central Europe. But to do this openly kills in Central Europe all hope of aid against Germany and thus merely speeds the process whereby Germany grows able to dictate to France and Britain. Berlin, moreover, can not trust that London and Paris, even if they promise Germany a free hand, will long resign themselves to the effects of such a policy or remain so blind as not to foresee them. Britain now as in 1914 and as in Napoleon's time is the real key-

stone of resistance to any country's desire for hegemony in Europe. Consequently, Germany though not desiring war with Britain must prepare above all either to overawe or overcome Britain. It is this set-up that made Stanley Baldwin call the Rhine Britain's frontier. German occupation of the Rhineland thus recreates the 1914 war danger for Britain.

Second, Locarno guaranteed Britain not only against France disturbing recovery by another Ruhr occupation, or becoming all powerful on the Continent, but also against France restoring her pre-war automatic alliance with Russia. Such an automatic alliance means that if Germany and Russia go to war, France must attack Germany. For France to have invaded Germany, unless authorized by the League or after a German attack on France, would have been a French violation of the Locarno treaty. This would have allowed Germany to demand that Britain and Italy should attack France. So long as the Locarno treaty stood France could make no automatic alliance wtih Russia without sacrificing its claim on Britain.

Again, an automatic Franco-Russian alliance risks putting Britain back in the dangerous position of 1914, where Russia really had the decisive role and could take initiatives bound to lead France and Britain into war. For if Russia decided that the moment had come for, say, a preventive war against Germany, the alliance would drag France in. That would confront Britain with this problem: If it stayed out it would face at the end a European continent controlled either by France and Russia or by Germany and company. If Britain went in it could determine the issue and maintain its position as the arbiter of Europe. That is, it could regain by war the position it was assured of without war so long as the Locarno-League system was maintained, and extended to include Russia.

By this system Britain kept the decisive role for, being under obligation to defend either France or Germany, Britain could defend whichever one suited British interests best and could thus keep both paying court to London. Moreover, as Britain's decision would take the form of a League Council vote to determine the aggressor, Britain, thanks to the rule excluding the votes of the parties but requiring unanimity in the rest of the Council, could always avoid being pushed into war on either side.

The unanimity rule allowed Britain, if it did decide for war, to enjoy from the outset—as in the Italo-Ethiopian war—the support of a vast ready-made coalition composed of all the other Council members whose votes had made its decision possible. Moreover, the vaguer the Locarno commitments remained, the easier it was for Britain to manoeuvre in the Council, and throw its great weight to one side or the other as it preferred. This situation required Britain to maintain the League and the prestige of the Council, for these provided the manoeuvring ground; if

they fell into decay Britain would fall back into its 1914 position, and become even more dependent on France than then by being more exposed than then to air attack.

Germany, France, Italy and Britain thus all had a strong national interest in the maintenance of the Locarno treaty. Yet they all were led inevitably by the principle of national sovereignty on which the treaty reposed to contribute to its ruin. The main lines of the Locarno tragedy are worth retracing for they show what is bound to happen with such pacts. It would take too long to tell the whole story here, but the following summary may show broadly how one thing led to another and make clear an extremely complicated chain of developments.

Because Britain could not underwrite blindly the foreign policy of the sovereign governments of France and Germany and remain sovereign, it had to limit itself to a general pledge to each and insist on its freedom to interpret this pledge in its own way when the time came. The French general staff therefore had to base its defense plans on the assumption it would have no British military aid with which to meet the first shock and on the possibility it might receive none thereafter. France thus had to rely primarily on French arms while French diplomats sought to manoeuvre Britain into a more definite pledge, make the most of the possibility of receiving British military aid, supplement this with help from allies more likely to act quickly, and still avoid anything weakening practically or legally either the French Locarno claim on Britain or its Covenant claim on all League members. Because the French could neither get a more definite pledge nor sacrifice the one Locarno gave them, they could neither reduce their armaments nor use them in preventive war, neither abandon military understandings with other neighbors of Germany nor develop these into automatic alliances.

Because France could not reduce armaments or military connections, and because Britain could give definite pledges to Germany even less than to France, Berlin could not feel safe or even sure that France and Britain did not mean to keep Germany down forever. Consequently Berlin had to make the most of France's difficulties in waging preventive war at this stage and build up Germany's military position. Berlin had to do this secretly (until strong enough to do it openly) in order to keep Germany's Locarno claim on Britain valid and prevent France strengthening its claim. Because of this whole situation and after it (together with its economic side, sketched in Annex 3) had brought Hitler to power in 1933 and after he had sacrificed Germany's treaty with Soviet Russia, France and Russia in 1934 started back toward their pre-war alliance. Because any alliance or pact with a non-League member weakened the Locarno claim on Britain, France insisted that Russia join the League and added to the French pact

with Russia the protocol which subordinated it both to the Locarno treaty and League and safeguarded Britain against the pact becoming an automatic alliance.

Because this pact was, even so, a step back toward the 1914 position Britain then sought to offset it by building up the prestige of the Council through which Britain kept the decisive rôle. The British pro-League policy began before and not, as many believe, after the Ethiopian conflict reached the League, and began for reasons of European instead of imperial policy. The time-table was: July, 1934, France arranges in London the entry of Russia into the League; September, France and Britain bring Russia into the League; December, Britain begins to throw her influence toward security through the League by taking the responsible rôle of mediator in the Yugoslav-Magyar conflict and by favoring—in fact proposing behind the scenes—the formation of the first League police force in Europe, the one sent to the Saar; 1935, January 3, Ethiopia appeals to the League against Italy.

Because Locarno kept the Russo-French agreement from being in fact an automatic alliance, France was the more encouraged to seek to supplement it with an agreement with Italy, including military staff plans for the execution of the Locarno treaty. Because of this Laval was led to encourage Signor Mussolini's Ethiopian ambitions and then, when these clashed with Britain's League, European and imperial interests, to play one Locarno guarantor against the other, in the hope of keeping the staff agreement with Italy and obtaining a staff agreement with Britain, or at least a more definite Locarno guarantee.

Because of this split among Britain, France and Italy, the opportunity rose for Germany to occupy the Rhineland. Because of this danger Paris refused to vote the oil sanction against Italy unless Britain gave France some staff guarantee against such German occupation. This pro-Italian policy weakened France's moral claim on Britain and the League. Because of this Germany, moving a few days before Paris could bring all its threads together by ratifying the Soviet Pact, obtaining a staff understanding from Britain and accepting the oil sanction, was able to occupy the Rhineland with impunity. While this German success cost the League authority in France, Italy (with the help of poison gas) was able to reach Addis Ababa, which cost the League prestige in Britain and elsewhere.

Because of this German blow to Locarno and the Italian blow to the League the main practical obstacle to the Franco-Soviet pact becoming what Germany and Britain both feared—a pre-war automatic alliance— was removed. Because of the German and Italian advances, London has ended by having its military staff make concrete war plans with the French staff and by committing Britain much more definitely than in 1914 to fight

if Germany attacks Belgium or France. And so Locarno's regional guarantee pact failed like the League's universal guarantee through the fatal flaw at the core of them both, and the world has been brought back appallingly near to 1914.

.   .   .   .

When I have seen what great men in France, in England and in Germany have written before me I have been lost in admiration, but I have not lost courage.—Montesquieu, Introduction, *De l'Esprit des Lois.*

.   .   .   .   .   .

As nature in her dispensation of conceitedness has dealt with private persons, so has she given a particular smatch of self-love to each country and nation. Upon this account it is that the English challenge the prerogative of having the most handsome women, of being most accomplished in the skill of music, and of keeping the best tables. The Scotch brag of their gentility, and pretend the genius of their native soil inclines them to be good disputants. The French think themselves remarkable for complaisance and good breeding. . . .

The Italians value themselves for learning and eloquence. . . . The Grecians pride themselves in having been the first inventors of most arts. . . . The Turks . . . pretend they profess the only true religion, and laugh at all Christians for superstitious, narrow-souled fools. The Jews to this day expect their Messias as devoutly as they believe in their first prophet Moses. The Spaniards challenge the repute of being accounted good soldiers. And the Germans are noted for their tall, proper stature, and for their skill in magic. But not to mention any more, I suppose you are already convinced how great an improvement and addition to the happiness of human life is occasioned by self-love.—Erasmus, *The Praise of Folly,* 1515.

ANNEX 5

My Own Road to Union

We are accepting this challenge of hostile purpose because we know that in such a Government, following such methods, we can never have a friend; and that in the presence of its organized power, always lying in wait to accomplish we know not what purpose, there can be no assured security for the democratic Governments of the world. . . . We are glad, now that we see the facts with no veil of false pretense about them, to fight thus for the ultimate peace of the world and for the liberation of its peoples, the German peoples included: for the rights of nations great and small and the privilege of men everywhere to choose their way of life and of obedience. The world must be made safe for democracy. Its peace must be planted upon the tested foundations of political liberty. We have no selfish ends to serve. We desire no conquest, no dominion. We seek no indemnities for ourselves, no material compensation for the sacrifices we shall freely make. We are but one of the champions of the rights of mankind. We shall be satisfied when those rights have been made as secure as the faith and the freedom of nations can make them.—President Wilson in his speech to Congress for declaration of war against Germany, April 2, 1917.

It may be useful to retrace briefly the road by which I have come to dissent now when "it is generally conceded that we should not have entered the last war" and were duped into it mainly for economic or even for sordid profit motives, when it is the fashion to jest bitterly of "making the world safe for democracy" as if it were "a matter of no overwhelming importance to the United States"—when "my brethren," as in the time of Job, are "ashamed because they had hoped." If I can not accept the basic premises and conclusions of the neutralistic school it is not from failure to give its arguments consideration. It is rather because I happened to go through long ago the evolution which many have undergone only recently, and because I have had more time and been under greater pressure to evolve further.

I have already mentioned one proof of the importance I attached to the profit motive in war when it was not so generally conceded. I would give other proof now that I did not wait till after the event either to stress this point publicly or to criticize our entry in the war.

On April 4, 1917, the Associated Students of the State University of Montana where I was then editor of the college paper, Montana Kaimin, sent this telegram to President Wilson:

Monster patriotic demonstration today by students of State University. A united student body, who, having faith and confidence in your wisdom and judgment pledges its enthusiastic support of your every undertaking.

The next day the college paper published under my signature the following:

BLIND DEMOCRACY

I have been asked why I voted against sending the telegram to President Wilson which was to say that the University students "stand behind him in whatever he undertakes." I was opposed to it because I object to the all-inclusiveness of the wording which I have just quoted.

When the war first began we condemned that very attitude among the Germans. We criticized severely their blind obedience to the Kaiser. Now at the first shadow of war, although we are not in the danger the Germans were with hostile countries on both sides, shall we lock up our brain and throw the key away?

To say that we are behind the President in everything he undertakes, especially at this stage of the international situation, is to undermine the very foundations of democratic government. It is an indication of mob-mindedness and is least to be expected and most to be deplored when found in our colleges.

Instead of being a "glittering generality" the telegram should have said something definite. If it had said, "We are behind you in every move you make to aid the cause of democracy against autocracy, and we urge you to make the entrance of the United States into the war dependent upon the definite agreement of the allies to establish a league to enforce peace after the conflict is over and while overpowering the German government to oppose dismembering and economically crushing that nation and thus sowing the seeds of future warfare"—if the message had been of that order, I would have been among the first to say aye.

The United States today has the opportunity of doing great service to the cause of democracy. The allies need our help, they are dependent upon us for munitions and other supplies. They are fighting the cause of democracy, but at the same time so many racial passions and other issues have entered into the war that it is doubtful whether the furtherance of democracy or the commerce of the allies will be uppermost in the minds of the men who gather around the council table when the war is over. We had a Platt amendment before we went into the Spanish war to keep us

to our purpose of making Cuba independent. We can do equal service for democracy and world peace if we make the condition of our entry in the war as definite as outlined above.

When the college term ended I volunteered in June, 1917, in one of the engineer regiments which Marshal Joffre on his visit to Washington urged the United States to organize and dispatch at once to France; it was called at first the 8th and later the 18th Railway Engineers. (I had been working summers as transitman in the United States Public Land Surveys in Alaska and the Rockies.) Six weeks after the regiment was organized we were sent to France where I remained until discharged from service June, 1919. In June, 1918, I was transferred to the Intelligence Service (G. 2, S.O.S.) and in December was attached in a confidential position to the American Peace Commission in Paris where I remained for six months.

I had access there to many highly secret official documents, not only the daily record of the secret meetings of Wilson, Lloyd George, Clemenceau, etc., but daily despatches between the President and American generals on all fronts, our diplomats, and Washington (on the home and Senate situation). I was in an unusual position to see daily what was really happening and how little the press or public knew of this, and to see too from the inside how propaganda was being handled abroad and at home. I was also one of those chosen to guard President Wilson on his return to Paris from Washington until the secret service men he brought with him could take over, my job being mainly to "smell" the bouquets sent him to see they hid no bombs. I mention these details to show the degree to which my functions encouraged a skeptical attitude—in one already born a Missourian.

My mental evolution during the war and armistice period does not need to be reconstructed now from memory; it can be followed in these excerpts from what I wrote then:

March, 1918. [*Letter published in the* Missoulian, *Missoula, Mont.*]

"I can not understand the wave of intolerance, with its determination to suppress the least expression of non-conformity, which seems to have spread over the country which has always acclaimed its freedom of speech and press," writes Private Clarence K. Streit, formerly of the Missoulian staff, from "Somewhere in France." "I suppose the country is only going through the same psychological stage as that experienced by England and France at the beginning of the war. May they pass through it quickly. When they have, they will realize that in a country fighting to make the world safe for democracy, intolerance, hate and forced conformity are among the enemies of the cause."

March 14, 1918 [*Letter*]

A good many of our newspapers understand the President's policy about as well as the German Junker class. . . . They have not caught that spirit of democracy which is abroad in the world. . . . The American who wants to know what our aims and those of our Allies are is denounced as a pacifist. The newspapers are keen to know more of our military operations over here—they don't give a continental damn, apparently, as to where we are going but they want to know how fast we're getting there. . . .

After Wilson's speeches of the past winter one has reason to believe that while Wilson remains President we will not be buying with our lives and limbs colonies for Great Britain, territorial gains for the other Allies and commercial special privileges for American big business. . . . His prestige over here is enormous, more than in the United States, I believe.

March 23, 1918 [*Published letter*]

In my opinion the Russians and President Wilson, backed up by the British Labor party and the French Socialists, have made this a war for democracy. Had the Russians remained under the Tsar and kept on fighting (which is rather doubtful) the Allies would probably have won the war already, but I do not think it would have been a victory for democracy, as it will be now. The Russian revolution at one stroke removed the primary *raison d'être* for German militarism. . . .

By its publication of secret treaties it showed how imperialistic were the aims of the Allies—making the Adriatic an Italian lake, giving France German territory to the Rhine, parcelling out supposedly neutral Persia, in fact, sowing the seeds of future wars on every hand. . . . I have noticed very little about those secret treaties in the American press. . . .

The despised Bolsheviks proceeded to demonstrate how imperialistic are the German war aims by the Brest-Litovsk conference. They got the first real show-down of those aims, a show-down which should convince everyone that the militaristic party is still in the saddle. . . .

The Russian military power is gone, it is true, but that has served to make the Allies really more than ever rely on help from the United States. It has made our position among the Allies much more important, in fact, I believe it has given us the leading position. And that, again, works toward a democratic peace. We are certainly a pacific people; we have no territorial ambitions and we have an idealistic and sincerely democratic president directing our great war power.

Oct. 26, 1918. [*Letter*]

It is going to be mighty easy to lose this war in winning it. By that I mean that I think the war will have been lost to democracy no matter

what the decision on the field if the prime motive in the making of peace
is not the safe-guarding of the world against another catastrophe such
as this war. If only a quarter of the zeal paid in each country to the
protection of its "national interests" were devoted to the interests of
humanity!

President Wilson has earned the everlasting gratitude of every democracy in the world by the policy he has pursued in this war, it seems to me.
Against all the pressure of "national interests" he has stood out firmly
for a peace on the broad lines necessary for the world's interest.

Against the decisions of the Paris Conference of 1915 and the "high
protectionists" at home and abroad he has emphasized the danger of economic wars after the war and called for the freedom of international trade.
I think that is one of the most important points in his policy. Commercial
rivalry between nations is one of the chief causes of war and if it is allowed
to continue after the war is over there will be little real hope for a durable
peace. And it is on this very point that the President is going to encounter
strong opposition at the peace conference.

Nov. 8, 1918 [Letter]

From what meager news we have received of the election results in the
States, it seems that the Republicans are in the lead. That's a pity. You
know I'm no Democrat, but in a time like this I want to see the President's hand strengthened in Congress. And electing Republicans now is
no way to help the President or democracy with a little "d." Of course,
the Republican and Democrat parties are hardly different, except in name.

Nov. 15, 1918. [Letter]

I am glad the President is coming over here for the peace conference.
His presence will be needed. He has shown himself the sanest and most
far-sighted of statesmen and with his enormous prestige he will have a
deciding voice at the peace table. And he will get a reception from France,
I will tell you. . . . Of course, the royalist and reactionary elements are
not pleased with his ideas, but he is unbelievably strong with the mass of
the people.

And as for our troops, well, I was talking with a fellow back from the
front while in Bordeaux. We were speaking of the recent election. He
said it was a shame the soldiers didn't get to vote, that the result would
have been different, for "the boys up at the front think President Wilson
is the greatest man in the world." I heard no rejoicing over here on the
Republican victory nor anything like commendation of the [Theodore]
Roosevelt tactics, though of course I am not acquainted with the sentiment in all parts of this big old AEF.

Dec. 22, 1918 [Paris, Letter]

I reached Paris about 9 a.m. Saturday Dec. 14th. . . . Soon came the boom of a cannon. The President had arrived. . . . I arrived at the *Champs Elysées* just in time to hear the cheers and see the handkerchiefs and hats waving. . . . He received a magnificent reception. . . . The French recognize the greatness of Wilson, even if a portion of the American public, perhaps too close to him and certainly too far distant from the late front, can't seem to appreciate him. . . .

If the Republicans really thought the President's policy was wrong, why didn't they say so when he first enunciated that policy?

Instead, Senator Lodge stated after the President's speech of April 2, 1917, in which he defined our aim in going to war, that Wilson had "expressed in the loftiest manner possible the sentiments of the American people." And [Theodore] Roosevelt, who now practically accuses the President of being pro-German, came out with this comment at that time on the President's speech: "The President's message is a great state paper of which Americans in future years will be proud. It now rests with the people of the country to see that we put in practice the policy the President has outlined." And now that . . . we are in a position to "put in practice the policy the President has outlined" this group is doing all it can to prevent the President's policy from being carried out to end.

The sickening feature of the situation is that the American public should have let itself be carried away with hysteria and elect a Congress hostile to the President in these critical times. And that the A.E.F. should not have had any voice in the proceeding.

The royalist propaganda papers and the reactionary press in France are playing up this group in the States for all, no, for a great deal more than it is worth. Fine bed-fellows. Meanwhile the liberal press of France and England is rallying strongly to the President's support.

Dec. 23, 1918. [Diary, Paris, Record Room, American Peace Commission]

I made the usual inspection to see what important papers had been left out. Found a great deal of valuable information lying around. Also all the keys to the filing cabinets. Among other things, a document dated Nov. 29, 1918, from the French Republic to U. S. Government giving plans for Peace conference drawn up by French Govt.

One learns a great deal at this station. Surprising the way things are left accessible. This record room contains all the files and documents of the Peace Commission. There are interests which would give a good deal to get hold of some of this information. My reports on all this carelessness are bearing some fruit, for conditions are slowly bettering. But I can easily

see why there were leaks in the State Department. Turned in a two-page report thereon this morning.

It is enough to give one an idea of the immensity of the problems confronting the coming conference—to see the universal scope of the documents and books in this room.

Dec. 24, 1918. [Diary, Paris]

Most important of all, saw notes taken by Col. House of meeting of heads of allied governments, Lloyd George, Clemenceau, etc., Nov. 4-7 (also the military—Foch, etc.) in which armistice conditions were framed.

Jan. 9, 1919 [Diary, Paris]

So many diverse peoples of the world are expecting so many diverse benefits from Wilson and America at the Peace Conference that the many inevitable disappointments are likely to have a boomerang effect in the world's opinion of the U. S. There is such a thing as setting up too great expectations.

It is reported that the first 100,000 miners have returned from the army to the coal pits of England. No doubt the super-patriots met them in the under-ground galleries with a band playing "Hail, the Conquering Hero Comes."

Before the Armistice the Allied press was filled with stories of the lack of food and raw materials in Germany, paper suits, etc. Since the Armistice the press is filled with stories of the comfortable situation of the Germans, of the plenitude of food in Germany, and no one has yet spoken of seeing a paper suit. The answer is—Propaganda. Germany is menaced by famine, yet the idea of feeding their enemies grates upon some Christian folk and they try to prove that said enemies need no food. . . .

No doubt German historians will prove the war was a victory for Germany or, at least, that she was not beaten. And millions of Germans will be brought up to believe that. Just as millions of other children will be brought up to believe another "truth." Each group of belligerents used its press for four years to instill into the majority of its people its own particular "truths," these "truths" being as absolutely opposed to each other as the soldiers of the two camps during a bayonet charge.

It would be idle to suppose that the effects of this persistent propaganda should die out with the Armistice and that now Truth should shake off her shackles, reveal herself to all people of the world so that no one could longer doubt her identity. Even in times of continued peace we cannot decide just what is this much referred to "Truth." What chance is there for her to be recognized now?

Jan. 18, 1919. [Diary, Paris]

The grand conference of Paris has at last opened, ushered in with some well chosen platitudes from the mouth of President Poincaré. . . . Surround the peace conference with a halo of high and noble thoughts, and then do your dirty work behind closed doors. Same old scheme that they worked in Vienna in 1815. . . . Read the stenographic report of the afternoon's session. What a beautiful frameup. Everything done unanimously after the slate prepared in advance. How long will that continue?

Jan. 25, 1919. [Diary, Paris]

Gave the peace conference the once over . . . from the outside. *Populo* is not very popular with the peace commissioners. He is useful as a background for the splendid limousines which roll by and up to the door of the Quai d'Orsay, carrying his "servants." . . . There were two or three hundred of *populo*, representing most of the Allied nations, many soldiers anxious to see the "fathers of the victory," the "premier poilus," the select few who "won the war."

Many of them, I gathered from phrases overheard, were waiting especially to see Pres. Wilson. . . . I recognized Balfour, and think I saw Winston Churchill. . . . Marshall Foch . . . drew a cheer. . . . The President . . . also drew a cheer, and the crowd pressed to the fence to see him descend from his car. . . . They could only get a glimpse of him. Cold weather, nipping wind. But crowd stuck. I see in the morning papers that Pres. Wilson made an important speech on the Society of Nations at this session.

Feb. 19, 1919. [Paris, Letter to a French girl]

President Wilson's speeches were all that reconciled me in the least toward this war as a war. The patriotic speeches only disgusted me. The men who were the strongest supporters of the United States entering the war "for democracy," why, they were all the worst reactionaries in America, men who all their lives had bitterly opposed democracy at home. And the men, most of them at least, who protested against our entering the war and were called traitors and maligned in the press—they were the men who had been abused for years by the same press because they advocated democratic reforms.

I detested the German government and the German idea, wherever I found it. And I found plenty of Prussianism in the U. S. I put little faith in the Allied protestations of democracy. And, in the last three months, I have seen enough of the secret inside workings to know that the heads of the Allied Governments are not sincerely democratic, they are only as

democratic as they feel compelled to be by public opinion. Some of them
are cynically un-democratic, though in their public speeches they usually
hide this.

[I would here give a general warning to the reader. I was only 21 when
I enlisted and had never been east of the Mississippi. I was much impressed in Paris by the fact that I was then in a better position to judge
what was really going on than most contemporaries, more impressed by
this than by the facts that the picture was, even so, very incomplete and
that I was young and inexperienced. I did not realize how I tended to
give more importance to what was unexpected or new to me, than to
what was true but not surprising.

Nor did I then realize what strange chameleons documents are. A passage
in a document read when it is fresh and in the light of one's impression
of the whole situation then may seem to one cynical and significant, while
if read years later when quite removed from the context of events it may
seem innocent and ordinary. Conversely, documents that raised no eye-
brows when written can take on a most sinister meaning when read years
after the contemporary atmosphere has gone but facts not common knowledge then have come to light or viewpoints have changed.

We tend to assume that the picture we get of a given event will be the
one the future will get of it or that the past got. Yet how many of the
factors that influenced President Wilson and other leaders of his day are
lost to us, and how many factors that we know now were unknown to
them? And, then, as Bishop Stubbs said apropos of Henry V:

"It is one of the penalties which great men must pay for their greatness, that they have to be judged by posterity according to a standard
which they themselves could not have recognized, because it was by their
greatness that the standard itself was created."]

March 3, 1919 [Paris, Letter]

Part of the Louvre museum is now open. . . . I've visited it twice. What
did I go back to see the second time? Especially the Venus de Milo. And
also the Victory of Samothrace. . . . The Victory of Samothrace has no
head. Did Victory ever have a head? Perhaps. But it always loses it. . . .

No doubt these letters of mine from Paris are rather disappointing to
you. So little about this epoch-making Peace Conference—this great historical assembly. Why, from the preceding four and a half pages [of this
letter], one would never know that the world's eyes were centered on this
city from which I am writing. Well, I could make a few remarks—but
this paper is not of asbestos and I don't know how well the fire department here is organized.

I might say, however, that this is not a Peace Congress but an inter-
allied Victory meeting, with indignation as the guiding general force and

Individual Economic Interest as the chief counselor of each nation. If you want to cling to your opinion of the greatness of a number of gentlemen much in the public eye, why, stay home and read the newspapers. Don't hang around here.

But still, this conference is an enlightened body compared to some of the vociferous Senators back home, for whom political thinking ended when the Constitution was written and the Monroe Doctrine enunciated. The world is moving mighty fast these days, but just where it is going I would not venture to say. Ah, these piping days of—the armistice. I'll wager some of the directing heads of the Allies long sometimes for the good old days when everybody had but one purpose—to lick the other fellow. Heigh ho! for the next last war.

But I'll re-iterate that President Wilson, in my opinion, is far ahead of the others. But he is handicapped by lack of support at home and I doubt if he will be able to accomplish much. It will be a pity, for there can be no doubt that the masses of Europe are trusting implicitly in him. It is touching the faith they show in him.

March 1919. [Paris, Letter]

The opinions of the American press these days show a lamentable ignorance of world conditions. To read the papers, and the speeches of . . . [various] . . . senators, one would think that they have been asleep for the last five or ten years. They talk about . . . keeping out of European affairs. Were we able to keep out of this war? The world isn't as big as it used to be. And it is getting smaller all the time. . . .

I don't think the proposed League of Nations is by any means perfect. . . . What discourages me with so much of American criticism of the League—it is so plainly caused by nothing more than personal or party hostility to the man Wilson. Or it is urged by a selfish nationalism and imperialism more closely related to Prussianism than to the old American idealism. It is not helping the cause of future world peace. The militarists and reactionaries of Europe are making capital use of our Lodges, Borahs and Co.

You seem to think that the government took over the cable lines to prevent American opinion hostile to Wilson from reaching France and England. If you could read the papers over here you would see that such is not the case. The reactionary newspapers and the royalist press are doing their best to weaken Wilson's position at the conference by playing up dispatches from the U. S. hostile to him.

March 20, 1919. [Paris. Letter to a French girl]

I think parents are rather under obligation to the child. . . . The same reasoning I apply to man's relation to the state. A man owes a state nothing because of the fact that he happened to be born in it. It was through

no choice of mine that I am an American. I could be naturalized now as citizen of some other country? True, but the state, in educating me, was fitting me for a life within that state, its object was to train me into being a good citizen of it. And the very accident of birth gave me dear associations, friends, memories in America, made me prejudiced in her favor. I would not change. With all her faults, I prefer America to any other country.

But—had I been born in France, say, of French parents—I would no doubt prefer to be French, would be proud of my French nationality just as you are. And if the fates had willed that I should have been born an Englishman, a Russian, a German, a Chinaman, a Turk or any other nationality, I would undoubtedly be just as happy in my state and prefer it to any other.

And yet, this simple accident of birth under one flag instead of another colors the mental attitude and distorts the intellectual processes of most men, including most of the men whom I used to look up to as intellectuals, men of science and philosophy, men whose sole concern was the truth. This war showed the stuff of which the world's "élite" or "intelligenzia" is made—and it is a sight enough to make one despair.

For my part, I love America—aside from the accident of birth—because of the ideals on which the Republic was founded (not all of them, however), I love American life for its boundless energy, its freedom from tradition, because it is facing the future and not the past. But that isn't going to keep me from trying to see things as they really are. I am an intelligent man first, an American afterwards. The United States is now undoubtedly the most powerful single nation on the globe. All the more need then for men in America whose allegiance is to the human race.

. . . .

My evolution, then, has not been from unthinking acceptance of the war to disillusioned belief that it was a monstrous mistake into which we the people were led through no fault of ours but through sinister influences. My evolution has been from doubtful acceptance of the war as being, on balance, more right than wrong, to a bitter feeling as early as 1919 that it had been botched. After this interlude of disillusionment I have slowly grown to the deep conviction that with all their mistakes Wilson and the American people chose the lesser evil in all their essential choices.

Though I went into the war favoring a league to enforce peace, I thought of it then only vaguely. When President Wilson talked of making the world safe for democracy I did not then understand that the real problem was not that of doing justice at once but of providing the means of doing justice, the machinery of world self-government. I lost interest in his League in 1919 because it was coupled with so bad a treaty

and because I thought it was too weak. I have since become convinced that, considering all he had to face and chose between, President Wilson showed high statesmanship in tying the Covenant to the Treaty of Versailles, and that he got as strong a world organization founded as was practically possible then. Though I have since come also to believe that the League is no solution for us because its basic working principle—which I never questioned then—is wrong, I am nonetheless convinced that this League was practically essential for the necessary transition to world organization on a sound basis. But when I left the army I was so disappointed with Woodrow Wilson and his works and so opposed to the irreconcilables that I took no part in the ensuing fight over the League at home.

I went to work as a reporter and then in January, 1920, returned to Europe as a Rhodes Scholar. After covering the Turco-Greek war, during vacation, for the Philadelphia *Public Ledger* I left Oxford in the Fall of 1921 to become the *Ledger's* Rome correspondent. My interest in the League had so ebbed that though I was in Lausanne for months in 1922-23 reporting the Turkish peace conference I never bothered to make the trip of only one hour needed to visit Geneva. I never saw the League in action, in fact, before *The New York Times* sent me in 1929 from New York to Geneva to be its correspondent there. Meanwhile, however, my life and work in many parts of Europe and especially in the territory of the Central Powers had helped persuade me that we had not made a mistake in entering the war.

I have had many occasions to note how advanced the British people are in the practice of political democracy and how the French people, if behind them as regards parliaments and courts, are ahead of them in practicing social democracy, above all in practicing the equality of man.

I have also had many occasions to see how retarded and inexperienced in democracy the peoples of Italy and of the Central Powers generally were, and the effects among them of their longer exposure to absolutism's degradation of the common man and insistence on blind obedience to state and church and all constituted authority. Such things (for one example) as finding even in Vienna in 1926 after six years of Socialism cooks and maids who still assumed as a matter of course that they had to go down on their knees and kiss my wife's hand when coming to receive instructions for the day. I have had many occasions to see how most of the democracy these people have has come from America, from England and, most directly of all, from the French Revolution.

Before seeing this I had already seen how close the abominable servile system of the Central Powers had come to triumphing over Europe's most advanced democracies. I had taken fifteen days zigzagging against

submarines to reach Britain in August, 1917, and feel there myself to what straits they had then reduced the British. I had seen soldiers reprimanded at Aldershot camp for throwing away a potato peeling, I had spent much of my first day in London (August, 1917) trying to find a place to eat amid all the padlocked restaurants. I had been among the soldiers convoyed across the Channel under cover of the night. I had witnessed how low French morale had fallen in 1917, how it rose with the arrival of the Americans—and how near to Paris the invaders still came more than a year after our entry in the war.

Long before Adolph Hitler rose to prove what bad habits the German people had got under their feudal lords, I had often had brought home to me how great were the dangers from which the old democracies had escaped, and how President Wilson had been much wiser than I had once supposed. I had come to understand better with each year why he had touched so deeply the hearts of common men and women all through Europe.

Then the Geneva assignment gave me a rare opportunity to follow continuously and at first hand the actual working not only of the League proper, but of the International Labor Organization and the Bank for International Settlements—all the chief machinery the world has organized for governing itself. The reasons that split Americans for and against the League in 1920 were, of course, paper reasons since the League then existed only on paper. Yet to this day only a relative handful of Americans have had or taken occasion to test their theories by studying on the spot how the League of Nations really works in practice. Most of the leading American opponents of the League have such faith in pure theory that they have never so much as laid eye or ear on a League meeting. My own theories about the League have had to face the facts directly year after year.

Unlike most of those who have been in close contact with the League and its problems, I have never been responsible for any part of the League machinery or for producing results in any of its fields for any government. My responsibility instead, has been that of reporting objectively, accurately and understandingly to all who cared to read what these others were doing. This function required close continual contact with the permanent officials of the League, I. L. O. and Bank, with the policies and special problems and delegations of all important member and non-member countries, and with all big world questions, political, economic, monetary, social—and yet sharp detachment always from each of these. No one present but the reporter had this function. Nor was any one under more pressure to see each day's development in every field in terms of living men and women, and to judge correctly the essen-

tials in it interesting laymen and experts far removed in distance or occupation. I have enjoyed the further and immense advantage of reporting
for *The New York Times*. Mr. Ochs said to me, as my only instructions on being appointed League correspondent ten years ago: "Remember always to lean backwards in being fair to those whose policies
The New York Times opposes."

A visiting correspondent once remarked as we sat together in the press
section during a Council meeting, "This post is a liberal education." I
have found it so. I could not help but come to see some things differently.
Nor could I help but be impressed with how difficult it was before the
League existed, and still is outside Geneva now, to enjoy that essential
for solving any problem correctly—a continued view of it as a whole. I
wrote in *The New York Times*, Sept. 13, 1931:

The world as seen from Geneva appears an Alice in Wonderland world,
devoted to the propositions that all nations are created superior, the part
is greater than the whole and the day is longer than the year. . . .

What is impressive in Geneva is that of sixty nations any fifty-nine
should realize so acutely the absurdity of the other's claim to be the only
one in step, and that none of them ever realizes that each is simultaneously
making that very same claim. . . .

What makes this loom big in Geneva is, of course, the very same thing
that keeps the world from seeing it. The near always seems greater than
the far, and only sometimes is. What is nearest to the observer in New
York, in London, Paris, Rome, Berlin, is a nation, a people, a way of
seeing, a way of understanding, a way of doing. What is nearest to him
at Geneva is the mixture of all these, the international thing. . . .

In Geneva day in and day out the observer's contacts, business and
social, are international. . . . There is no major issue that does not come
up here. And always from an international if not a world viewpoint. You
are hearing in Geneva not merely the views of the various nations on all
sorts of questions but, what is far more illuminating, you are hearing
what they think of each other's arguments. It doesn't matter in Geneva
if you can't see the beam in your own eye: While the American is pointing unerringly to the motes in the eyes of the Frenchman, the Englishman, the German, the European in general, all these are revealing the
motes in the American's eye, and all the motes in the eyes of the others
that he has missed.

You have the politicians, the businessmen, the professors, the admirals,
the bankers, the jurists, the scientists, the poets, the doctors to correct
each other similarly. They come and go and come back again, dipping in
and out of this atmosphere, but the observer living in Geneva is in it all
the time. With everyone and everything continuously forcing upon him a
world viewpoint, he is naturally struck by the lack of it elsewhere.

The discovery that the world does not see the world for the nations is so new to him that he is likely to think that it is something new. The world, of course, has never seen the world for the nations. What is new about the world is that in the last of its ten thousand years it has at least and at last begun to try to see itself as a world. What is new is the world observatory that the world itself has started in Geneva.

Such is the road I took at the age of 21 and by which I have come in 21 years to propose Union now.

. . . .

To understand the true greatness of Man one must first understand how infinitesimal he is.

. . . .

Man is certainly stark mad; he cannot make a worm, and yet he will be making gods by dozens.—Montaigne.

. . . .

What I call virtue in the republic is the love of country, that is to say, love of equality.—Montesquieu, opening *De l'Esprit des Lois.*

. . . .

Surely our twentieth century civilization can not be so helpless that it is out of its power somehow to obtain what is the common desire of all nations and peoples . . . *We may surely believe that whole-hearted cooperation for a common aim must eventually be crowned with success.* —Beaumont Pease, Chairman, Lloyds Bank, London, 1936 Report.

. . . .

Whatever the fears and forebodings of those who hold their own faith weakly, there is no reason to fear that the world, having known the joys of freedom and enlightenment, is destined to relapse into the brutish obscurity of another Dark Age.—Harold Butler, Director, International Labor Organization, in his valedictory Report, April 25, 1938.

Last Word

On all great subjects much remains to be said.—Mill.

One must not always finish a subject so completely as to leave nothing for the reader to do. The object is not to make others read but to make them think.—Montesquieu, *De l'Esprit des Lois,* Book IX, Chapter 20.

When Aristide Briand proposed his European Federation the similarity of many of the responses to it impressed me. They applauded, they said: "This is noble, this is what we all want," and they added, "But there is this difficulty and that difficulty, and how is he going to meet them?" They acted as if the veteran French statesman, though in a much better position than they to see the difficulties his proposal faced, had not foreseen them and needed their help in seeing rather than in solving them. They implied that all these difficulties were for him to overcome; they assumed the role of spectators who would not be affected if his project came to naught through his failure to overcome every difficulty himself. Even the depression that followed could not persuade these waiters-for-a-perfect-plan that this was an enterprise in which they were willy-nilly involved, that they too would be punished—swiftly, mercilessly, increasingly—for failure to solve in time the problems on which Aristide Briand had made so brave a beginning.

I am aware of many of the difficulties confronting the Union, and I have no doubt that there exist more than I realize. I know that this book has led me into fields where others have a much greater knowledge than I. No one needs take time to convince me that this book falls far short of what it should be, that it is weak indeed compared to the great enterprise it would promote. I regret that this book is not as clear, short, complete, well organized, free from error, easy to read and hard to controvert on every page as I—perhaps more than any one—desire it to be. I feel, however, that I have reached the point of diminishing return for isolated work on its problem, and that time presses for an agreed if imperfect answer. My hope is that the book can now make at least the friends it needs, for if it can then I am sure that they can do far more than I to correct its faults and advance its purpose.

One can not believe as I do in democracy and fail to believe that the surest way to bring out the true from the false and to accomplish any great enterprise is to get the greatest number of individual minds

to working freely on it. The variety in our species is so rich that one can be sure in any such undertaking that one can do almost no detail in it so well as can some one else.

Democracy taps this rich vein. It does so by recognizing that Man can not foresee which obscure person or lowly thing may suddenly become of the greatest value to Man, by setting therefore an equal value on every man and every thing, and by seeking to give equal freedom to every man to do the thing he best can do and trade it in the commonwealth for all the billion things he can not do so well. That is the meaning of democracy's great declaration, *All men are created equal,* and the reason why democracy's spread has led to the discovery of more and more truths and to the doing of greater and greater enterprises.

And so I ask you not merely to make known any error you have found in this book but to try yourself to solve the problem that it leaves. Since it was you who found the fault how can you know that you are not the one who can overcome it better than I, better than anyone?

After all, are not your freedom, your prosperity, your security, your children at stake as well as mine? Is not the problem of world government your individual problem as well as mine? Can I alone organize the world for you any more than you for me? Can any dictator do it for us? If you and I and the other man and woman working freely and equally together can not gain our common end, then how on earth can it be gained?

For Man's freedom and vast future man must depend on man. It is ours together, or no one's and it shall be ours.

Index

(Abbreviations: Am.—American, Br.—Britain, Confed.—Confederation, Const.—Constitution, Fr.—France, Ger.—Germany, It.—Italy, Jap.—Japan, U.—Union.)